D1290033

LIBERTIES & COMMUNITIES IN MEDIEVAL ENGLAND

LIBERTIES & COMMUNITIES IN MEDIEVAL ENGLAND

*Collected Studies in Local Administration
and Topography*

BY

HELEN M. CAM, Litt.D., F.B.A.

PROFESSOR EMERITA
HARVARD UNIVERSITY

MERLIN PRESS

To

MY FIRST AND BEST TEACHERS

MY FATHER AND MOTHER

We begin our public affections in our families. No cold relation is a zealous citizen. We pass on to our neighbourhoods and our habitual provincial connections. These are inns and resting-places. Such divisions of our country as have been formed by habit, and not by a sudden jerk of authority, were so many little images of the great country, in which the heart found something which it could fill.

EDMUND BURKE

FIRST PUBLISHED IN THIS EDITION
1963
BY THE MERLIN PRESS LTD
112 WHITFIELD STREET
LONDON WI

PRINTED IN GREAT BRITAIN
BY D. R. HILLMAN & SONS LTD
FROME

CONTENTS

vi CONTENTS

MAPS

PREFATORY NOTE

These articles, written between 1923 and 1942, with their introduction, are reprinted substantially unaltered from the edition published by the Cambridge University Press in 1944. A few necessary corrections have been made, and a few references to later work added. New notes are indicated as such by square brackets.

H. M. C.

March 1963

October 1942

ABBREVIATIONS

Ass.R. Assize Roll. (Public Record Office.)

C.A.S. Cambridge Antiquarian Society.

C.R.C. Calendar of Close Rolls. (H.M. Stationery Office.)

Cal. Misc. Inq. Calendar of Miscellaneous Inquisitions. (H.M. Stationery Office.)

D.B. Domesday Book. (Record Commission 1834.)

Eng. Hist. Rev. English Historical Review. Cited by year and page.

F.R.C. Calendar of Fine Rolls. (H.M. Stationery Office.)

Inq. Post Mortem. Calendar of Inquisitions post mortem. (H.M. Stationery Office.) Cited by volume and page.

O.H.S. Oxford Historical Society's publications.

Plac. Quo War. Placita Quo Warranto. (Record Commission 1818.)

P.R.C. Calendar of Patent Rolls. (H.M. Stationery Office.)

P.R.O. Public Record Office.

Rot. Cart. Rotuli Cartarum. (Record Commission 1837.)

Rot. Hund. Rotuli Hundredorum. (Record Commission 1812–18.)

Rot. Lit. Claus. Rotuli Litterarum Clausarum. (Record Commission 1833–44.)

Rot. Parl. Rotuli Parliamentorum. (1767–77.)

R.S. Rolls Series.

Vict. Co. Hist. The Victoria History of the Counties of England.

Trans. R. Hist. S. Transactions of the Royal Historical Society. Cited by the year.

INTRODUCTION

In Defence of the Study of Local History

The sixteen studies in local history here gathered together may seem to the reader a somewhat miscellaneous collection with a distinctly antiquarian tinge. They are, for the writer, bound together by the belief that medieval local government can only be understood through much short range study of particular places and institutions. An inveterate dislike of scrapping the obsolete or obsolescent has left in this country an enticing variety of survivals, affording innumerable clues for the investigator to follow up, and though he cannot expect the reader to share with him all the excitement of the chase, he may at least defend his choice both of subject and of technique as being very closely associated with major historical and even political issues.

The history of local institutions has suffered at times from the unequal knowledge and ill-balanced zeal of the antiquary, but he is awake to one great truth that historians do not always keep in view. He starts from a present-day objective reality, whether building, boundary, name or custom; he holds the live end of an unbroken thread running back into the past that he is exploring. He takes for granted the continuity of history, and it is in that continuity that not only the fascination but the justification of such researches as the following lies. The discovery in the Parks Road at Oxford of a stone inscribed 'Here endeth Northgate Hundred' may start a train of inquiries running back past Robert Plot and Anthony Wood to the Pipe Rolls of Henry II and the charters of Ethelred the Unready.[1] The watercourses of Cambridge lead back to the days when 'East Angle and Mercian glared at each other across Magdalene Bridge', and Etheldreda's sister sent her men up the Granta to find a worthy sarcophagus for the Saint's relics among the remains of the little ruined chester, the line of whose earthworks can be traced to-day on Mount Pleasant.[2] The name of Chequers Farm at Stokenchurch records that stage in our national history when government office was hereditary and government salaries were paid in land;[3] while that of the Shire

[1] pp. 107–123. [2] pp. 1–18. [3] pp. 136–149.

Manor at Madingley registers alike the relation of the medieval knight of the shire to the constituents who paid his expenses, the interlocking of the franchisal and royal administrative systems, and the instinct for compromise and adjustment that produced the unique composition of 1430 between the Bishop of Ely and the gentlemen of Cambridgeshire.[1]

English local history abounds in such oddments. We are not alone, as a nation, in the mongrel character of our origins[2]—

> A medley canton'd in a heptarchy,

as Defoe said,

> Where with easy search you may distinguish
> Your Roman, Saxon, Danish, Norman, English—

but we are surely unique in the obstinate affection with which we cling to our old clothes. 'The relics are so lasting and so strong' that we find ourselves, for instance, forced to go back to the tenth century to explain why there are to-day two separate County Councils for Cambridgeshire north and south of the Ouse.

This diversity in continuity must needs be reflected in the character of our institutional research. To take one instance, it has long been a commonplace with students of English urban origins that each borough has its own constitutional history. The recent attempt to apply a great Belgian scholar's formula to the evolution of 'the' English borough[3] has been stoutly resisted by the natives who know only too well how Norwich and Gloucester, York and Leicester, Hastings and Bristol differ from each other, though at the same time they recognize the great value of Mr Stephenson's application of the continental technique of comparative topography to English problems, for he has shown us how much remains to be done, in spite of all the pious labours of municipal historians in the past. The harvest, again, that is beginning to be reaped from the work of the English Place-Name Society is evidence of the soundness of the piecemeal method in evoking the contribution of philology and topography to history, and the same may be said of the achievements of the Romano-British and Anglo-Saxon archaeologists. But such a procedure is above all necessary for the student of institutions, where some facile generalization on legal, social or administrative matters, passed on from pen to pen, may, without such checking by the facts, destroy both the life and the truth of pictures of the past.

Antiquarianism, then, can be defended on sound scientific grounds, but local history is more than a pursuit of origins. The historian is concerned not with detached threads, but with the seamless web of which Maitland spoke. It is not even simply a question of forms and techniques; it is a question of the men who used them, and of their attitudes and assumptions in using them. Institutionally speaking, the chief English contribution to western civilization has been parliamentary government. The discussions and researches of continental and English scholars in the last decade have thrown into strong relief the unique nature of the English development of a widespread European device.[1] The Cortes of the Spanish kingdoms, the Estates of France, Italy and the Low Countries, the Diets of the Empire all failed to meet the needs of the modern world; only in England did a medieval House of Commons move from strength to strength, adapting the traditions and forms of the fourteenth and fifteenth centuries to the needs of the seventeenth, eighteenth and nineteenth. Stubbs' contention that our representative institutions owe their durability to the foundations laid in the medieval communities of shires and boroughs is not invalidated by A. F. Pollard's vindication of Henry VIII as the architect of parliamentary power. It would not have been worth the Tudor dictator's while to exploit the parliamentary machine for his great revolution had it not been so intimately involved in the structure of English society. The *patria*—the neighbourhood—the country-side—was the key to the mastery of England, and just as the autocratic Edward I had found it expedient to get into direct touch with the knights of the shires, so Henry VIII and Elizabeth after him found that conciliar government exacted a body of loyal J.P.s to be the eyes and ears and hands of the central executive, all the more effective because on occasion they might, as M.P.s, become the voices of the communities they managed. We may admit with Stubbs that the toughness and the elasticity of our representative institutions may be traced in large measure to the preservation of the shire court by the statesmanship and common-sense of William the Conqueror; and we may attribute the extraordinary proliferation of juries for every kind of legal, fiscal and administrative purpose in part to the governmental genius of the Plantagenets, but Maitland has pointed out that the ground had been

[1] pp. 223-250.

prepared by the customs and habits of Saxons and Danes before the Frenchmen came,[1] and 'the jury flourished in the fertile ground of consent' in England, while on the Continent it developed along inquisitorial lines that matched the bureaucratic character of local administration. 'Self-government at the King's command', as A. B. White has called it, was the foundation of our durable parliamentary institutions, and the House of Commons began as the *communitas communitatum*.[2]

We have long been familiar with these notions, but the medieval country-side has made another contribution to our political traditions which is perhaps less fully appreciated.

Feudalism is generally regarded as the antithesis of democracy. It originated in military necessities and was the child of force; it depended on the exploitation of human labour; it consecrated inequality and privilege.[3] All this is true, but there are other truths that should be borne in mind. Feudalism rested on a conception of contract, and by medieval canon law an oath taken under compulsion was not binding; free consent, in theory at least, underlay the relationship of lord and vassal. This theory was not totally divorced from fact. G. B. Adams pointed out many years ago, that the right to repudiate the relationship if the contract was broken involved the vassal's right of resistance and provided a recognized technique for such resistance in the *diffidatio*, used in 1214 and 1264 by 'His Majesty's opposition', but it did not need a political crisis to bring out the democratic element in feudalism. In the day to day concerns of the fief and the honour and the manor, consultation and discussion between lord and man was the normal and indispensable procedure. F. M. Stenton has built up for us a picture, anticipated to some extent by the imaginative genius of Kipling, of the 'barons' barons' in the feudal courts up and down eleventh-century England tackling the problems of conflicting customs and competing property rights, and hammering out rough principles and practices of law which paved the way for the great reforms of Henry II's legists. Not only in the shire and hundred courts but in the courts of earls and barons, in honours and liberties, the determination to reconcile order and justice, to find some working compromise between English and Norman customs, to see, in fact, that 'the king's government was carried on', produced a working system in which both authority and responsibility were distributed between lord and man, and not

[1] pp. 49–63.   [2] pp. 27–48, 236–250.   [3] pp. 205–222.

concentrated solely in the superior to whom deference and loyalty were owed by the inferior. The returns of 1166 to the royal inquest into knights' fees contain such expressions as 'My men tell me that I owe the King the service of fifty knights'; and if the latest theory as to the procedure of 1086 is valid, the Domesday inquest was held in the honour courts of the barons with their Frenchmen, as well as in the hundreds by the reeve and priest and four men of the old communities. In both types of court the rule of law obtained; in both 'give and take' was the established technique.

If feudalism demanded the co-operation of lord and vassals it also involved a correlation of privilege and duty which made it a political education for the privileged. The contractual principle could be and was applied to the grant of governmental functions. When the kings parted with fiscal, judicial or administrative functions to a subject, with the grant went an obligation. The holder of a liberty who enjoyed all those rights which the king had had within it, accepted the responsibility for keeping the king's peace and doing the king's justice within it. In the early days of the Norman Conquest the lord of a franchise might be free, as he was not later, to delegate his regalian privileges to another, but he could not strip himself of the responsibility attaching to the privileges he held. As the royal machinery of government developed, so his duties grew. The privilege of returning royal writs in the sheriff's place involved a steadily increasing burden of activity; the franchise-holder, by virtue of his franchise, became a royal official, liable like a royal official to censure, punishment, and in the last resort displacement. The lord of a liberty had to show not merely by what warrant he claimed to hold the liberty, but whether he had exercised it in accordance with the terms of the grant, and for the public welfare, and in the royal interest. Thus, to quote F. M. Powicke, the feudal baron had, by virtue of his dignities and privileges, become 'part of an administrative machine from which he could not, even if he wished, escape', whilst conversely the king had no need nor desire to remove him so long as he fulfilled his functions and discharged his duties efficiently.[1] Feudalism was neither the rival nor the enemy of royal government; it was part and parcel of the system. And at the same time it was bequeathing an invaluable tradition to later generations of Englishmen; that no privilege should exist without a corresponding duty, and that high social standing and extensive lands

[1] pp. 173–204.

entailed upon their holder 'a great and continual labour'. Disraeli said of feudalism, in 1870: 'Its main principle, that the tenure of property should be the fulfilment of duty, is the essence of good government', and it is significant of our commonwealth that this doctrine should be common ground to-day for the parties of the right and the left, who differ not so much on the existence of this responsibility as on the authority which in the twentieth century should have the feudal monarch's right to declare the tenure forfeit if the duty is not fulfilled.

The history of our constitutional progress is indeed the story of the extension of political responsibility, spreading downwards and out-wards from the aristocrats to meet the tradition of local responsibility, growing upwards from the communities of villagers, squires and burgesses, unimpeded by any watertight social barriers;[1] the class 'liberties' of Magna Carta, each with its corresponding obligation, expanding towards the human liberties of the Atlantic Charter, with their exacting demands upon the conscience and the pertinacity of those descendants of the men of Runnymede and Philadelphia who have accepted them as their standard of political conduct. It is the writer's conviction that if we in this country are to be granted the honour of helping to vindicate the principles of democracy in the world of the twentieth century, we shall owe it to the age-long habit, transmitted through Anglo-Saxon, Dane and Norman, of accepting responsibility for the order, liberty and justice of our own neighbourhoods. 'These are but inns and resting-places', but we need not lose the lesser when we gain the greater, nor forget our village communities and local liberties in honouring the awe-inspiring obligations of world citizenship.

[1] pp. 18–26, 124–135, 163–172.

I

The Origin of the Borough of Cambridge:
A consideration of Professor Carl Stephenson's theories[1]

It should be made clear from the outset that this paper does not pretend to throw any new light on this ancient question. All that I hope to do is to review once more facts that have been accumulated or established by the long labours of scholars whose pupils we all are: and whose work is to a very large extent recorded in the former proceedings and communications of this society. If one follows in the footsteps of Babington, J. W. Clark, McKenny Hughes, Maitland, Canon Stokes, Arthur Gray (the Master of Jesus) and Dr Cyril Fox one cannot hope to have much chance of discovering evidence that has been overlooked: and I should never have thought of bringing the subject forward but for the recent appearance of a work[2] by an American scholar, which challenges, as he himself says, the 'weighty opinion of Maitland and Mr Arthur Gray' as to the origin of the Borough of Cambridge. It is clear, as I hope to show, that Mr Stephenson has not taken all the evidence into consideration; but it must be remembered that whilst all general historians are risking a great deal when they invade the realm of local history, topography and archaeology, scholars from another country are at a special disadvantage, and Mr Stephenson must therefore be regarded as particularly valiant in venturing on to such ground, and asserting as he does, very rightly, that the evolution of the borough must be approached from the side of topography. He is taking risks, and he knows it; and not the smallest is the risk of missing some invaluable article tucked away in the files of the proceedings and communications of some local association or club. This paper incurs the same risk; but the fact that the evidence is so scattered was a second reason for reopening the question: a synthesis of the work done over so many years by so many hands seemed worth attempting for its own sake, and not merely as an answer to a challenge.

[1] Read to the Cambridge Antiquarian Society 27 November 1933, and reprinted from their *Communications*, vol. xxxv (1935).

[2] *Borough and Town, a study of urban origins in England*, by Carl Stephenson (Cambridge, Mass. 1933).

Mr Stephenson is a pupil of the great Belgian scholar Pirenne, whose work on the towns of the Netherlands has revolutionized the study of urban origins on the Continent. Mr Stephenson considers, possibly with justice, that research into the early history of English boroughs has suffered from insularity; Pirenne's first study appeared in 1891, and, until the appearance of Mr Stephenson's book, we have had no serious attempt to test the applicability of his theory to English urban beginnings. That theory is, briefly, that town life is due above all to economic factors, and that the origin of the medieval town is 'a mercantile settlement freshly produced by contemporary economic changes'. In the eleventh century the revival of European commerce, practically extinct in the Dark Ages, produced colonies of merchants, planted outside the walls of an old Roman city, or, as in Flanders and Germany, of a *burg* of more recent origin, and from these new extra-mural settlements developed both urban life, and urban self-government. Pirenne, according to his pupil, had discovered 'an explanation for all medieval towns'.[1] If the formula 'a trading settlement which began as a stockaded quarter beside some older fortification'[2] accounts for the medieval town abroad, will it not also account for the English borough? In his recent book, *Borough and Town*, Mr Stephenson replies that it does.

Following Pirenne's example, Mr Stephenson looks for evidence in England of a commercial activity sufficient to provide such colonies. The traditional view, upheld by Cunningham and most subsequent writers on economic history, is that the Danes provided the stimulus, and that the first development of town life is to be associated with their colonization of north-eastern England and their seafaring activities, though a second and more powerful stimulus was supplied by the Normans after 1066. To Mr Stephenson the Danes are mainly pirates and fighters,[3] and though he allows that they were responsible for the growth of York and of Lincoln, he denies them any widespread and general influence on English commerce. Nothing worthy of the name of commerce, he maintains, existed in England before the eleventh century; the first general impulse to town life was given by the Norman Conquest, after which a whole crop of trading settlements and 'new boroughs' come into existence. Domesday Book is his main source for these conclusions.

---

[1] *History*, XVII. 10.   [2] *Borough and Town*, p. 8.
[3] 'It seems unlikely that the invading Danes established trading towns as a by-product of devastation and piracy.' *History*, XVII. 14.

The general scope of Mr Stephenson's theories has been adequately examined already by Professors Tait and Stenton;[1] I only propose to discuss their application to the history of Cambridge. He very rightly insists on the necessity of detailed topographical study as a means of testing his hypothesis, and gives a series of plans of English towns—York, Lincoln, Nottingham, Norwich, Bristol and Cambridge—seeking to show that, in each case, a mercantile settlement outside an older fortress produced the medieval borough. In Norwich, Nottingham and Northampton Domesday definitely speaks of a new borough: a post-Conquest, French mercantile settlement outside the old Anglo-Saxon centre. To Mr Stephenson Cambridge offers a problem that 'involves the same fundamentals'.[2]

Across the river from the modern town, he says, lie the remains of a considerable earthwork, inclosing some 28 acres. Whether it is Roman or Danish in origin does not affect his theory, which is as follows. Within this earthwork lay the ten wards of the Domesday borough. Cambridge south of the river was mainly a Norman development. The Conquest probably produced as great changes here as elsewhere; an expanding mercantile settlement absorbed an earlier village, and by the thirteenth century Cambridge centred to the south. The King's Ditch was evidently a new work constructed (in 1215) for the defence of a town that was hardly old.[3]

This theory is the same that Freeman, Babington and T. D. Atkinson supported; Maitland, who examined it closely in his *Township and Borough*, considered that 400 houses could not well be packed into so small an area—an area that contained only 70 or 80 houses in 1279, and only 209 in the eighteenth century.[4]

Mr Stephenson replies that the houses are packed as tight as this— 14 houses to the acre—in Domesday Lincoln, and nearly as tight in Domesday Norwich,[5] and that the Domesday record in saying 'There are 10 wards in the borough—*in burgo*' settles the question, for the phrase *in burgo*, or *in civitate*, as used in Domesday Book,

---

[1] *Eng. Hist. Rev.* 1933, pp. 642–8; *History*, XVIII. 256–7.
[2] *Borough and Town*, p. 200.   [3] *Ibid.* pp. 200–202.
[4] *Township and Borough*, pp. 99–100.
[5] In each case Mr Stephenson arrives at his figures by comparing the number of houses destroyed to make room for the castle with the area of the (later) castle; at Lincoln the ratio is 166 houses to 8 acres (p. 193), at Norwich 98 houses to 8 acres (p. 199). From Mr Stephenson's own figures a lower *average* might be deduced for Lincoln, but he believes that the 'lower (Roman) city in part lay vacant'. As in Cambridge, it is not clear that all his premises are warranted.

invariably means 'inside the walls'—'within a fortified area', and the only fortified area in Cambridge was the earthwork on Castle Hill. These two words *in burgo* are in fact the sole piece of positive evidence adduced by Mr Stephenson in support of his theory, just as the Lincoln figures form the sole piece of new presumptive evidence which he brings against the 'weighty opinion' of Maitland and the Master of Jesus. The real reason for his assertion that the 'weight of the evidence' is with him [1] is his conviction that the theory he is supporting is always valid unless the contrary can be proved.

Is it possible to prove a contrary? Is there evidence to show that in 1066 or 1086 'the borough of Cambridge' was located on both sides of the Cam, and that cispontine Cambridge did not come into existence as a result of the Norman Conquest? I am not sure that it can be proved; but I am prepared to maintain that 'the weight of the evidence' goes the other way; that it is on the side of Maitland and against Mr Stephenson.

The general criticism to be brought against Mr Stephenson's picture of the evolution of Cambridge is that he fails to take into account both the archaeological and the fiscal evidence for the early existence of Cambridge south of the Cam, whilst he also ignores several slight but significant indications of the economic importance of Cambridge before the Norman Conquest.

Let us then examine the evidence for the early history of Cambridge.

With regard to transpontine Cambridge, there is to-day practical unanimity amongst scholars. In the earthwork on Castle Hill we have a Roman station, to be identified with the 'little ruined city called Grantchester' which Bede describes under the year 695, when the first recorded archaeological discovery in this county was made by the monks who found under its walls the stone coffin that they needed for enshrining the bones of Etheldreda. Stukely in 1736 saw 'a vast collection of coins and antiquities dug up in the old Roman city of Granta, north of Cambridge river'.[2] In 1794, according to Bowtell, walls were still traceable to the north-west, by the Histon and Huntingdon Roads, and foundations of what he held to be the Decuman gate were found on the east side in 1810. According to Dr Fox, the finds point to occupation from Nero to Honorius;[3]

---

[1] *Borough and Town*, p. 201.
[2] *Surtees Soc. Proc.* no. 76, p. 36. See Map 1.
[3] C. F. Fox, *Archaeology of the Cambridge Region*, p. 174.

whilst excavation in the bank in Magdalene gardens by R. G. Walker in 1910[1] suggested that it was thrown up between A.D. 320 and 420.

That this area was inhabited in Anglo-Saxon times is proved by the Anglo-Saxon gravestones discovered in 1810 in the castle precincts, suggesting that an Anglo-Saxon churchyard was encroached upon for the throwing up of the Norman castle mound, which chronicle evidence places in the year 1068. The Master of Jesus has given reasons, accepted by Dr Fox, for attributing to Offa's time the building of the bridge which changed the name of the town from Grantchester to Grantebrigge.[2] The Roman Road, he believes, crossed the river at the *hard* or ford formerly traceable to the east of the present bridge, in the direct line of Hills Road, from which Bridge Street to-day diverges at the Round Church: the bridge, that is, took a new line. It was probably, then, in this existing fortification that the three Danish kings placed themselves when, as the A.S. Chronicle tells us, they 'sat in' Cambridge in 875.

Let us now cross the river and consider the antiquity of cispontine Cambridge. The first kind of evidence to be considered is the geological, meticulously studied by Professor Hughes.[3] Before men attempted to level up the low-lying areas east of the river, the ground sloped down from the gravel ridge along which the Roman Road ran, through a belt of gault to the alluvial deposits that were constantly submerged by the river in flood time. The names Peas Hill and Market Hill to-day reflect this stage of history; and examination of the soil shows that the whole area west of King's Parade, now occupied almost entirely by Colleges, is made land—built up from the rubbish dumps of the older period. Thus the few finds of the Romano-British period south-east of the river are mostly along the gravel ridge near the Union Society and the Round Church.

In the age following the Romano-British period, archaeological evidence indicates several small settlements in the area south-east of the river as well as in that north-west of it. There was a pagan cemetery south-east of Castle Hill, in ground that has now been encroached on by the Cam, and another in what is now St John's cricket field; these, Dr Fox considers, served a settlement inside the *chester*, whilst the cemetery at Newnham Croft is to be associated with a settlement near Ridley Hall. South and east of the river,

[1] *C.A.S. Proc.* XV. 178 ff. (1911).   [2] *Ibid.* XIV. 130 (1910).
[3] *Ibid.* IX. 370–84 (1897); XI. 393–423 (1906).

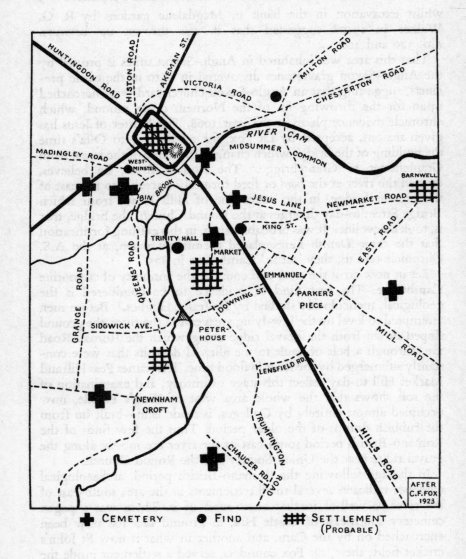

Map 1. The archaeology of pre-Norman Cambridge

interments near Jesus Lane and in Rose Crescent belong to a settlement south of the market-place, and there was another settlement out
at Barnwell.[1]

The evidence of archaeological finds, Dr Fox considers, corresponds in a striking manner with the theories worked out by the
Master of Jesus in his paper of 1908 'The Dual Origin of the Town of
Cambridge'.[2] That paper maintained that Cambridge originated
from two settlements, the southern town being separated from the
northern by the river and by a belt of uninhabited land represented
to-day by the parishes of All Saints, St Radegund, Holy Trinity and
St Andrew. Mr Gray also traced the lines of certain old watercourses
called king's ditches, existing, to a comparatively late date, on both
sides of the river, partly artificial, partly old branches of the Granta,
and argued that these represented ancient bridgeheads formerly
existing on both sides of the river to guard the crossing. When the
southern or East Anglian town was the stronger it held the bridgehead north of the river known in the twelfth century as the Armeswerk, and bounded by the watercourse called Cambridge in the
sixteenth century. The probable date of the ascendancy of the
southern town was the reign of Redwald, the East Anglian king who
was Bretwealda at the beginning of the seventh century.[3] Later,
when the Middle Anglians or Mercians triumphed, and Offa built
the bridge, a southern bridgehead may have been constructed, defined by the ditch that ran across the land of St John's Hospital to All
Saints Churchyard, ran under All Saints Passage, and joined the main
King's Ditch at Jesus Lane.[4]

If the twelfth-century writer of the *Liber Eliensis* was right in his
statement that the Armeswerk where Etheldreda's coffin was found
was already in existence in 695,[5] it would follow that the East
Anglian settlement south of the river was established and had dug its
ditches before the little waste city on the hill was reoccupied. That is
perhaps more than we are justified in inferring; but the evidence of
the artificially constructed bridgehead does undoubtedly point to a
settlement of some importance south of the river in the seventh
century, since after that date the dominant power was undoubtedly

[1] Fox, *ut supra*, pp. 246, 296; and see Map 1.
[2] *C.A.S. Quarto Publications*, 1908. See also the Master's paper, 'The Ford and
Bridge of Cambridge', *C.A.S. Proc.* XIV. 126–39 (1910).
[3] Fox, *ut supra*, pp. 276 f., 295 f.   [4] See Map 2.
[5] *Liber Eliensis*, ed. Stewart, p. 64.

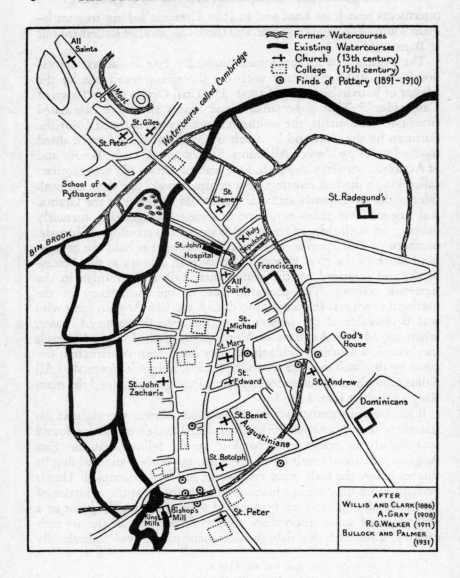

Map 2. Churches, ditches and watercourses

that of the Middle Anglian kings. It may be doubted if Mr Stephenson has fully grasped the significance of the watercourse called Cambridge—that *ripam de Caunt*' [1] up which, as Dr Palmer has shown, the barges brought stones to build the Edwardian castle in the year 1289, the stream mentioned in Magdalene deeds of the sixteenth century, indicated on Lyne's map of 1574,[2] and crossed by a bridge still remembered in 1792 as the ancient bridge called Cambridge.[3]

Even if we set aside the evidence of pagan cemeteries and of the old town ditches, still, as Maitland says, 'the tower of St Benet's church raises its protest' against the idea of an Anglo-Saxon Cambridge of purely transpontine character. It is late Anglo-Saxon work, but definitely pre-Norman, being dated about 1040 by Baldwin Brown,[4] and the community that could build a church like that was a wealthy one. If, as Mr Stephenson maintains, it was merely 'a village' that 'existed south of the river' it is for him to show us the Domesday entry that describes that village. As Maitland says, 'the houses which that church implies were a part of Grentebrige or they are not accounted for. The Survey of Cambridgeshire has no name to spare for the vanished village'.[5]

The archaeological deposits, the evidence of the watercourses and the tower of St Benet's are all ignored by Mr Stephenson. But there is evidence other than archaeological which he has overlooked.

The Ely chronicler who records so many moots held at Cambridge in the tenth century, speaks on one occasion of Irish merchants there, who had brought cloaks and other goods and set them out for sale.[6] At an earlier date, as Dr Fox shows,[7] wares from Kent and even from France had reached Cambridgeshire, and Cambridge itself; but here in the tenth century we have exactly that foreign trade the existence of which Mr Stephenson denies. The Irish merchants, as the Master of Jesus says,[8] were probably Danes from Dublin or Wexford, who came up the Cam (we must remember that Cambridge was reckoned a sea port as late as 1295) and landed their wares on one of the wharves or hithes in the quarter known for long after this date by the distinctively Danish name of the Holm, where the church of St Clement,

---

[1] *C.A.S. Proc.* XXVI. 84 (1924).
[2] Clark and Gray, *Old Plans of Cambridge*, no. 1.
[3] Willis and Clark, *Arch. Hist.* II. 356.
[4] *Arts in Saxon England*, II. 446 (1925 edit.).
[5] *Township and Borough*, p. 99.   [6] *Liber Eliensis*, p. 148.
[7] Fox, *ut supra*, pp. 245, 274, 290.   [8] *Town of Cambridge*, pp. 21–2.

a favourite Danish saint, now stands. We have thus good reason to think that the Danish occupation of Cambridge which the chroniclers report under the year 875 left other than purely military traces. The *Liber Eliensis*, again, classes Cambridge in the tenth century with Thetford, Norwich and Ipswich,[1] all of them definitely trading centres in pre-Norman days. And lastly, the evidence of coinage is, as Professor Stenton points out,[2] highly significant. What need has a self-contained agrarian settlement of money? Yet from the reign of Edward the Martyr down to the time of Edward the Confessor coins continued to be struck at the Cambridge mint bearing the legend *Grant*.[3] Pirenne's contrast between gold and silver coinage is not valid in England; silver pennies were adequate for all purposes there for centuries after the Norman Conquest. The Cambridge of the tenth century, then, knew commerce—whether that Cambridge was confined to the 'Chester' or not.

Another bit of evidence is that afforded by the records of the Cambridge churches. Maitland has shown that nearly all of those south of the river seem to be the foundation of townsmen. Whilst none of their records are older than the twelfth century, there are indications of a previous existence of some duration. The Round Church was founded in 1114–30 *on the site of a previous Church*—St George's.[4] A church owned by Ely is mentioned in the *Inquisitio Eliensis*; it seems highly probable that this is St Andrew's,[5] which was held by Ely from 1225 on. If the church held by Ely in 1086 was not St Andrew's it may possibly have been St Botolph's, which was given to Barnwell Priory by the bishop of Ely. The dedications St Botolph and St Edward strongly suggest a pre-Norman foundation, just as the dedication St Clement suggests a Danish foundation. The earliest date to which documentary evidence points, however, is that for St Peter's outside Trumpington Gate, the church that was rededicated in the fourteenth century and that is now known as Little St Mary's. In 1207[6] a jury found that the patronage of this church had formerly been in the hands of a certain Langlin who had held it as parson, and had bestowed it on a relation of his, one Segar by name, who had held it for 60 years in the same way, as

[1] *Liber Eliensis*, p. 140.   [2] *History*, XVIII. 258.
[3] Cooper, *Annals of Cambridge*, I. 14–15.
[4] *Township and Borough*, p. 174.
[5] H. P. Stokes, *Cambridge outside Barnwell Gate*, pp. 9–10.
[6] *Curia Regis Rolls*, V. 39.

parson and patron, and had given it to his son Henry who had also held it for 60 years, and ultimately bestowed it on the Hospital of St John. These transactions, pointing back to a very early stage in the law of patronage which was no longer canonical in 1207 and which was then described as 'the ancient custom of the city of Cambridge', would take back the date of foundation of St Peter's to *at least* 1087 and probably earlier, if confidence could be placed in the figures given by the jury.[1] It seems a fair inference that by the end of the eleventh century, whilst the Castle End contained the three churches of St Giles, St Peter and All Saints, the cispontine area contained, certainly, the churches of St Benet, and either St Andrew or St Botolph; probably St Clement's and St George's and St Peter's; and possibly St Edward's.[2]

Another form of evidence discussed by Maitland is that of the tithe payable to the churches of Cambridge. The open fields that lay round the town fell, he showed, into two systems. The four open fields across the river to the north and west were known as the Cambridge fields and the four south and east of it as the Barnwell fields. Roughly speaking, the tithe of the Cambridge fields went to the three churches north of the river, and to St Clement's; and the tithe of the Barnwell fields to the other nine churches. If the origin of Cambridge is dual, the dividing line seems to be rather St John's ditch[3] than the main stream of the Cam to-day: certainly not the line of Chesterton Lane under the Roman earthwork.

The evidence for the early existence of a cispontine Cambridge, then, is manifold; burial grounds, ditches, one ancient building, the lay out of the town fields, the dedication and patronage of churches. The evidence for the commercial importance of the dual town rests on the stories of chroniclers and on a series of coins minted here. It is time to reconsider the Domesday evidence.

'There are, and were', says Domesday, '10 wards in the borough.' *In burgo*, according to Mr Stephenson, means inside the earthwork on Castle Hill with its area of 28 acres—that is, the Domesday borough does not even extend to the river. It may be noted that in at least one other case his generalization that *in burgo* or *in civitate* means 'within the walls'[4] will not hold; for at Hereford Domesday says '*In civitate*—in the city of Hereford—there are 103 men dwelling

[1] Both Canon Stokes and Dr Tait are sceptical as to their trustworthiness.
[2] See Map. 2.   [3] Gray, 'Dual Origin', p. 22. See Map 2.
[4] *Borough and Town*, p. 77.

inside and outside the walls'.[1] In Cambridge there were in 1066 400 house-plots, distributed fairly evenly between the ten wards. In 1086 27 houses have been pulled down to make room for the castle, and this has led to two wards being thrown into one called in 1086 the first ward. But Mr Stephenson considers that the 35 houses described as waste in the third and fourth wards were also destroyed to make room for the castle, which he thus considers takes up the space of four 1066 wards. He identifies the *enceinte* of the Norman castle with that of the Edwardian castle, which occupied 4½ acres, shows that the ratio of 62 houses to 400 is almost identical with that of 4½ acres to 28, and considers that the theorem is proved.

That *destructe* and *waste* do not mean the same seems clear from the statement that in the first ward 27 houses were destroyed and two are waste. Mr Stephenson further asserts that Domesday tells us that the ward that has disappeared is the sixth. Atkinson did indeed draw this inference, but it is merely an inference; Domesday in fact tells us that there are *still* ten wards; therefore if two 1066 wards have been thrown into one 1086 ward there must have been a rearrangement, and the sixth ward in 1086 is probably the new one, containing houses subtracted from the old sixth and seventh wards of 1066. The point is worth making, because if Atkinson or Mr Stephenson were right the sixth ward would be near the first, and the probability of all ten being on the Castle Hill side of the river would be stronger. In fact neither the extension of the castle area into four wards, nor the identification of the missing ward with ward VI, nor the assumption that the small wooden Norman keep of 1068 had as much land attached to it as the grand Edwardian structure whose building accounts have been expounded to us by Dr Palmer, is really justified.

But the weakest part of the hypothesis that all the Domesday borough lay north of the river is its failure to account for certain other features of the survey.

Firstly, the Ely Inquest calls the second ward Bridgeward. This would fit well either the Armeswerk quarter, or the part round St Clement's; but there was no bridge inside the earthwork.

Secondly, the Ely Inquest speaks of three gardens belonging to the church of Ely. We have no reason to think that Ely had a monopoly of the garden sites, but unless she had, room has to be found for a number of garden plots as well as the 400 houses in the borough and this makes still further demands on our 28 acres.

[1] *D.B.* I. 179.

Thirdly, there are the mills of Cambridge. The Domesday entry runs 'Picot fecit ibi iij. molend. q' aufer. pasturam et plures domos destruunt. Et molendinum unum Abbatis de Ely. Et alterum Alani comitis.' In the *Inquisitio Eliensis* Picot is said to have two mills *in burgo de grantebrigge*,[1] and the natural inference is that one of the three had been destroyed before 1085 in obedience to the royal command of 1082, 'Molendinum de Grantebrigge quod Picotus fecit destruatur si alterum disturbat'.[2] Canon Stokes,[3] reading *iij* as *tercium*, believed that Picot only built one mill in addition to the two already existing belonging to the abbot of Ely and Count Alan, namely the one later called the King's Mill, which stood next to the Bishop's Mill above the millpool near Queens' College, and was only destroyed, with the Bishop's Mill, in 1927. The two mills of the *Inquisitio Eliensis* he thought were just the two that did not belong to Ely, Count Alan's also being carelessly attributed to Picot.[4] Canon Stokes argued from the difficulty of finding room for five mills on the river, owing to the slight fall of the water; but it is difficult to get over the plural verb *destruunt* in the Domesday entry, and on the whole the older view which he rejected seems the more tenable. The abbot of Ely's mill, then, can be identified with the later Bishop's Mill; Count Alan's is Newnham Mill;[5] one of Picot's two mills is the King's Mill and the other may have stood north of the river, and have given its name to the Milne Lane noted by the Master of Jesus as formerly existing in St Peter's parish.[6] For our purpose two facts are significant: firstly the statement of the *Inquisitio Eliensis* that Picot has two mills *in burgo de grantebrigge*. As windmills were not yet known in England in 1086, these must have been watermills, and as no water to turn a mill could be found within the earthwork on Castle Hill, this one statement invalidates the equation, '*In burgo* = within the *chester*'. The second fact is that if the King's Mill and the Bishop's Mill could be described in 1086 as being in the borough of Cambridge, that borough must then have extended to a point at the extreme south end of the thirteenth-century borough.[7]

There is, moreover, another form of evidence, the significance of which Maitland has developed with great care, and which, for

---

[1] *Inquisitio Comitatus Cantabrigiensis*, ed. Hamilton, p. 123.
[2] *Ibid.* p. xxii; H. W. C. Davis, *Regesta Regum Anglo-Normannorum*, no. 151.
[3] 'The Old Mills of Cambridge', *C.A.S. Proc.* xiv. 180–233.
[4] *Ibid.* p. 182.   [5] *Ibid.*
[6] Gray, 'Dual Origin', p. 13.   [7] See Map 2.

Professor Tait, is quite conclusive. This is the evidence of the burgage rents. These customary dues, payable to the king in 1086, became payable to the town after the borough had bought from John the *firma burgi*, that is the right to deal direct with the exchequer, and they are still paid to the borough to-day,[1] by the name of hagable—in medieval form hawgafol or hawgavel. Working backwards, we find that in the reign of Richard III there is a rent roll of hawgavel amounting to £7. 10s. 5¾d.;[2] and that the amounts payable in 1279 add up to between £7 and £8. Many items are unchanged; in 1483 the scholars of Merton pay 4s. 10d. and in 1279 they pay 4s. 10d.; but in 1279 the payment is 'for hawgavel and landgavel'.[3] Domesday Book tells us that the *landgablum* due from the borough amounts to £7. 3s. 6d.[4] The permanence of the amount from 1086 to 1483 does appear to indicate that the *landgablum* of Domesday Book is the same as the *hawgavel* of 1483, and includes rents chargeable on land in the open fields, as well as rents chargeable on the haws or house-plots.

This is an assumption, strengthened by the continuity traced by Maitland of individual items in the hawgavel roll. If we accept it, certain other consequences follow.

The marvellous survey of 1279, recorded in the Hundred Rolls of that year, contains statements of the holdings of every burgess in Cambridge, with the dues incumbent on them. Maitland has analysed the survey in the appendix to *Township and Borough*. It indicates the holdings from which the rents were due. According to medieval practice, the customary dues were a charge on specific lands, and reassessment was not thought of. Of course the hawgavel rents made up only a small fraction of the town revenues: the farm payable at the exchequer was £60, and the rents, as we have seen, come to just over £7. If the assessment really goes back to Domesday, then we can fairly assume that there was in 1086 a house paying hawgavel and landgavel on the spot where the house was standing which paid it in 1279. That is to say, that from the distribution of the holdings paying hawgavel we can tell where there were houses standing in 1086.

In 1279 hawgavel is paid from houses all over the town. In the transpontine parishes there are 73 houses, from 22 of which hawgavel

---

[1] W. M. Palmer, *Cambridge Borough Documents*, p. 75.
[2] *Ibid.* p. 65; Cooper, *Annals of Cambridge*, 1. 227, gives the total as £7. 1s. 3¼d.
[3] Maitland, *Township and Borough*, p. 180.
[4] If the *ore* were reckoned at 16d. instead of 20d., the sum would be £7. 2s. 10d.

is due, totalling 2s. 3½d. In the parishes of St Benet, St Mary the Great, St Edward and St Botolph—the region round the market—there are 159 houses and 69 shops, paying hawgavel to the amount of 12s. 10d. from 63 holdings. The localization of the payment of hawgavel, that is, fits in exactly with the other indications of an early nucleus of population near St Benet's and the market-place; and if the proportions are any indication, it was a wealthier and denser settlement in 1086 than the settlement on Castle Hill, with three times as many chargeable holdings and five times as much money payable. The same reasoning confirms the belief in an early settlement just south of the Bridge; St Clement's parish contains 15 holdings paying altogether 1s. 5½d.; whilst the gap between the two towns described by the Master of Jesus and by Maitland is revealed by the fact that only 3 holdings pay hawgavel amounting to 3½d. in the parishes of St Sepulchre and All Saints. That the growth of Cambridge beyond the ditch is a recent development in 1279 is indicated by the fact that St Radegund's, Barnwell, St Andrew's outside Barnwell Gate and St Peter's outside Trumpington Gate, though they contain 159 houses, only have 9 holdings paying hawgavel, which amounts only to 1s. 3½d.

The evidence of the burgage rents then, if it can be accepted, points the same way as the other evidence. A southern settlement, more wealthy and more populous in 1086 than that north of the river, seems to be indicated.[1] The continuity of terminology and amount, the distribution of incidence and the correspondence with other indications do seem to constitute a body of evidence which ought to be taken into account in weighing the pros and cons of Mr Stephenson's theory.

Lastly, there is the question of the King's Ditch. Mr Stephenson says of it: 'The King's Ditch, in spite of all argument, was evidently a new work in the thirteenth century, constructed for the defence of a town that was hardly old.' The course of the King's Ditch in the sixteenth century is clearly indicated in the maps of Lyne and of Braunius,[2]

[1] Dr Tait, to whose kind criticism I am much indebted, considers that Cambridge, as described in Domesday, belongs tenurially rather to the East Anglian type of borough, like Ipswich or Norwich, than the the Midland type like Northampton or Leicester. He points out that the *Liber Eliensis* (p. 140) describes Cambridge as enjoying like liberty and dignity with Norwich, Ipswich and Thetford. If transpontine Cambridge was Mercian, this is an additional argument for the preponderance of the southern town before 1086.

[2] Clark and Gray, *Old Plans of Cambridge*, nos. 1 and 2. See Map 2.

and can be verified from many other sources; it is its antiquity that is in question.

Now we have unshakeable evidence as to the digging of ditches and the building of gates in the year 1267. The Barnwell chronicler tells us that in 1267, when the last adherents of the barons were holding out in Ely, 'The king came to Cambridge with a great army and there lodged...he caused gates to be made and ditches dug all round the town, so diligently that the workmen were not allowed to rest even on saints' days'.[1] The chroniclers' account is confirmed by a contemporary entry on the Liberate Roll providing for the compensation of those whose houses were pulled down to make room for the ditch and for the eight-foot wide walk that ran alongside it,[2] as well as by the reports of the Hundred Rolls Inquest 12 years later as to the digging of the ditch and the later encroachments on the walk beside it.[3]

On the other hand there is equally unequivocal evidence of the existence of both ditch and gates before that date. In 1268 the king orders 'the great town ditch' to be cleared out, so that the water can flow freely;[4] this can hardly be a ditch not yet a year old. In 1250 Henry III granted to the nuns of St Radegund land lying between their church and 'the ditch of Cambridge',[5] and a deed at Jesus College, witnessed by Hervey Fitz Eustace who died before 1240, mentions the King's Ditch, by that name.[6] Again, St Peter's is described as 'St Peter outside Trumpington Gate' long before 1267;[7] St Botolph's goes back to the twelfth century, and St Botolph was the stock dedication for churches near a gate;[8] and there are townsmen bearing the surname *ad portam* as early as 1211.[9] The Close Roll for 1215 refers to the expenses incurred for enclosing the town of Cambridge,[10] and this is taken by J. W. Clark, by Hughes and by Atkinson as the first beginnings of the Ditch.[11] The evidence in fact points in two directions. The fact that the King's Ditch cuts in two

---

[1] *Liber Memorandorum de Bernewelle*, ed. Clark, p. 122.
[2] Liberate Roll, 52 Hen. III, m. 6. See Cooper, *Annals of Cambridge*, I. 51. The entry, which is undated, appears to belong to the end of April 1268.
[3] *Rot. Hund.* II. 392.   [4] *P.R.C.* p. 196 (20 Feb. 1268).
[5] A. Gray, *Priory of St Radegund*, p. 78.   [6] *Ibid.* p. 93.
[7] Clark and Gray, *Old Plans of Cambridge*, p. xxiii.
[8] H. P. Stokes, *Cambridge outside Trumpington Gates*, p. 2.
[9] Maitland, *Township and Borough*, p. 169.
[10] *Rot. Lit. Claus.* p. 234.
[11] *Liber Memorandorum de Bernewelle*, p. xxviii.

the land of the Franciscans (given them in 1228),[1] the parishes of St Botolph and St Benet,[2] points to a late date, yet other references, as we have seen, suggest the existence of the ditch in the twelfth century. Professor Hughes believed in an earlier ditch on an inner line, and thought that the traces of a channel with fresh-water shells in it discovered near Hunnybun's premises in 1891[3] indicated the line of this ditch near Barnwell Gate, just as the remains found in Mill Lane and Silver Street in 1893 indicated a double line of ditch there.[4] Canon Stokes disputed the Hunnybun evidence, identifying the channel found in 1891 with a running watercourse mentioned in 1633.[5] No one seems to have attempted to trace the history of the watercourse that ran through the second court of Christ's College, before the Fellows' Building was erected,[6] but this watercourse might also represent the line of an earlier channel which if continued to meet the Jesus brook would run outside the Franciscan lands. It is clear that the line drawn in 1267 was drawn for strategic reasons, across an area partly built over. It is not clear that the whole course of the ditch from the Mill Pool to Jesus Green was new. Indeed it seems highly probable that parts of it were far older.

In excavations in Hobson Street, Mill Lane and Silver Street in 1892 and 1893 large quantities of potsherds were found in the bottom of two ancient ditches. Professor Hughes considered that the fragments represented a transition from Roman to medieval pottery, and that they might belong to any date between A.D. 800 and 1300.[7] Miss O'Reilly, to whose assistance I am deeply indebted, tells me that the dating of medieval pottery is as yet largely a matter of conjecture, but points out that Dr Fox, in a paper read to the Prehistoric Society of East Anglia in 1924, definitely attributes the pottery found in Mill Lane to the Anglo-Saxon period.[8] If he is right there is no doubt that the first town ditch is older than the Norman Conquest. This is the last piece of evidence to be here considered. Like so much of the evidence it is equivocal. If we could be certain

---

[1] But it also cuts in two the lands of the Augustinians, given them in 1290. See Map 2.

[2] H. P. Stokes, *Cambridge outside Trumpington Gates*, p. 1.

[3] *C.A.S. Proc.* VIII. 40–3 (1892).

[4] *Ibid.* VIII. 255 ff. (1893); see also IX. 370–84 (1897).

[5] H. P. Stokes, *Outside Barnwell Gate*, p. 3.

[6] Willis and Clark, *Arch. Hist.* II. 189–90.

[7] *C.A.S. Proc.* VIII. 43–6 (1892); 255–83 (1893) (with illustrations of pottery).

[8] *Proc. of Prehistoric Society of East Anglia*, IV. 227–30.

of the Anglo-Saxon date of the pottery which has been found in the market-place, in St Andrew's Street, at Christ's College, in Hunnybun's ditch, and under the foundations of the Archaeological Museum in Tennis Court Road,[1] we should have evidence of widely distributed Anglo-Saxon settlement in the southern town to match that in the northern town, and evidence that the southern settlement was already protected by ditches as the northern was by an earthwork. As it is, we can merely say that the opinion of so good an expert as Dr Fox is on the side of an early date for this part of the ditch, and that it appears to agree with other evidence.

It may be worth while, in conclusion, to indicate the directions in which further investigation might possibly extend our knowledge of the early history of Cambridge.

(1) Investigation of the date at which the castle was taken out of the borough, and attributed to Chesterton parish. The shift of importance to the cispontine quarter must have been greatly accelerated by this, but when did it take place?

(2) A search for some more exact evidence as to the dates of the foundation of the churches in cispontine Cambridge.

(3) A reinvestigation of evidence bearing on the old town ditches and, above all,

(4) A closer dating of the pottery found in them.[2]

I fear that only along the last line is there much hope of new knowledge. The field has been too well harvested by the great Cambridge antiquarians in the past for there to be much left for any gleaner to gather. But in spite of the ambiguity of so much of the evidence that has been adduced, I think the cumulative effect does entitle us to deny that Mr Stephenson has the weight of evidence on his side. The evidence of the burgage rents, of the churches, of the mills, of the ancient watercourses, of the burial grounds, of the pottery, all together tips up the scale against him; we may still admit the protest of St Benet's tower and continue to believe in the dual origin of the town of Cambridge.

[2] [Since 1944 new finds of pottery have been made in Cambridge and old finds re-examined. See articles by J. E. Hurst in *C.A.S. Proc.*, Vols. XLIX, L and LI. Whilst precise dating is impossible, there is a strong presumption that some of the sherds found in the King's Ditch are of pre-Conquest date.]

II

The Early Burgesses of Cambridge in relation to the surrounding country-side [1]

The borough of Cambridge lies in the centre of what is, even to-day, a purely agricultural district. In the county south of the Ouse, which still forms a parliamentary constituency and a local government unit distinct from the Isle of Ely, that ancient liberty whose boundaries go back to the tenth century, there are 120 villages and no other town than Cambridge itself. On Saturdays, when the narrow streets are choked with the carts of the market-gardeners, the country buses bringing the housewives in for their weekly shopping, and the motor-cars of the farmers of the country-side coming in to do business with each other, the university is temporarily lost in the market town. Moreover, as in the tenth century, when the rural hundreds were first grouped around the borough to form the shire of Cambridge, it forms the administrative as well as the economic centre of the county; to the Town Hall in the market-place correspond the Shire Hall and the Assize Court on the Castle Hill, on the site where the 'placita hundretanorum et civium' were held in the days of King Edgar [2] and where the county courts met right down to the eighteenth century. And as in the eighteenth century, when the noblemen and squires of the county met in Cambridge and settled the affairs of the town and the country-side at quarter sessions and at political dinners at 'The Rose Tavern', 'The Black Bull' or 'The White Bear', so in the eleventh century the thegns of Cambridge had their gild in the town, with provision for religious observances for keeping the peace, for feasting and for funerals.[3] It is not surprising, therefore, that there should be a close relation between the burgesses of Cambridge and the surrounding country-side; that we should find country dwellers acquiring land in the borough and burgesses acquiring property in the county. It is to material bearing on this relationship that I desire to call attention.

[1] Reprinted from *Wirtschaft und Kultur; Festschrift zum 70.Geburtstag von Alfons Dopsch*, Vienna, 1938.   [2] Maitland, *Township and Borough*, p. 212.
[3] Cooper, *Annals of Cambridge*, I. 15. Liebermann held that these thegns were in fact burgesses. *Gesetze der Angelsachsen*, I. 358; II. ii, 501.

The evidence of Domesday Book is slight. Of those who held land in the borough in 1086 only those privileged persons are mentioned whose subtenants were exempt from paying geld. Count Alan of Brittany was a great tenant in chief holding many manors up and down the county. More interesting are the three tenants of the earl of Mortain who succeeded to Judichel the huntsman, who under Edward the Confessor had held land not only in the borough but also in Barton and Grantchester.[1] Erchanger the baker was less eminent; he held land at Hardwick, Toft and Comberton[2] and was almost certainly the ancestor of that Robert of Hardwick who held by the serjeanty of supplying a hot loaf every day for the King's dinner, and sold his land at Comberton to the prior of Barnwell before 1249.[3] Ralf de Bans, the lord of three burgesses, was the Ralf de Bancis or de Scamnis who also held land at Barrington, Orwell, Kingston and Pampisford, where his descendants were still holding in 1230.[4]

In the twelfth and, above all, in the thirteenth century the material becomes fuller. At Cambridge, as at Oxford, the fact that the colleges become the heirs both of the burgesses and of the religious houses has led to the preservation of a marvellously rich collection of deeds registering the transfer of small holdings of land. In addition to the cartularies and original deeds preserved at Peterhouse, Pembroke, Corpus Christi, Trinity, St John's and Jesus Colleges, Cambridge, there is an important series of deeds at Merton College, Oxford, whose founder Walter de Merton acquired property in Cambridge in the reign of Henry III, 'for reasons', says Maitland, 'that I dare not guess'.[5]

For Cambridge, again, as for Oxford, the survey of 1279 is extant, with its minute details of the burgesses' holdings.[6] To these can be added the *Liber Memorandorum de Bernewelle*[7] with its list of the tenants of the Priory in Cambridge and the county, and the *Pedes finium* of the county of Cambridge, preserved at the Public Record Office, which go back to the reign of Richard I.[8]

This wealth of material still awaits adequate exploitation, and the notes which follow are based on a very cursory examination.

[1] *D.B.* I. 193.   [2] *Ibid.* I. 202; *Inquisitio Eliensis*, p. 192.
[3] *Liber Memorandorum de Bernewelle*, pp. 93–4.
[4] *Ibid.* pp. 245, 255; *Pedes finium*, 29 Hen. III.
[5] *Township and Borough*, p. 6.   [6] *Rot. Hund.* II. 356–401.
[7] Edited by J. W. Clark, Cambridge, 1907.
[8] The Cambridgeshire *Pedes finium* have been calendared by W. Rye, Cambridge, 1891.

It may be as well, at this point, to indicate briefly the main stages of municipal progress in Cambridge. The first royal grant, recognizing the jurisdiction of the town court and giving the borough the monopoly of waterborne trade in the county, belongs to the period 1120–31. Henry II made a temporary grant of the *firma burgi* to the burgesses in 1185–86. John recognized the gild merchant, with various trading privileges, in 1201, and made the grant of the *firma burgi* permanent in 1207, granting also to the burgesses the right to choose their own reeve. The first official document directed to a mayor of Cambridge is dated 1231, and the grant of return of writs in 1256 gave the borough administrative self-government and freed it finally from the intervention of the county officials.[1]

As to the tenurial relations between town and county in the thirteenth century, if we leave on one side those non-resident landlords who, as the Hundred Rolls show, are receiving rent from their burgess tenants, the 'Pyrots, Argentans, Troubelvilles, Colvilles and Cockfields',[2] two types of landholders may be distinguished, the burgess who acquires land in the county, and the country dweller who acquires houses or lands in the borough.

The cartulary of St John's Hospital, now at St John's College, supplies the names of a number of Cambridge burgesses, largely benefactors to the Hospital, who in the first half of the thirteenth century were holding land elsewhere than in the fields of Cambridge itself, that 'rural commonwealth' eloquently described by Maitland.[3] In the neighbouring hamlet of Newnham lands were held by William Seman, of a family that produced one of the first mayors of Cambridge. At Chesterton, in the opposite direction, lands were held by Thomas Tuillet, William fitz Geoffrey and Richard Crocheman, the last 'prepositus' of Cambridge before 1232, whose son William also held land at Trumpington, and his nephew lands at Histon and Impington.[4] In the fourteenth century the family became lords of a manor at Trumpington called after them 'Crouchmans'. John le Rus, of whom more will be said later, and Martin Brihtnoth, important burgesses in the southern extremity of the borough, held land at Grantchester, as did Thomas Tuillet, Nicholas Childman, John Wombe, William the Goldsmith, Peter le Rus and Thomas Wulward in 1246, as tenants, along with a number of villagers, of

[1] F. W. Maitland and M. Bateson, *The Charters of the Borough of Cambridge* (Cambridge, 1901).   [2] Maitland, *Township and Borough*, p. 177.
[3] *Ibid.* pp. 4–5.   [4] Jesus College deeds.

Simon de Montfort.[1] Baldwin Blancgernoun, of a leading family at the northern or Castle end of the borough, held land at Coton two and a half miles out, in 1235, and Simon le Pescur and Reginald Sherewynd, bailiff in 1260,[2] held land at Barton, three miles out. Farther afield were the holdings of Robert son of Hugh the merchant at Toft, of Richard the merchant at Comberton, and of Hamo the merchant at Teversham; whilst Guy le Spicer, bailiff in 1294 and mayor in 1299, held land at Hungry Hatley in 1298. Altogether six mayors of Cambridge and many more bailiffs can be shown to have held land in the county before 1307.[3]

We have now to consider those burgesses holding land in the borough who have come into the town from the surrounding country. The chief evidence is their names; if a burgess is called Reginald of Cottenham or Andrew of Wimpole it seems fair to argue that either he or his ancestors come from the village in question. The immigrant may be a younger son who has severed his connection with his native village, but even so the wide field from which the population of the borough was being recruited, has its interest. Within three or four miles of Cambridge there are Trumpington, Newnham, Barton, Madingley, Impington, Teversham; between four and ten miles Hauxton, Wimpole, Toft, Bourn, Childerley, Lolworth, Swavesey, Cottenham, Swaffham, Wilbraham, Fulbourne, Abington, Shelford; more than ten miles away Fordham and Isleham to the east, Ickleton to the south and Gamlingay and Eltisley to the west of the county.[4]

In a few cases we know a little more of the newcomers to the borough than their mere names. John Butt, who was mayor of Cambridge for twelve of the years between 1277 and 1296, was only holding two acres of land in Cambridge in 1279,[5] but he had 20 acres at Swaffham, where his widow made a fine of land in 1298. The Cayleys, who were at Trumpington in 1086, had several members of their family in the town by 1279,[6] and Philip Cayley was mayor three times and parliamentary burgess twice under Edward III. Better known and of higher standing were the two families of le Rus or Ruffus and Dunning.

John le Rus,[7] who was mayor c. 1260–70, was the great-grandson

---

[1] *Pedes finium.*   [2] Ass. R. 82, m. 31.   [3] See subjoined Table I.
[4] See subjoined Table II.   [5] *Rot. Hund.* II. 367, 494.   [6] *Ibid.* II. 357, 376, 378.
[7] A full account of the Le Rus family is given by H. P. Stokes, *Cambridge outside the Trumpington Gates* (Cambridge, 1908), pp. 35–43.

of Eustace of Madingley, and the grandson of Alberic Ruffus who was settled in the borough by 1177, when he contributed to an amercement imposed upon the borough;[1] he was a benefactor to St John's Hospital. Maurice le Rus, the mayor's father, who also held lands in Oakington, had a large stone house with a chapel dedicated to St Lucy in Trumpington Street, just south of the present site of Peterhouse. John himself, who had inherited his property encumbered with debts to the Jews, was forced to let his house and live in a 'parvum messuagium', and his nephew and heir, Hugh le Rus from Oakington, had to sell most of the town property that remained.

Most notable of all the landed burgess families of Cambridge, how-ever, are the Dunnings.[2] It does not seem possible to determine whether Cambridge or Gamlingay, on the borders of Huntingdon-shire, was their first home. The Dunninc who held land at Southoe in Huntingdonshire before the Norman Conquest had lost it by 1086, and, if, as Mr Gray thinks, the Dunning family was occupying before 1066 the Anglo-Saxon *Sael* that gave its name to Sale piece on Castle Hill,[3] we have no positive proof of their presence in Cambridge before about 1150, when Dunning the father of Eustace gave 50 acres in the fields of Cambridge to Barnwell Priory. Dunning's son Gilbert held a hide of land at Gamlingay, and Eustace, the other son, lived in the stone manor house at Cambridge which still stands below the Castle Hill on the land belonging to Merton College and is known by the misleading name of 'The School of Pythagoras'. Hervey, the son of Eustace Dunning, was alderman of the gild merchant and probably the first mayor of Cambridge;[4] he held land at Babraham, Girton, Cheveley, Chesterton and Madingley as well as his uncle's land at Gamlingay.[5]

This wealthy burgess claimed knightly rank. His seal bore a mounted warrior, and he twice demanded wager of battle in a plea of land in the county court. It should be noted that the 'lagemanni' of Cambridge, as described in Domesday Book, paid a heriot which included a palfrey and a knight's armour, thus ranking as thegns.[6]

[1] Maitland, *Township and Borough*, p. 171.
[2] The following account is based upon that in J. M. Gray, *The School of Pytha-goras* (Cambridge, 1932).
[3] Dr Reaney does not consider this derivation tenable, however.
[4] St John's Cartulary and Jesus College deeds (undated).
[5] See subjoined Table I.
[6] See J. Tait, *The Medieval English Borough* (Manchester, 1936), p. 43.

If the Dunnings were in Cambridge before 1066 they may well have been members of the Cambridgeshire gild of Thegns.

Hervey fitz Eustace died at some date between 1232 and 1240, and his son Eustace fitz Hervey became involved in several rather dubious transactions, and was driven, like John le Rus, first to borrowing and then to leasing, mortgaging and selling his land. Mr Gray has traced the stages by which most of the lands and the capital messuage of the Dunnings came into the hands of Merton College, so that in 1279 their manor house figures in the Hundred Rolls as 'the stone house of the Scholars of Merton'. Hervey's grandson Richard, who had actually surrendered the house in 1271, retired to his Gamlingay estate, which was ultimately divided between his two daughters.

Hervey's second and third sons remained in the borough, and the family supplied several bailiffs, two more mayors, an alderman of St Mary's gild and a member of parliament to the borough, as well as an active ally of the 'disinherited' barons in 1266 and the ringleader of an attack upon the scholars of the university in 1322. In 1338 John Dunning sold his last holding in Cambridge and the connection of the family with the borough was severed.[1]

The curious parallelism between the histories of the Le Rus and Dunning families provokes the question whether the experiment of blending the career of burgess and squire was economically unsound. It is possible that closer researches may produce further examples of the decline and fall of a borough magnate, but the normal contacts of town and county in the thirteenth century are less spectacular, and Maitland's formula appears adequately to summarize most of the instances here collected: 'Younger sons "go into business", and thriving burgesses buy land in the neighbouring villages.'[2]

---

[1] It is possible, but has not been proved, that the eighteenth-century founder of Downing College who gave his name to Downing Street in Cambridge was a member of the same family. [2] *Township and Borough*, p. 177.

Table I. *Cambridge burgesses holding, acquiring or transferring land in county*

(*=Mayor of Cambridge, †=Bailiff of Cambridge)

Date	Name of Burgess	Name of Village	Miles from Cambridge	Source
1196	*Hervey son of Eustace (Dunning)	Newnham	1 S.W.	*Pedes finium*
1196	,,	Girton	3 N.W.	,,
1199	,,	Gamlingay	14 S.W.	,,
1200	,,	Chesterton	1½ N.E.	,,
1203	,,	Cheveley	15 E.	,,
1232	,,	Madingley	3 W.	,,
1235	Baldwin Blancgernoun	Coton	2½ W.	,,
Early 13th century	†William Seman	Newnham		St John's Cartulary
,,	*John le Rus	Grantchester		,,
,,	Martin Brihtnoth	,,		,,
,,	Robert son of Hugh the Merchant	Toft	5 W.	,,
,,	Richard the Merchant	Comberton	4½ S.W.	,,
,,	Hamo the Merchant	Teversham	3½ E.	,,
,,	Thomas Tuillet	Chesterton	1½ N.E.	,,
,,	William son of Geoffrey	,,		,,
,,	*Richard Crocheman	,,		,,
,,	Robert son of Laurence	Babraham	6 S.E.	,,
1246	Thomas Tuillet	Grantchester		*Pedes finium*
1246	Nicholas Childman	,,		,,
1246	John Wombe	,,		,,
1246	William the Goldsmith	,,		,,
1246	Peter le Rus	,,		,,
1246	Thomas Wulward	,,		,,
1258	†Reginald Sherewynd	Barton	3 S.W.	,,
1260	Simon le pescur	,,		,,
1279	William Crocheman	Trumpington	2½ S.	,,
1286	Godfrey the Merchant	,,		,,
1288	†John Porthors	Chesterton		,,
c. 1290	*†John Goldring	Newnham		,,
1295	*†John Butt	Trumpington		,,
1297	†Richard Crocheman	Impington	3 N.	,,
1297	,,	Histon	3½ N.	,,
1298	Cecilia, widow of John Butt	Swaffham	8 N.E.	,,
1298	*†Guy le Spicer	Hatley	12 S.W.	,,

Table II *Men from the country who held land or houses in Cambridge*

(★=Mayor of Cambridge, †=Bailiff of Cambridge)

Date	Name of Burgess	Name of Village	Miles from Cambridge	Source
c. 1150?	Dunning	Gamlingay	14 S.W.	*Rot. Hund.* II. 356, 360
c. 1177	Alberic le Rus	Madingley	3 W.	St John's Cartulary
1177	William of Swavesey	Swavesey	8 N.W.	Pipe Roll
1209	Reginald of Fordham	Fordham	14 N.E.	*Pedes finium*
1211	Reginald of Abington	Abington	8½ S.E.	Pipe Roll
1239	Stephen of Hauxton	Hauxton	5 S.	*Pedes finium*
1241	John of Barton	Barton	3 S.W.	St John's Cartulary
Early 13th century	†Peter of Wilbraham	Wilbraham	6 E.	Jesus College deeds
,,	John Baldwin	Cottenham	6½ N.	,,
,,	Andrew of Wimpole	Wimpole	9 S.W.	,,
,,	Robert of Fulbourne	Fulbourne	5½ S.E.	,,
,,	Geremias of Eltisley	Eltisley	11 W.	,,
,,	Gilbert of Childerley	Childerley	7 N.W.	,,
,,	Alexander of Isleham	Isleham	17 N.E.	,,
1253	Alan of Ickleton	Ickleton	10 S.	*Pedes finium*
1266–67	Stephen of Shelford	Shelford	4½ S.E.	Assize Roll 83
1269	Walter of Wilbraham	Wilbraham		*Pedes finium*
1269	Hugh of Bourne	Bourn	8 W.	Assize Roll 83
c. 1272	†Reginald of Comberton	Comberton	4½ S.W.	Corpus Christi College deeds
1273	John le Moyne	Shelford		Merton College deeds
c. 1274	Hugh le Rus	Oakington	5 N.W.	Peterhouse deed
1279	Thomas of Impington	Impington	3 N.	*Rot. Hund.* II
1279	Warin of Teversham	Teversham	3½ E.	,,
1279	Thomas of Cottenham	Cottenham		,,
1279	John of Westwick	Westwick	5 N.	,,
1279	Simon of Trumpington	Trumpington	2½ S.	,,
1279	John Cayli	,,		,,
1282	†Robert of Madingley	Madingley		Corpus Christi College deeds
1289	†John of Camps	Camps	15 S.E.	College deeds
1292	Reginald of Lolworth	Lolworth	6 N.W.	*Pedes finium*
1295	†Richard of Bottisham	Bottisham	6 N.E.	,,
c. 1300	★Simon of Stocton	Hauxton	5 S.	Corpus Christi College deeds

III

Cambridgeshire Sheriffs in the Thirteenth Century[1]

In a recent article in the *English Historical Review* Dr Round asks, almost desperately, 'How can we combine the learning of the historical specialist with the indispensable knowledge of the local antiquary?'[2] One might almost retort with the inquiry, 'How do you do it yourself?' for his own articles in the *Victoria County History* are outstanding examples of such a fruitful combination, and he himself admits that Cambridge furnishes the conspicuous exception of Maitland; but broadly speaking, there is no doubt that his lamentation is justified. There is an enormous field for co-operative effort along some such lines as those of the Place-Name Survey. In economic history, as in archaeology, the value of studies of local conditions, not only for their own sake but as leading to a general survey, is well established, but in administrative history the thing is far less common. The historian is content with a dry and stale generalization, repeated, it may be, at third or fourth hand from some sixteenth- or seventeenth-century writer like Coke or Madox; the antiquarian is too much concerned with the personal, the episodic, the exceptional to dwell on the normal routine of the system. Studies like Mr Lapsley's recent paper on the parliamentary representation of Cambridgeshire and four neighbouring counties under Edward II,[3] which may have little or no anecdotal interest, must be accumulated laboriously before we are in a position scientifically to reconstruct the actual method of medieval administration.

It is worth while, then, to indicate the relation of our subject—Cambridgeshire Sheriffs in the thirteenth century—to general constitutional and administrative history. The position of the sheriff in the evolution of our constitution is like that of some essential cog or pin in a great machine. Take him out and the whole thing falls to pieces. The task of the Normans, Angevins and Plantagenets—that of making one England, with one law, out of the congeries of provinces which Harold left, was only made possible by their

[1] Read to the Cambridge Antiquarian Society on 12 February 1923. Reprinted from their *Communications*, vol. xxv (1924).

[2] *Eng. Hist. Rev.* 1921, p. 211.

[3] *Ibid.* 1919, pp. 25, 152.

adaptation and transformation of the Anglo-Saxon official called the sheriff whom the Conqueror found in England when he arrived. That official—in origin a royal steward, in theory the subordinate or substitute of the earl, in practice a magnate well on the way to becoming hereditary and therefore independent—had become by the thirteenth century an individual who might almost be called the king's maid-of-all-work in the shire; not merely a connecting link between the central and local systems, but the pivot upon which all governmental activities turned. The general constitutional historians, more concerned in this period with the source of power than with the channels through which it flowed, lay their chief emphasis upon the diminution of the sheriff's political power. We are told that he had passed the zenith of his powers before the reign of John; that coroners, escheators, keepers of the peace were encroaching on his sphere of activity and that his vested interest in his office was a thing of the past, except in some few outlying counties. All this is true, but it is only half the truth. Those very reforms which had bit by bit brought the sheriff into strict subordination to the crown had added to his local importance the weight of the royal authority. Instead of the tyranny of an irresponsible magnate the men of the county were up against the active arm of a great and growing organism—the whole system of royal administration and justice. In the hundred and fifty years between the Conquest and the accession of Henry III the scope of royal activity had widened immeasurably, and every extension of the central government's field of action automatically increased the work of the sheriff. If his powers were less, his activities were more in the thirteenth than in the eleventh or twelfth century.

From the administrative point of view, the thirteenth century is the sheriff's golden age. I called him the king's maid-of-all-work in the shire. I am not going to attempt to describe his duties systematically, but a few instances, taken at random, of the jobs that fell to the lot of the sheriff of Cambridgeshire, will illustrate their immense variety. There is enough of the steward about him still for him to be expected to furnish supplies on occasion for the royal table. In 1257 William of Stow is ordered to supply luces, eels, one crane, four peacocks and four swans for the feasts of St Edward and of Christmas, and may write off £15. 15s. 10d. of his account at the exchequer by way of compensation.[1] When it comes to the Scottish campaigns of Edward I orders are sent, year after year from 1298 to 1303, for corn

---

[1] Memoranda Rolls (L.T.R. series), 32, m. 19.

for the army—for instance, in 1300, 1000 quarters of wheat, 1000 of oats, and 500 of malt—the wheat to be ground into flour, well bolted, placed in new clean strong barrels, well salted so that it may keep a year or two at need, and three hazel rods placed in the top of each barrel, and so to be sent to Berwick upon Tweed to be there by a given day.[1] Again, the sheriff acts as the king's almoner. In 1244 Ralph de Bereford is told that Richard Irontooth, the king's pensioner, being dead, he is to pay his twopence a day henceforth to William Coynturel.[2] In 1285 Thomas of Belhus is instructed to send 10 live bucks and 20 live does to stock the park of Roger Lestrange.[3] He is generally responsible for the condition of roads and bridges, ways and watercourses. It is his duty to set up clear landmarks to show the boundaries of Huntingdonshire and Cambridgeshire as defined by the special commission of 1284–86.[4] In the eyre of 1272 the jurors report that the whole community of Cambridge has been digging gravel in the king's highway near Trumpington ford, so that those who could come and go on their way to and from Cambridge cannot pass, to the damage of the whole county. The offenders are fined, and the sheriff has to repair the road at their charges.[5] Out along the Huntingdon Road, at the town's end, men and women have been encroaching on the road, probably with stalls and booths, for one is a fish wife, so that carts cannot get by; the sheriff must put this right.[6] In Fulbourne, in Fleamdyke hundred, a watercourse which drained the town is blocked up, and the resulting floods prevent horses and carts from passing; also a wall has been built that takes off a large part of the road. The sheriff is to reopen the ditch and pull down the wall—at the expense of the offenders.[7] He is, of course, responsible for the upkeep of the castle, where extensive works are going on in the reign of Edward I.[8] It is possible that these works and repairs account for the fact that for eleven years of Edward's reign the sheriff of Cambridgeshire pays in nothing to the exchequer.[9] They may also explain why the prisoners taken at Dunbar in 1296 and distributed all over the counties of England, are in Cambridge-

---

[1] *Patent Roll Calendar* (henceforth cited as *P.R.C.*), p. 487.
[2] *Close Roll Calendar* (henceforth cited as *C.R.C.*), p. 204.
[3] *Ibid.* p. 309.   [4] See *P.R.C.* pp. 140, 201; *C.R.C.* pp. 415, 416.
[5] Ass. R. 85, m. 12.   [6] *Ibid.* m. 14.   [7] *Ibid.* m. 7.
[8] See *Ecclesie de Bernewelle Liber Memorandorum*, p. 167, n. 2, and W. M. Palmer, 'Cambridge Castle Building Accounts', in *C.A.S. Proceedings* for 1925.
[9] I owe this information to Miss Mabel H. Mills; cf. *Eng. Hist. Rev.* 1923, pp. 337, 351.

shire confined in the bishop of Ely's castle at Wisbech instead of Cambridge Castle. The sheriff is ordered to meet them, escort them to Wisbech, and pay 3*d*. a day for each of them and their keepers while they are there.[1] This is an emergency duty, as is the order to remove all alien clerics from the waterside and dismantle their boats in September 1295, lest they should leave the kingdom.[2] The warden of Chesterton church, a Lombard by birth, is exempted from this regulation, which is of course connected with the French war.[3] Again in 1297 the sheriff has to take steps for enforcing the king's measures against the clergy who, in obedience to the bull *Clericis laicos*, refuse to pay taxes.[4] He has military and naval duties: in April 1297 he is to send all ships arriving in his shire to be at Winchelsea by Midsummer;[5] and in 1300 he is instructed to persuade all men of a certain income to arm themselves and be at Carlisle by Midsummer to fight the Scots.[6] He has to back up the university authorities in the maintenance of discipline: if the chancellor and masters appeal to him he must go and arrest any scholar indicated, or expel him from the university.[7]

Apart from emergency orders there is a steady and unbroken stream of routine administrative duties. The sheriff is for ever receiving orders to hold inquests—into the age of heirs; as to whether so and so, now lying in Cambridge gaol, killed so and so of intent or by misadventure; as to whether the king will suffer if the Carmelites enclose a plot of the king's land between their house and the water of Granta,[8] and so on. For all such extraordinary inquests as those of 1255, 1258, 1268, 1275 and 1279 he will have to provide juries, as he does for the general eyres, of which some nine or ten occur in the century. He has to see to the election of coroners and representatives of the counties for all sorts of business.[9] He may not himself try criminals of any importance, but he has an immense amount of police work connected with criminal and civil justice; serving writs, distraining beasts, taking charge of the goods and chattels of felons, arresting accused persons, and either bailing them or providing for their custody, and collecting fines and amercements imposed by the king's justices. On the fiscal side he collects all sorts of dues on behalf of the exchequer, to which he renders his account every year. At the

---

[1] *C.R.C.* p. 483.   [2] *Ibid.* p. 459.   [3] *Ibid.*
[4] *P.R.C.* pp. 239–40; *C.R.C.* p. 19.   [5] *C.R.C.* p. 100.   [6] *Ibid.* p. 295.
[7] 3 May 1231, *C.R.C.* p. 586; 28 Oct. 1294, *P.R.C.* p. 101.
[8] *P.R.C.* p. 474 (1292).   [9] *C.R.C.* pp. 499 (1301), 559 (1302).

monthly shire-moot on Castle Hill he publishes the king's proclamations, whether they concern new statutes, or the terms of the
truce with France, or the sale of provisions or export of wool, or the
holding of tournaments within three miles of Cambridge.[1] Lastly, he
has a petty criminal jurisdiction in the six-monthly courts, his tourns,
which he holds in the hundreds.

In the majority of duties that have been mentioned the sheriff is
acting under orders and is accountable to the central government—
most often to the exchequer; but it will be seen that however much
the government has the whiphand of him, to the average subject in
his two shires of Cambridgeshire and Huntingdonshire this ubiquitous
activity will make him both mighty and terrible. The importance to
the king of this official is also clear, and the dependence of good
government upon a close control over his person and activities.

The questions that arise in one's mind in connection with the
thirteenth-century sheriff concern the nature of this control. How
were the sheriffs appointed? For how long did they hold office?
What manner of men were they, socially and politically? By
what machinery were they brought to book for their conduct?
What is proposed here is to make some attempt to answer the
first three questions, more specially that on social status, for this
one sheriffdom of Cambridgeshire and Huntingdonshire during
the reigns of Henry III and Edward I. The question of account-
ability will be touched on incidentally but is too large to be dealt
with now.

In regard to the appointment of the sheriff, Cambridge presents no
special peculiarities. As in the large majority of counties, the position
was dependent upon the king's will. In the Angevin period the
office might be and was bought; in 1208 Fulk Fitz Theobald paid
120 marks and two palfreys to have the counties of Cambridge and
Huntingdon for seven years, with the castle;[2] but this practice of
John's, who sold anything for which a purchaser offered, was not,
I think, followed under his son and grandson, with whom we are
mainly concerned.[3] The form of appointment of John le Moyne in
October 1253 may be taken as typical. He is to keep the counties of
Cambridge and Huntingdon and the castle of Cambridge *during the
king's pleasure*, and his predecessor Simon de Houghton is simply

[1] C.R.C. p. 197.   [2] Madox, *Exchequer*, p. 319.
[3] After 1236 the office was, financially, a liability rather than an asset. See
M. H. Mills, *Trans. R. Hist. S.* for 1927, p. 126.

ordered to hand over to him.[1] The sheriff has no right of tenure as against the king.

Simon de Houghton himself is a case in point. We are not given the details of his offence, but we gather that he has been summarily removed, from a notice on the Close Roll. On 4 July 1253 the king informs the treasurer and barons of the exchequer that he has removed Simon de Houghton from his office of sheriff of Cambridge and Huntingdon and that they must have another appointed in his place to account at the exchequer for the issues of the counties.[2] Three weeks before two justices had been ordered to inquire how Simon de Houghton bore himself as sheriff, and their report must have been unfavourable.[3] From other counties, notably from Northamptonshire, we hear lurid and detailed stories of the misdeeds for which sheriffs were deprived of their offices; most of these instances fall between 1250 and 1260, and are probably to be associated with the general movement for reform. It should be noted that Simon de Houghton remains responsible till his successor is appointed on 17 October 1253. As to the machinery of appointment there are some slight variations. Up to 1278 the appointment is normally made in the chancery; after that date in the exchequer,[4] a change which reflects the increased fiscal pressure being brought to bear on the shires. In the reign of Edward I the farms of the Cambridgeshire hundreds were practically doubled:[5] by 1307 the sheriff is almost certainly regarded primarily as a fiscal agent.[6] There are one or two special occasions, however, when the procedure is varied for political reasons. In the crisis of 1258–60, when the kingship was for the moment put into commission, the sheriffs were chosen by the king in council, and ordered to come up to the exchequer to take an oath the form of which had been fixed by the council. For those years the appointments are enrolled in the memoranda rolls of the exchequer and not in the chancery rolls; and the formula instead of 'during the king's pleasure' is 'as the king's council has provided'. William le Moyne is the sheriff who goes up to Westminster to take his oath before the treasurer and barons in the form provided by the council.[7]

---

[1] P.R.C. p. 223.   [2] Close Roll, 37 Hen. III, m. 7.
[3] P.R.O., Lists and Indexes, IX. iii.   [4] Ibid.
[5] See Assize Rolls, 82, 85, 86, 95, and Hundred Rolls of 1275.
[6] See Trans. of R. Hist. S. for 1896, p. 52.
[7] P.R.C. p. 655. For evidence of nomination of the sheriff by a local panel of knights during these years, see E. F. Jacob, Baronial Reform and Rebellion, pp. 50 ff.

In 1261, in some counties at least, the county courts were invited to send up names to the exchequer,[1] and the Annals of Dunstable assert that the magnates provided and appointed sheriffs almost all over England, against the authority and will of the lord king, rejecting and refusing to obey the sheriffs whom he had appointed.[2] In Cambridgeshire they did not succeed in ousting the king's nominee, John Luvel, but they did succeed in reducing his power to a shadow. In 1268, after the final overthrow of the baronial party, the barons of the exchequer were directed to hold a special inquest of four knights of Cambridgeshire into the condition of John Luvel's tenure of office, and they found that Hervey of Evesham and Ralph Pirot had prevented him from taking the profits either of the shire-moot or of his tourns in the hundreds during the summer and autumn of 1261.[3] Saer de Freville, who held office for six months of 1262, seems also to have been a royalist.

This episode illustrates well the connection between party changes and administrative appointments. Every political crisis almost inevitably produced a clean sweep and appointment of new sheriffs throughout the country. Not only in 1258, but in 1264 after Lewes, in 1265 after Evesham, and in 1274 when Edward I returned from the Holy Land, such general clearances occurred.

Another variation in the method of appointment, not so important as one might think, occurs sporadically under both Henry III and Edward I—the election of sheriffs in the shire. In 1300, by the Articles on the Charters, Edward I granted his subjects the right of electing the sheriffs of their own shires, provided the office were not hereditary.[4] This right, which was withdrawn in 1311, does not appear to have been regarded as very valuable. In the absence of any clear knowledge as to how elections in the shire-moot were conducted, it seems possible that in practice this worked out at the sheriff's nominating his successor—merely another form of royal nomination. The Cambridgeshire sheriffs of 1300–7 do not appear in any way less dependent on the central government than those before 1300, and there is a great deal of passing from shire to shire if the country be considered as a whole, which strongly suggests inspiration from headquarters. For instance Robert Hereward, sheriff here 1300–1, goes on to Norfolk and stays there till 1306; and his successor, Robert of Bayouse, here from 1301–6, is sheriff of Leicestershire and Warwickshire 1306–7.

[1] *P.R.C.* p. 328 (1261).   [2] *Ann. Monast.* [R.S.], III. 217.
[3] *Royal Letters* [R.S.], II. 322, 297.   [4] Art. super Cartas, c. 8.

Closely bound up with the question of appointment is that of duration of tenure. The ideal of the reforming party in 1258 was an annual appointment; the Provisions of Oxford laid down that none should hold office for more than a year.[1] How far this standard was observed can be seen from the accompanying list, which is based on that published by the Record Office. We begin Henry III's reign with

CAMBRIDGESHIRE SHERIFFS IN THE 13TH CENTURY

9 March	1216 Fawkes de Bréauté.	8 Oct.	1262 John Luvel.
18 Jan.	1224 Richard de Argenteuin.★	18 June	1264 John de Scalariis.★
23 Jan.	1224 Geoffrey de Hatfield?★	24 Aug.	1265 John le Moyne.★
10 May	1232 Jeremy de Caxton.	Michaelmas	1265 Almaric Peche.★
7 July	1232 Peter de Rivaux.	23 Nov.	1267 Baldwin de St George.★
1 May	1234 Jeremy de Caxton.	Christmas	1267 Saer de Freville.★
24 Oct.	1236 Henry de Colne.★†	5 Aug.	1270 Robert del Estre.
16 Dec.	1242 Hugh de Hodeng.	19 Oct.	1274 Walter de Shelfhanger.
26 June	1244 Ralph de Bereford.†	Michaelmas	1275 William le Moyne.★
15 Feb.	1246 Philip de Stanton.★	25 Oct.	1278 Baldwin de St George.★
19 April	1249 John de Scalariis.★	8 Oct.	1279 William de Rothing.
11 May	1249 Henry de Colevile.★	28 Oct.	1281 Thomas de Belhus.
6 Oct.	1251 Simon de Houghton.	20 Oct.	1289 Hugh de Babington.★
17 Oct.	1253 John le Moyne.★	10 April	1296 William de Mortimer.★
17 May	1255 John de Marines.	19 Oct.	1297 William de Sutton.
11 May	1256 William de Stow.★	4 Oct.	1298 Thomas de Gardinis.
3 Nov.	1258 William le Moyne.†	6 Oct.	1300 Robert Hereward.★
Michaelmas	1259 John de Scalariis.★	17 Oct.	1301 Robert de Bayouse.†
9 July	1261 John Luvel.	11 Nov.	1306 Robert de Hoo.★
26 Feb.	1262 Saer de Freville.★		

★ Holding land in Cambridgeshire.   † Holding land in Huntingdonshire.

the two long shrievalties of Fawkes de Bréauté and Geoffrey de Hatfield; and Henry de Colne holds office for six years; after that the normal length of office is about two years, till up to the date of the Provisions of Oxford, when political convulsions produce short and broken terms of office. After 1265, the year of Lewes, there is greater calm; we have three years of Saer de Freville, four of Robert del Estre, three of William le Moyne, eight of Thomas de Belhus, seven of Hugh de Babington, whose term of office is only ended by his death, and five of Robert de Bayouse. If the reformers of 1258 believed in rotation, the civil servants at headquarters had a very different view. We get an expression of it in Bishop Stapleton's

[1] See also King's Letters [R.S.], II. 365, for the royal proclamation on the subject.

admirable ordinances of the exchequer of 1325, where it is laid down 'Let not the sheriffs be so often changed as they have been, for by the more often changing of the sheriff it frequently happens that the king is ill served and his mandates not executed and the people vexed in divers ways'.[1] Lack of continuity in administration, lack of experience in the administrators are the evils suggested. It is probably to escape the latter evil that the exchequer officials transferred men from one shire to another, a practice commoner at the end of our period than at the beginning. Six of the twelve sheriffs appointed by Edward I held sheriffdoms in other counties: Walter of Shelf-hanger was in Lincolnshire 1273–74, Cambridgeshire 1274–75, Norfolk and Suffolk 1275–77; William of Rothing went from Cambridgeshire to Norfolk in 1281, and was sheriff there till 1289; William de Sutton was sheriff of Essex, 1294–97, of Cambridgeshire 1297–98, and of Norfolk 1298–1301, Thomas de Gardinis was sheriff of Gloucestershire 1293–98, and of Cambridgeshire 1298–1300; Robert Hereward was appointed sheriff of Essex in 1299, though the appointment was cancelled; he was sheriff here from 1300–1, and of Norfolk 1301–6; and Robert de Bayouse, as we have seen, went to Leicestershire after five years in Cambridgeshire.[2] It will be noted also that in the more peaceful and stable days of Edward I the appointment is always made in October, in contrast to the scattered dates of Henry's reign, the sole exception being caused by the death of Hugh de Babington in office.

We are now in a position to discuss a question for which detailed individual examination is necessary; what manner of men, socially speaking, were these sheriffs? Again the Provisions of Oxford supply a standard: 'Let there be provided as sheriffs loyal people and substantial men and holders of land; so that in each shire there be a vavasour of the same shire as sheriff.' Substantial country gentlemen, not necessarily tenants in chief; men who will not be dependent on the favour of the crown for a livelihood, or without a local interest to counteract the official, clerkly interest of a civil servant, are the kind the reformers desire.

The demand is reiterated throughout the century, from 1222, when the men of Cornwall agree to pay 1300 marks to have a sheriff from among themselves,[3] down to 1325, when it is endorsed officially by

---

[1] *Red Book of the Exchequer* [R.S.], p. 961.
[2] See P.R.O., *List of Sheriffs*, for all except last instance, for which see *C.R.C.* p. 515 (1307).   [3] Madox, *Exchequer*, p. 283.

the exchequer in Stapleton's ordinances. The sheriffs are to be 'sufficient persons, with good estates in land in the counties where they shall hold office'.[1] For, from the king's point of view, it was desirable that the sheriff should have immovable property, which could be confiscated in lieu of arrears if he made default in his account. Yet the very characteristics which commend a man to the baronial party or to his own shire might make him less eligible from the point of view of departmental efficiency, which would include the knack of extracting money from his shire. Which type, one asks, will predominate; the country squire or the king's clerk? That is the problem upon which a biographical study of the Cambridgeshire sheriffs, incomplete as it is bound to be, sheds much light. We will examine the record of these men with reference to these points—Are they landholders? Are they Cambridgeshire men? What are their relations to the government?

We begin with the foreigner Fawkes de Bréauté, appointed by John in the last months of his reign, almost certainly for strategic reasons—to secure the control of the important military point of Cambridge Castle. Similar reasons probably led to his being appointed sheriff of Oxfordshire, Buckinghamshire and Bedfordshire, Northamptonshire and Rutland, of all of which counties he was the nominal sheriff at the same time. This sort of pluralism belongs rather to the past age; we have only one other instance of it to note. For ordinary administrative purposes, it is probable that the sub-sheriff, Ralph de Bray, was the man who mattered. Fawkes was the captain who controlled the military resources of these midland shires in the campaign against Louis of France.

Richard of Argenteuin, whose appointment was revoked in five days, was a Cambridgeshire landholder, holding four knight's fees of the honour of Richmond in Melbourne and elsewhere.[2]

Geoffrey de Hatfield had a house in Cambridge, and conferred land on Barnwell Priory;[3] so, although his name probably indicates residence in Essex or Hertfordshire, he may be regarded as a Cambridgeshire landholder.

Jeremy de Caxton is a more interesting figure. From his name one would judge him to be a Cambridgeshire man, but there is no evidence of his having held land in Caxton. He is the king's clerk

---

[1] *Red Book of the Exchequer* [R.S.], p. 959.
[2] Farrer, *Feudal Cambridgeshire* (henceforth cited as F.F.C.), p. 28; *C.R.C.* p. 84 (1224).   [3] F.F.C. p. 244; *C.R.C.* p. 247 (1229).

par excellence. He appears first as Geoffrey de Hatfield's clerk, accounting for him at the exchequer in 1231. The office of sheriff's clerk was undoubtedly most responsible; the clerk probably had a great deal of the fiscal business of the county in his control, acting as treasurer of the revenue collected on behalf of the king's exchequer in the shire. Then he is sheriff for two months in 1232, and we may safely assume that he carried on as sheriff's clerk under the great pluralist Peter de Rivaux, who was nominal sheriff of eighteen other counties besides Cambridgeshire and Huntingdonshire in 1232.[1] The fall of Peter des Roches in April 1234 meant the dismissal of his supporter Peter de Rivaux from his many offices, and the disappearance from the Cambridgeshire list of sheriffs of political magnates like himself and Fawkes de Bréauté. Jeremy de Caxton resumes the title of sheriff and exercises the office till 1236. That seems to be the end of his connection with the county, but not by any means of his career. He is acting in various official capacities, as guardian of empty sees, as assessor of a tallage of the Jews, as justice of the forest and as justice of assizes up to 1253, when he is holding pleas with Bracton *Coram Rege*.[2] One seems to see some young villein of Caxton getting his freedom through his brains, his education through his order, and his career in the king's service through efficient local work for the royal favourite: but this is, of course, pure imagination.

Of his successor Henry de Colne there is little to relate, but it is interesting to notice that he held 80 acres of land in Caxton of John de Scalariis, himself thrice sheriff, besides the 60 acres at Colne in Huntingdonshire from which his name was derived.[3]

Hugh de Hodeng offers another example of the sub-sheriff becoming sheriff; in 1243 he is allowed to account at the exchequer both for his predecessor Henry de Colne as his clerk, and for himself as sheriff.[4] It is possible that he is a landholder in Essex, and that the Hugh de Hodeng who held manors in Burnham and Eton in Buckinghamshire and Hedingham, Wanstead and Ham in Essex, and died in 1242, was his father.[5] Anyway, there is no evidence of his having held land in Cambridgeshire.

[1] For the significance of this pluralism, see M. H. Mills, 'The Reforms at the Exchequer, 1232–1242', in *Trans. R. Hist. S.* for 1927, pp. 111–33.
[2] *P.R.C.* pp. 176, 247, 289, 442; Foss, *Dictionary of Judges*, p. 160.
[3] F.F.C. p. 178.   [4] *C.R.C.* p. 120.
[5] *Inq. Post Mortem*, I. 829; *C.R.C.* pp. 75, 200.

Ralph de Bereford held land in Huntingdonshire, at Needingworth and Holywell, just over the Cambridgeshire border.[1] He went to law with the abbot of Ramsey in 1241 as to his right of cutting rushes in Warboys marsh, but lost his case.[2] He was present, as sheriff, at the inquest held at Huntingdon on 7 January 1244, before special commissioners, to determine the boundaries between Northamptonshire, Huntingdonshire and Cambridgeshire.[3]

Philip de Stanton is a very typical respectable country gentleman. He held land in Long Stanton and Lolworth.[4] In 1242 he was one of the two men appointed for Cambridgeshire to swear men to the keeping of arms.[5] He had been elected and was serving as one of the two coroners of the county when in February 1246 he was made sheriff.[6] But like so many other sheriffs his official duties brought him to prison. Before his successor had been appointed he was being detained in custody at the exchequer for the arrears of his account with the king.[7] In January 1251 he was in the Tower of London, and was to be released so that he might provide for a survey of his lands to be made.[8] Later in 1252 he pays a mark of gold to be pardoned for all his trespasses as sheriff.[9] He died about 1268.[10]

Henry de Colevile held land both in Histon and Long Stanton.[11] He had served as assessor of a tallage in the county before he held office,[12] and he paid the king ten marks for the privilege of acting as custodian and not farmer of the counties,[13] which probably means that he was held responsible only for actual receipts and not for uncollected debts, at the exchequer. He also safeguarded himself, like his predecessor, by securing a pardon for all trespasses he and his bailiffs might have committed during his term of office.[14] This canniness suggests the professional rather than the amateur, and when we find him acting in 1252-53 as justice in eyre in seven counties, including Cambridge and Huntingdon,[15] and inquiring into the conduct of his successor in the sheriffdom,[16] we feel disposed to write him down as

[1]   *Cartularium Mon. de Rameseia* [R.S.], I. 193.
[2]   *Ibid.* III. 36-7.   [3]   *Ibid.* III. 39.
[4]   F.F.C. pp. 194, 203.   [5]   C.R.C. p. 485.
[6]   *Ibid.* p. 418.   [7]   *Ibid.* p. 142 (1249, Feb.).
[8]   *Ibid.* p. 397 (1251).   [9]   P.R.C. p. 128 (1252).
[10] F.F.C. p. 203.   [11] *Ibid.* pp. 38, 203.
[12] Foss, *Dictionary of Judges*, p. 182.   [13] C.R.C. pp. 323, 502 (1250-51).
[14] P.R.C. p. 125. A special inquiry into the conduct of local officials was being held in 1252.
[15] *Ibid.* pp. 161, 227.   [16] *Ibid.* p. 233.

belonging rather to the class of royal clerks than of country squires. He is our first indication that that classification is not a sound one; the two classes are not mutually exclusive.

Simon de Houghton may have come from Houghton in Huntingdonshire, but I have found out nothing about him beyond his removal, presumably for misconduct, after the inquiry held by Henry de Colevile, and the fact that his accounts were not yet settled at Michaelmas 1255[1]—a perfectly normal delay.

John le Moyne with John de Scalariis I will leave for the moment; of John de Marines I have found few notices; the charges against him in the eyre of 1261 do not throw any light on his social standing. In 1274 the treasurer and barons of the exchequer ordered a jury of the county to be summoned to inquire whether John de Marines had taken money in the hundreds and vills of Cambridgeshire contrary to the customs of the county when he was sheriff, and from the command that these men are not to have any affinity with him or with the two other Cambridgeshire men involved,[2] one would infer that John de Marines belonged to the county. I have failed to locate him, however.

William de Stow held land in Bourn and also in Long Stow, of the abbot of Ramsey.[3] He, like Philip de Stanton, was coroner of the county, either before or after he was sheriff.[4] He probably supported the baronial cause, as he gets protection after Lewes.[5]

We come on now to the times of disorder. Cambridgeshire suffered longer, perhaps, than any other county of England; we have heard John Luvel complaining of the disorders of 1261 and 1262, and the records of 1268,[6] when William de St Omer sat at the Castle and at Barnwell to inquire into the doings of the islanders of Ely and their abettors, give a lively picture of the unsettlement of the country, and the settlement of private grudges carried on under cover of the civil war. A more prosaic testimony is to be found in the Pipe Rolls, where the sums paid in from Cambridgeshire drop from £217 under John de Marines in 1255 to £53. 6s. 8d. in 1258, £40 in 1264, the year of Lewes, £26 in 1265, the year of Evesham, and nothing at all in 1267, the year of the island war.[7] It took years for the exchequer to recover from the strain; John Luvel was still haggling over

---

[1] Mem. Rolls (K.R. series), 29, m. 5.   [2] Mem. Rolls, L.T.R. 32, m. 3.
[3] F.F.C. p. 155.   [4] Ass. R. 82, m. 23 (1261).   [5] P.R.C. p. 538 (1264).
[6] Ass. R. 83. A few extracts are printed in Hunter's *Rotuli Selecti*. See also the inquests *De rebellibus, Cal. Misc. Inq.* I. 194-5 [and *V.C.H., Cambs.,* II. 390-6].
[7] I owe these figures to Miss M. H. Mills.

his arrears due for 1261–62 in 1274;[1] and the persistence of the habit of lawlessness is reflected in Robert del Estre's claim in 1270 for £40—the expenses involved in keeping the peace in the teeth of the many malefactors 'who came out of the University of Cambridge and committed depredations and other enormities both within the town and without'.[2]

The first undoubtedly political nomination is William le Moyne, who comes up to the exchequer to take his oath in November 1258, in the new form provided by the council. He had been one of the four knights appointed for Cambridgeshire in the previous August to hold the special inquests into grievances ordered by the Provisions of Oxford.[3] He is described on the Patent Rolls as 'of Raveley' and therefore probably belongs to Huntingdonshire; the family of Le Moyne is freely distributed over both counties in the thirteenth century.[4] He may possibly be the same William le Moyne who was sheriff from 1275–78, and was still alive when the justices in eyre came round in 1286, but on the whole it is more likely that that William was on the king's side, as was John le Moyne of Shelford.

John de Scalariis or des Chalers was sheriff thrice; in 1249 for a month only; in 1259 for a year and three quarters, and in 1264, for the period between Lewes and Evesham. From the dates of his two last appointments it is clear that he was on the baronial side; after Lewes all the county is exhorted to assist him in the task of restoring peace.[5] The family was at Caxton and at Dullingham;[6] Henry de Colne was a tenant of theirs, and the de Frevilles were connected with them by marriage.

John le Moyne of Great Shelford, who held his manor by the serjeanty of making or mending the king's crown,[7] is clearly a royal adherent. He served as sheriff from 1253–55; he goes to Gascony twice on the king's business; he is sheriff again from August to September 1265, and from that date onwards we find him holding various official positions, as justice of the Jews, guardian of vacant bishoprics, commissioner to inquire into the sea walls of Lincolnshire

---

[1] Mem. Rolls, L.T.R. 48, m. 2 d.
[2] Exchequer Miscellanea, 1/47. Mr E. F. Jacob kindly pointed out the passage.
[3] P.R.C. p. 646. Most of the new sheriffs had been put on the inquests for their own counties.
[4] See Rot. Hund. II. 607, 627, etc.   [5] P.R.C. p. 264 (1264).
[6] F.F.C. pp. 110, 111.   [7] Inq. Post Mortem, II. 73.

and so on. He was a benefactor both to the scholars of Merton and to the friars preachers of Cambridge, and died in 1275.[1]

John Luvel, sheriff from 1261-62 and 1262-64, is again a typical royalist. He appears as a personal adherent of Edward the king's son, serving him in Gascony in 1255. A series of grants to him are to be found on the Patent Rolls, of hunting and other privileges. In the military crisis of the spring of 1264 Northampton Castle is committed to him, he is taken prisoner at Lewes, he sits on the inquests into the conduct of the rebels in Northamptonshire in September 1265; he is granted the lands of one such rebel and sells them back to him; he sits on the inquests of 1267-68 into the disposition of the confiscated lands in eleven counties (those inquests which in Cambridgeshire were held by William de St Omer); he goes on crusade with Edward in 1270, leasing for his expenses the three manors in Oxfordshire, Wiltshire and Northamptonshire which his son inherits in 1287.[2] There is no sign that he had any land in Cambridgeshire or Huntingdonshire. He is described in the inquests of 1267-68 as 'a magnate of the lord king',[3] but that did not save him from having to render a strict account at the exchequer, where he was still in arrears in 1274, ten years after the close of his last term of office.[4]

In connection with his sheriffdom there is a remarkable story that seems to have escaped the attention of the historians of the university. The date is not given, so it may have occurred at any time during Luvel's two terms of office. It was reported to the justices of the eyre of 1272. 'Certain clerks of Cambridge beleaguered the house of Stephen de Hauxton, in Hauxton, but as they could not get into it they returned to Cambridge and associated with themselves the clerks John de Weston and William de Burnham, and they took an oath among themselves to plunder that house and fixed a certain day for the deed. Meanwhile they' (the last two clerks) 'came to John Luvel the sheriff and told him and asked aid from him that they might take the said clerks in the act. John Luvel told the whole thing to Jordan de Daventry, seneschal of the Bishop of Ely' (who was, of course, partly responsible for the discipline of the university) 'and

---

[1] P.R.C. pp. 409 (1255), 553, 657 (1266); *Abbreviatio Placitorum*, p. 186; C.R.C. p. 214 (1276).

[2] P.R.C. pp. 402 (1255), 202, 300 (1262), 306, 410 (1264), 491, 537 (1265-66), 113, 160 (1267), 425, 514 (1270); *Inq. Post Mortem*, II. 377.

[3] Hunter, *Rotuli Selecti*, p. 174. [4] Mem. Rolls, L.T.R. 48, m. 2 d.

both John and Jordan sent to the court of Stephen on the night for which the said clerks (planned their attack), together with the said John de Weston and William de Burnham, John de Helecumb and John de Evere, servants of the said sheriff, and the sheriff handed over to them men both of the vill of Hauxton and of his own household, (and they placed them) everywhere in the outhouses. At length the aforesaid clerks with others associated with them came to Hauxton on the night fixed, and burgled the house, and bound the men in it, and made a heap of all the goods they found in it, and then feasted there and whilst they were feasting the said John de Weston and William de Burnham and John de Helecumb and John de Evere fell upon them and took them and killed one of the said clerks, with the assistance of the men hidden in the courtyard. The jurors, asked what became of the clerks, say that the four mentioned kept guard over the surviving clerks till next morning, and at break of day the four departed, and afterwards came John Luvel and Jordan of Daventry to the house and found the dead clerk and the surviving clerks, and raising the hue and cry took their heads to Cambridge Castle. And as to William de Burnham, he is now prior of Norwich: and John de Helecumb and John of Evere are now in Bucks.'[1] There, like so many judicial records, the story stops—we do not know if any of these *agents provocateurs* were ever produced before the justices at Cambridge Castle in 1272, or whether John Luvel and Jordan of Daventry appeared there or elsewhere to explain their disciplinary methods with Cambridge undergraduates. But we do know a little more about William de Burnham, who reported his fellows' designs to the sheriff. In August 1272, four months after the justices were at Cambridge, the citizens of Norwich attacked the abbey and burnt down most of the church. The gentle Henry III, roused to fury by this sacrilege, came himself to Norwich to punish the offenders, calling for the support of all loyal Christians. A special commission inquired into the matter. Cotton, a devoted adherent of the monks, declares that the judges and juries were bribed, but the fact remains that in October William de Burnham, who had been chosen prior in 1268, was deprived of the priory 'for divers transgressions', by Henry himself—almost his last act, for he died in November. William de Burnham died in the following February. One wonders what John Luvel, still presumably on

[1] Ass. R. 85, m. 12d. The words in brackets are added, the Latin being very careless.

crusade in the East, thought of his former protégé's fate when the news reached him.[1]

Saer de Freville must belong to the family whose tombs are at Little Shelford. Its history is traced by Dr Franks in the *Proceedings* of this Society for 1848,[2] but his conjecture as to Saer's place in the genealogy does not fit the dates. Saer de Freville was acting as coroner in 1260,[3] before he became sheriff for the first time, and between 1272 and 1286, by which date he was dead.[4] The fact that he holds office in 1262, between John Luvel's two terms, and again in 1267 after the troubles are over, suggests that he was a moderate royalist. He is ordered in 1263 to hold an inquiry into an attack upon the lands of the royalist John le Moyne[5] of Great Shelford; possibly his neighbour, though the only reference to Saer's lands that I have found is to land held at Bourn by the courtesy, which suggests that he married a Peverel.[6] The social relationships of the different sheriffs are well illustrated in his career. Connected by marriage with the des Chalers family, in 1281 he witnessed some deeds for Simon de Insula to which two other ex-sheriffs, Baldwin de St George and Walter de Shelfhanger, are also witnesses.[7] Here we have to do with typical county families, it seems.

Almaric Peche also belongs to a historic Cambridgeshire family, though besides his lands in Wickham he also held lands in Suffolk, Norfolk and Essex.[8] Some of these were bestowed on him by Henry III, who also appointed him after Evesham to hold the inquests for Cambridgeshire concerning the lands of rebels, which were rendered necessary, there as elsewhere, by the tendency of the winning side to grab whatever they could get.[9]

Baldwin de St George held land not merely in Hatley St George, but in half-a-dozen villages about the county.[10] There is nothing remarkable about him; he does the usual jobs of a country gentleman, helping to assess the fifteenth of 1275 and serving as a justice of oyer and terminer in 1285.[11]

---

[1] Full documents and details are given in W. Rye's *Norfolk Antiquarian Miscellany*, II. 17–89. The legal records give evidence that the Prior's conduct was highly provocative, and largely accounted for the citizens' violence.

[2] *Proceedings* (quarto), XIV. p. 21.
[3] Ass. R. 82, m. 23.
[4] Ass. R. 86, m. 38.
[5] P.R.C. p. 287.
[6] *Rot. Hund.* II. 520.
[7] C.R.C. p. 130.
[8] *Inq. Post Mortem*, II. 407; F.F.C. pp. 58–9.
[9] P.R.C. p. 490.
[10] F.F.C. pp. 136, 137, 167, 223, 230, 253, 269.
[11] C.R.C. p. 250 (1275); P.R.C. p. 153 (1285).

With Robert del Estre again we come to an outsider, and a zealous adherent of Edward. Our first picture of him is drawn by Giles de Goushill, sheriff of Yorkshire, who writes in 1268 to the justice, John de la Lind, to say that he cannot answer for the county of York if Robert del Estre is to have the West Riding in complete independence of him. He says that Robert has possession of the castle and demands to be put in possession immediately of the West Riding, but declares he will not give an account to anyone but the king at the exchequer or to Prince Edward. 'And', Giles says desperately, 'I shall be the loser by 140 marks, for it is a full third of the shire.'[1] Unfortunately, the answer to this letter is not extant, but as Giles carried on for another year, presumably a *modus vivendi* was arrived at. In 1268 and 1269 Robert is acting as the king's taker of wines throughout the country, until April 1270;[2] in August 1270 he becomes sheriff of Cambridgeshire and is at once involved, as we have seen, in restoring peace among the turbulent scholars of Cambridge, at a cost of £40. Of his tenure of office the Hundred Rolls of 1275 give us some idea. His most picturesque achievement was in connection with the great bridge of Cambridge, which had been broken down, probably by floods. The customary pontage or bridge tax was 6d. the hide on those lands that owed it; Robert del Estre took it from the whole county at 2s. the hide,[3] promising that he would build them a fine bridge of stone and mortar. But he did not spend the third part of what he took on it, but made a bridge at a low price of hurdles and timber.[4] Thus when the commissioners of the inquest of 1279 came round four years later, they found the bridge broken down and badly needing repair.[5] To add insult to injury, Robert's underling, the keeper of Cambridge prison, used to pull planks out of the bridge by night and so delayed its completion for three months, during which the country folk coming in to the town had to pay him for ferrying them across in Robert's boat,[6] by which he made 100s.[7]

By 1276 Robert, like most sheriffs, is in arrears with his accounts at the exchequer. He has been trying to collect his own personal debts, and he complains bitterly that his son John has been getting

[1] *Royal Letters* [R.S.], II. 325.
[2] *P.R.C.* pp. 297, 422.
[3] *Rot. Hund.* I. 50.
[4] Hundred Roll, Cambridge, no. 2, m. 3 (unprinted). Hundred Roll, Cambridge, no. 4, *in dorso* (unprinted).
[5] *Rot. Hund.* II. 407.
[6] *Ibid.* I. 49.
[7] *Ibid.* II. 407.

hold of his lands behind his back. Whilst Robert was acting as sheriff of Cambridge and Huntingdon, the sheriff of Northampton seized his lands at Abthorp in Northamptonshire for debt, and John del Estre asserted that his father had made them over to him, and by a packed jury, consisting of enemies of the father and friends of the son (so Robert asserts), the land was awarded to the son, and the sheriff delivered it to him.[1] Special justices are appointed to hear and determine the matter; and there the story stops abruptly. After all the squeezing of other folk by Robert del Estre one is not sorry to think of his being squeezed in turn. He is acting as justice of Gaol Delivery in London in 1277, and appears to be still alive in 1283.[2] As a type, he seems to have most in common with John Luvel.

From Robert del Estre on, it is noticeable that an increasing proportion of the sheriffs are not Cambridgeshire landholders. One might almost say that the office is becoming more professionalized. As I pointed out, the sheriffs are passing from county to county. Of these outsiders, Walter de Shelfhanger is lord of the manor of Shelfhanger in Norfolk,[3] but he is described in 1281 as 'the king's clerk'[4] and is sheriff in Norfolk and Lincolnshire as well as Cambridgeshire; William de Rothing held land in Suffolk and Essex, and was also sheriff in Norfolk;[5] Thomas de Gardinis held land in Oxfordshire and served as sheriff in Gloucestershire also.[6] The general pardon issued to Walter de Shelfhanger for trespasses committed while in the king's service, in which the fines for three failures to serve writs amount to £28. 6s. 8d.,[7] gives one some idea of the financial risks for a man and his heirs involved in taking on the office of sheriff; and the assumption of three sheriffdoms in succession seems a brave deed.

Thomas de Belhus is another outsider and man of substance. He belonged to a family which held land in Essex, Suffolk and Norfolk. His own manor was at Stanway, near Colchester.[8] The canon of Barnwell's tale of him helps to explain the force of the requirement that a sheriff should have lands in the county he governed.[9] 'Thomas of Belhus', he says, 'was sheriff of Cambridgeshire for many years,

[1] P.R.C. p. 151.
[2] P.R.C. p. 233 (1277); C.R.C. p. 231 (1283).
[3] Rot. Hund. i. 472 b.
[4] P.R.C. p. 5.
[5] Rot. Hund. i. 147, 148.
[6] Inq. Post Mortem, ii. 411.
[7] C.R.C. p. 508 (1288).
[8] Rot. Hund. i. 140; ii. 147.
[9] Note also Stat. West. i (1275), c. i.; Art. super Cartas, c. xiii. 'They shall choose such sheriffs as shall not lodge too long in one place, nor with men of religion.'

and he greatly loved the canons of Barnwell, and with good reason, since they bestowed many benefits and honours upon him; and he frequently stayed there with his wife and an all too extensive household.' (This was the time, when, as we saw, repairs were going on at the castle.) 'At last, having stayed there for three days and nights, with his wife and children and household and twenty-two horses, when he departed he begged the loan of a cart to carry a load of wine to his manor of Stanway. And when they replied that there was no cart about the place that would take so heavy a load, but that they would hire one and pay for it themselves, Thomas went off in a rage, talked everywhere of the outrageous behaviour of the canon who had given him that answer, and did all that he could from that time on to annoy Barnwell Priory'.[1] The sequel was an interference with the prior's judicial rights in Chesterton, and a writ brought against the sheriff by the prior in the King's Bench—and eventually a loveday or compromise out of court. The canon, however, tries to score the last laugh by relating how Thomas' lands were seized by the king on his death, and his widow had to pay a vast sum to redeem them. I have not found documentary confirmation of this last statement. When his term of office expires Thomas does business for the king in Ponthieu as his seneschal,[2] as well as holding a great many commissions of oyer and terminer and gaol delivery in the eastern counties.[3] In April 1292 we hear that he is going to Rome on the king's affairs, and is to have respite till Michaelmas for his debts at the exchequer.[4] In September he is back, serving as a justice in Cambridgeshire again; and in July 1293 he is dead, and others must fill his place in the commissions.[5]

Hugh de Babington holds land in Gamlingay,[6] though also in other counties.[7] He is the only sheriff on our list who seems to have died in office.

William of Mortimer is an elusive figure, because his name is so common—there are at least three contemporaries so called who figure on the chancery rolls. But he is officially described as William de Mortimer of Freckenham, which is half in Norfolk and half in Cambridgeshire, and I think he may be the William Mortimer who dies in 1304, whose lands at Soham and Fordham escheat to the

[1] *Liber Memorandorum*, pp. 180–1. [2] *P.R.C.* p. 321 (1289).
[3] *Ibid.* pp. 489, 513 (1292). [4] Mem. Rolls, L.T.R. 63, m. 13 d.
[5] *P.R.C.* pp. 520, 521 (1292); 113 (1293).
[6] F.F.C. p. 177. [7] *Inq. Post Mortem*, III. 251.

crown because he is himself illegitimate and has no heirs of his body.[1] His record in the eyre rolls of 1299 gives us a good idea of the local tyrant brought to book. In conjunction with a special commissioner, William had been ordered to purvey corn for the king's Scottish campaigns in 1297.[2] Now in hundred after hundred men complain that he made them pay large sums of money to escape this requisitioning, that he took more than the king's clerk had assessed them at and kept the balance, that he compelled them to buy corn to make their contribution and so on. Again and again William denies the charge and puts himself on a jury; but the jury always find against him, and eventually he has to pay 50 marks in amercements, as well as a large sum for replacing the corn unjustly taken.[3]

With William de Sutton we are back at a busy servant of the central government. Besides being sheriff in three counties in turn, he acts as justice in Wales, serves on a commission for perambulating the forests and acts as guardian of the vacant see of Ely.[4] He has lands in Essex and also it would seem in Norfolk—apparently not in Cambridgeshire.[5]

Robert Hereward seems to have begun his public career as seneschal of the bishop of Ely;[6] as such he would be exercising functions practically the equivalent of the sheriff's in the Isle of Ely—all Cambridgeshire north of the Ouse. In 1300 he is acting on a commission *de walliis et fossatis* in Cambridgeshire and Norfolk, and inspecting wines in Bedfordshire and Buckinghamshire, Cambridgeshire and Huntingdonshire.[7] He acts as guardian of the vacant see of Ely in 1302; he assists in purveying corn in Norfolk, Suffolk and Cambridgeshire.[8] He is appointed sheriff of three counties in succession. He is the king's clerk *par excellence*—and yet he holds land in Cambridgeshire—half a knight's fee in Gilden Morden of William de Kirkby.[9] Robert de Bayouse, who holds lands in Huntingdonshire,[10] and Robert de Hoo,[11] who holds land in Eversden, need not detain us; Robert

---

[1] *Inq. Post Mortem*, IV. 131–2.
[2] See M. H. Mills, in *Eng. Hist. Rev.* 1923, p. 351; J. G. Edwards, *ibid.* 1943, p. 159.
[3] Ass. R. 95, mm. 52, 55, 59 d, 61 d, 62, 63.
[4] *C.R.C.* p. 62 (1303); *ibid.* pp. 170, 396 (1298–1300).
[5] *Ibid.* pp. 74 (1296), 287 (1298), 377 (1300).
[6] Ass. R. 95, m. 64; cf. *P.R.C.* p. 178 (1295).
[7] *P.R.C.* pp. 545, 551 (1300).
[8] *C.R.C.* p. 540; *ibid.* pp. 498 (1301), 68 (1302).
[9] *Ibid.* p. 41 (1303).   [10] *Ibid.* p. 437 (1301).   [11] F.F.C. p. 169.

Hereward will do as a test case to examine this question of king's clerk *versus* country squire.

I think one thing emerges from the cases we have been considering. The normal sheriff is a landholder. In many cases he is really the country squire, taking his turn with his neighbours at the opportunities for profit and risks of loss, the privileges and responsibilities that the position of sheriff entails. Such men are Philip de Stanton, William de Stow, John des Chalers, Saer de Freville and Henry de Colne, the forerunners of the Elizabethan J.P. Three of them, you will remember, had been elected coroners in the county court. Alongside of these is the man of county family who goes farther afield and serves the king in different capacities in various regions. Here one might place men like Henry de Colevile, John le Moyne, Thomas de Belhus, Thomas de Gardinis, perhaps William de Rothing and John Luvel. Then come the efficient administrators, the all-round civil servants of no ancestry—Jeremy de Caxton, Robert del Estre, William de Sutton, Robert Hereward. In the case of all these but Jeremy de Caxton we leave them settled on the land; but are not their estates the reward of service? A generation later contemporaries thought it noteworthy that a knightly family like the Scropes should have sons who followed the law. In the case of Robert Hereward one seems to see how it may have happened. John de Kirkby, the great treasurer and bishop of Ely,[1] grants a holding to an efficient subordinate. In some such way Robert del Estre may have acquired his lands in Northamptonshire and William de Sutton his in Essex and Norfolk. But that is in the nature of guess-work. What has been established by this examination is that although Edward I fell far below his father's standard in appointing natives of the county, the large majority of the Cambridgeshire sheriffs in the thirteenth century did at least conform to the standard of the Provisions of Oxford and the Articles on the Charters so far—that they were 'loyal people, substantial men, and holders of land'.

[1] William de Kirkby was his brother and heir. See *Inq. Post Mortem*, vols. II and IV. Unfortunately the 1279 returns for Gilden Morden are lacking.

IV

Suitors and Scabini [1]

The history of local government in France and England might be
compared to the course of two rivers which rise near together and at
first flow in almost parallel channels, until some apparently trifling
natural obstacle diverts their streams, and they flow farther and
farther apart, ultimately reaching two different oceans. The Mediter-
ranean and the North Sea are not farther apart than are the two
systems in the eighteenth century: on the one hand, the despotism of
Louis XV, controlling from one centre the thirty-three *généralités*
and *intendances*; on the other, the parliamentary monarchy of
George III, controlled by the sovereign representatives of the shires
and boroughs. Nor does the contrast end there; the French system
was jettisoned in 1789 by the National Assembly, when they remade
the map of France and created the departments of to-day, while the
reformers of 1832 in England left the shires intact, so that the county
members and county councils of to-day represent units of local
government that were already in existence a thousand years ago.

An attempt to compare the history of local jurisdiction in France
and England during the three centuries from Charlemagne to Philip
Augustus and from Alfred to Henry II thus involves a question of the
very greatest importance in the development of the national con-
stitutions. On the fate of the Anglo-Saxon shire-moot, it might
almost be said, the whole future history of the English monarchy
was to turn. Why had the Frankish *mallus*, comparatively speaking,
so little influence on the development of the French monarchy?

I

It will be as well to recall the points of resemblance between the
English and the Frankish local courts of the ninth and tenth centuries.
The Frankish unit was the *pagus* or *comitatus*, subdivided into *centenae*;
the English unit was the shire, subdivided into hundreds. The court

---

[1] Read at the International Congress of Historical Sciences at Warsaw, 1933.
Reprinted from *Speculum*, April 1935.

of the *pagus* was called the *mallus*, and the *centena* also had its court.
The shire had a shire-moot and the hundred had a hundred-moot.
In these courts the bulk of the legal business of the two countries was
conducted; both Frankish emperors and Anglo-Saxon kings dis-
couraged appeal to themselves for justice. At these courts, it would
seem, all the freemen of *pagus* and shire had originally to be present,
whether they had business there or not.

In both *pagus* and shire there were two great meetings in the year;
in Francia certainly[1] and in England probably there were lesser
meetings in between. The English hundred-moot met every four
weeks, while we do not know how often the Frankish *centena* met.
As to the procedure followed in these courts, there has been much
controversy in the case of the Frankish *mallus*. But certain matters
are beyond dispute. The count, the emperor's official, or his deputy,
the viscount, presided over the court, and promulgated the judgments, and with him there acted in many, though not all cases, a
number of men known up to the end of the eighth century as the
rachinburgi, after that date as the *scabini*. In the records of lawsuits in
the *mallus* we are repeatedly told that the judgment was found or
given by these men, who are sometimes called *judices*, sometimes
boni homines, sometimes *legislatores* or *juridici*. Fustel de Coulanges,
though he considered their authority was far outweighed by the
count's, yet pointed out their indispensability.[2] Men who knew the
local customs were needed to help the count, often a stranger to the
district, to do justice according to local law and the custom of the
country, as he was bound by oath to do. The great variety of laws
in the Frankish kingdom, and the rule that each man could claim
to be judged by his own law, still in force till the middle of the
tenth century, made such assessors especially necessary. In a case in
Languedoc in the year 918, for instance, we hear of Roman, Salic and
Gothic *scabini* as acting together in finding the judgment pronounced
in the *mallus publicus*.[3] Till about the end of the eighth century, it
would seem, the *rachinburgi* have no professional status; any freeman
of the court may act and probably different men are called on,

[1] A. Boretius, *Capitularia Regum Francorum* (Hanover, 1883), 1. 46. (Capitulary
of 769, cl. 12.) Almost certainly this distinction between greater and lesser courts
was introduced by Charles the Great.
[2] *Recherches sur quelques problèmes d'histoire* (Paris, 1885), p. 447.
[3] M. Thévenin, *Textes relatifs aux institutions...mérovingiennes et carolingiennes*
(Paris, 1887), p. 179.

whether by the count or by their fellows, to act at the different sessions of the court. But though the composition of the body may vary, their position is authoritative; they are more than assessors or witnesses; they are *Urteilfinder*, who declare the law and decide how it applies in the case before the court; and the count, though responsible for holding up the judgment if he believes it to be bad law, cannot act without them in all cases involving customary law. And the judgment found by the *rachinburgi* and promulgated by the count has the authority of the whole body of the *pagenses* behind it, as is clear from the names enrolled on the records of the cases. But the count undoubtedly had the overriding influence in the court.[1]

Between 769 and 780 Charlemagne increased the number of *generalia placita* of the *pagus* to three: released the ordinary freeman from the duty of attending the lesser *placita*: and ordered the creation for each *pagus* and *centena* of a board of judges, known henceforth as *scabini*—the later *échevins*, *schöffen*, or *scepene*.[2] These did the work of the *rachinburgi*, but differed from them in holding office for life. Charles' aim was both to lighten the burden on the small freeman, who could ill afford the heavy fine for non-attendance, and to lessen the personal influence of the count by creating a body of judges whose life tenure would make them independent of him, and whose appointment had to be approved by the *missi* and reported to the king. But in the event, when such control was lost, the *scabini* came to be known as the 'Count's *scabini*', and the way was opened for the transformation of the *mallus publicus* into the 'count's *mallus*'.

Turning to England, we have very much less material for an account of the working of the shire-moot. To the large body of ninth- and tenth-century legal deeds enrolled in French cartularies, and to the collections of Frankish legal formularies there is no Anglo-Saxon parallel. Only a few chronicles and a few charters describe proceedings in shire-moots, and these charters are far less carefully drafted than the Frankish deeds, omitting the date, and the names of the presiding official and the scribe, and giving comparatively few names of witnesses. All the same, the similarity of procedure is obvious; to the count or viscount corresponds the ealdorman or

---

[1] The fullest accounts of the system are those given by Beaudouin, *Nouvelle revue historique de droit français et étranger* (henceforth cited as *NRHD*), XI (1887), 450–523, 556–651; XII (1888), 121–239; and Saleilles, *Revue historique*, XL (1889), 286–304.

[2] *Capitularia Regum Francorum*, I. 210, cl. 14; cf. I. 116, cl. 20, and I. 290, cl. 14.

sheriff; the judgments are found by the men of the shire, clearly guided by the opinions and pronouncements of the leading men, on whose nod, as Bracton was to say three hundred years later, the views of the others depend. In the shires of the Danelaw Domesday Book reveals an institution which bears some resemblance to that of the *scabini*, though we have no evidence whether it is popular or royal in origin—twelve doomsmen or lawmen, known after the Norman Conquest as *judices*, who are especially responsible for the judgments, though it is not clear that the ordinary freeman is debarred from taking his part. The twelve senior thegns of Athelstan's law may be this same board of judges. Domesday suggests that the office was hereditary; and later records show that they served for both shire and hundred courts, and some survived into the fourteenth century.[1]

In both France and England, then, there is an official president, representing the emperor or king, appointed by and responsible to him, at any rate in the earlier period. In both countries the judgments are found by the men of the country-side, who declare the customary law applicable to the case: in both countries the evidence points to the dominance of the local notables in this process of judgment-finding, but their judgment is endorsed and witnessed by the whole body of *pagenses* or men of the shire, and pronounced by the president—*comes* or *vicecomes*, ealdorman or sheriff, who, in both countries, is enjoined to know and observe the law, and thus has more than a purely formal part to play. The greatest contrast is in the records; in the Frankish kingdoms still drafted in a workmanlike style derived from Roman tradition; in England informally, almost casually worded. For in England it is the witness of the shire rather than the written deed that counts in matters of folk law. The well-known record of a Herefordshire case in Cnut's reign well illustrates this characteristic:

This writing is to declare that a shire-moot sat at Aegelnoth's stone in the days of King Cnut. There sat Bishop Aethelstan and Ranig the ealdorman, and Eadwine the ealdorman's son, and Leofwin Wulfsig's son and Thurkil the White, and Tofig Pruda came there on the king's errand and there was Bryning the sheriff and Aegelweard of Frome and Leofwin of Frome and Godric of Stoke and all the thegns of Herefordshire. Then came Eadwine, son of Eanwene, to the moot, and made claim against his

[1] *Eng. Hist. Rev.* 1926, pp. 33–4.

mother for a piece of land....And they appointed three thegns from the moot to ride to the place where she was...and when they came to her she was vehemently angry with her son,... and said,...'Here sits Leofled my kinswoman, the wife of Thurkil the White, to whom after my death, I grant my land and my gold...and all I possess', and she said to the thegns 'Act like thegns, and duly announce my errand to the moot before all the good men, and make known to them to whom I have granted my land, and ask them to be witness to this'. And they did so; they rode to the moot and made known to all the good men what she laid on them. Then Thurkil the White stood up in the moot and asked all the thegns to give his wife clear the lands her kinswoman granted her, and they did so. And Thurkil rode to St Aethelbert's minster, by leave and witness of the whole people, and caused this to be recorded in a gospel book.[1]

The importance of the witness of the shire is as clear as the fact that there is no clerk present at the moot, so that the successful party to the case has to ride to the nearest monastery to get the case enrolled, and incidentally preserved for us, by the abbot.

II

If we pass from the ninth and tenth centuries to the twelfth, we find that the divergence between the lines of development in France and England has become marked. In both countries alike a great many courts held not by royal officials but by feudal magnates have come into existence. In France the main body of judicial business is being conducted in the courts of dukes, counts, viscounts, barons and *seigneurs* of all sorts. In England every lord holds a court for his men, at which feudal justice is administered, and these courts range from the great honours of fifty knights' fees and upwards, to the smaller courts where, as Stenton has shown, so much useful work had been done in the century after the Norman Conquest by the baron's barons.[2] And alongside these strictly feudal courts are the great franchises like the palatinate of Durham or the Soke of Peterborough, where the lord of the liberty holds courts for men who are not his feudal tenants at all, but subject to his jurisdiction by royal grant. It is probably true in England as in France to say that more justice is being done in the lords' courts than anywhere else. But in

[1] J. M. Kemble, *Codex Diplomaticus aevi Saxonici*, no. 755; A. J. Robertson, *Anglo-Saxon Charters* (Cambridge, 1939), no. LXXVIII.
[2] F. M. Stenton, *English Feudalism 1066–1166*, p. 45.

England, alongside the lords' courts the courts of shire and hundred still exist and still function, and though a large number of hundreds are in private hands, no shire has become feudalized, even if Durham and Cheshire may look like it. The earl, the successor of the ealdorman, is as completely a noble as the count; but he has lost all part in the administration and jurisdiction of the shire from which he takes his title. The sheriff, the equivalent of the French *vicomte*, has not, like him, become a hereditary magnate, though in one or two counties he comes near it; he is in the twelfth century at least as much of a royal official as the Frankish count had been in the ninth century.

In France the *pagi* have almost completely disappeared. They have been parcelled out by usurpation, by family arrangement or by royal grant, and are replaced by the hereditary fiefs of those dukes, counts and viscounts who are the descendants of the Carolingian officials, but are now bound to the crown by the tie of vassalage only. These fiefs may be fragments or amalgamations of the tenth-century *pagi*; they are very seldom identical with them.

In both France and England, again, a system of royal administration is being built up, which in the long run will starve out the feudal magnate and recapture the system of justice for the king and for his officials. But the process will be very different in England and in France, as far as the machinery of local government is concerned. In France the kings build up a sound system on the royal demesne, of administration by *prévôts* and by *baillis*, and extend the system to fief after fief as they are recovered; while in England the Norman and Angevin kings have a royal agent, the sheriff, in every shire from the first, and build up their system of local administration within the old traditional framework. It is significant that in England the royal agent takes his name from the old district, the shire, while in France the royal agent gives its name to the new district, the *bailliage*.

In France, then, the *mallus* and the court of the *centena* seem to have disappeared, while in England the shire-moot and the hundred-moot are very much alive, and the sheriff, though essentially a royal official, under the thumb of the exchequer, with the whole central machine of royal government behind him, is, in the shire-moot, dependent on the suitors, those knights of the shire who make the judgments and who can at their pleasure hold up the course of justice if the sheriff outrages them by departing from local custom.[1]

[1] F. Pollock and F. W. Maitland, *History of English Law*, I. 549 f.; G. T. Lapsley, 'Buzones', *Eng. Hist. Rev.* 1932, pp. 177 ff., 545 ff.

Now this sort of relationship between the president and the suitors of a local court is not unknown in twelfth-century France. In Flanders, in Artois, in Normandy, in Vermandois, to go no farther, we meet the popular judges finding the judgments which are promulgated by the official judge. Nowé and Ganshof have recently drawn for us the picture of the *vierschaaren* of Flanders [1] where the men find the judgment and the *châtelain* (later the *bailli*) pronounces it, neither being able to act without the other. The actual terminology of the Carolingian courts survives; the *échevins* or *scepene* find the judgments; in one or two instances, as at St Omer,[2] the court is still called the *mallus* in the twelfth century; the three great sessions are still held; the boundaries of the judicial districts even can in some cases be identified with Carolingian *pagi* or *centenae*. The *pagus* may have disappeared, but something very like the *mallus* has survived, with the *châtelain* of the count of Flanders playing the part of Charles the Great's count.

In Normandy the name *scabini* has died out except in the towns, but the *Très ancien coutumier* and the records of cases show the men and the knights of the duchy acting as *judicatores* with the king's *justiciarii* and *vicomtes* in the local courts.[3] De Fréville's thesis [4] that this co-operation was introduced by Philip Augustus cannot be admitted; Vinogradoff in his latest contribution to legal studies [5] maintained the antiquity of the procedure and its inevitable connection with customary law. Génestal has shown that the *vicomtes* of Normandy are the descendants of the Carolingian *vicecomites*;[6] the judgment of the peers in the Norman *assises* would appear also to be inherited from the older courts, whether of *pagus* or of *centena*.

Beaumanoir's treatise has familiarized us with the judgment by the men—*les hommes jugeurs*—in Vermandois. Writing towards the end of the thirteenth century, he describes in detail the cases in which

[1] H. Nowé, *Les baillis comtaux de Flandre* (Brussels, Lamertin, 1929), pp. 258–328, F.-L. Ganshof, *Les tribunaux de châtellenie en Flandre* (Paris, Champion, 1932).
[2] Ganshof, *op. cit.* pp. 82–3.
[3] *Très ancien coutumier de Normandie*, ed. E. J. Tardif (Rouen, 1881, 1903), cc. XXVI, XLIV; *Summa de legibus Normannie*, ed. E. J. Tardif (Rouen, 1896), IX. § 2; *Arresta communia scaccarii*, ed. E. Perrot (Caen, 1910), no. 45; L. Delisle, *Jugements de l'échiquier de Normandie* (Paris, 1864), no. 793, *Recueil des historiens de France*, XXIV (Paris, 1904), *Preuves*, nos. 10, 14, 23, 30, 31, 34, 40, 53, 68, etc.
[4] *NRHD*, XXXVI (1912), 681–736.   [5] *NRHD*, L (1926), 195–212.
[6] *NRHD*, XXVIII (1904), 766–75.

they should be left to act and those in which the model bailli will act without them.[1] The working of the system has been admirably described and documented by Waquet.[2]

In Vermandois, as in Normandy and in several other districts, we are dealing with a fief that has been recovered by the monarchy, and the process of jurisdiction by the men of the fief has often been described as the 'feudal' judgment of the peers.[3] To describe the process as feudal is, however, to beg the question. The process is older than feudal theory and needs no vassalage to explain it. As the personality of law died out, the procedure of popular judgment became the natural means of safeguarding the rights of the different social classes, and the greatly diminished class of freemen and the growing class of knights will cling to the traditional method of up-holding customary law.[4] In England, when the writer of the *Leges Henrici Primi* insists that peers are to be judged by their peers in the shire court,[5] he is not thereby implying that it is a court of vassals, but merely that it is the natural tribunal where each man's right is secured to him by his neighbour's backing. So with the judgment of the *hommes jugeurs*—the *homines regis*—in the local courts of northern France where public justice is exercised in the twelfth century.

In regard to the feudatories' courts, where both feudal and seig-norial justice is exercised, it has been often held that lords who had acquired the rights of justice imitated the procedure of the public courts.[6] This may cover some, but not all cases; for Ganshof has actually traced in concrete detail the stages by which the *mallus* of the *Pagus Matisconensis* was transformed into the court of the count of Mâcon and the 'count's *scabini*' became the 'lord's vassals'.[7] In Flanders, as he admits, the materials for bridging the gulf are lacking; but the presumption is overwhelming that in those districts where in the thirteenth century the judgments are found not by *échevins* but by men of the fief the same thing has occurred.[8] We seem safe in

---

[1] Beaumanoir, *Coutumes de Beauvaisis*, ed. A. Salmon (Paris, 1899), pp. 27–9, 36–8.

[2] H. Waquet, *Bailliage de Vermandois* (Paris, 1919), pp. 55–63.

[3] E.g., by O. Tixier, *Les baillis et sénéchaux royaux* (Orléans, 1898), pp. 77–8; by J. Declareuil, *Hist. gén. du droit français* (Paris, 1925), pp. 275 ff.

[4] P. Vinogradoff, *ut supra*, pp. 205, 207; A. Luchaire, *Manuel des institutions* (Paris, 1892), pp. 201–2, 575.   [5] *Leges Henrici*, c. 31, § 7.

[6] E.g., by P. Guilhiermoz, *Origines de la noblesse* (Paris, 1902), pp. 260, 317–18.

[7] *NRHD*, LII (1928), 644–65.   [8] *Tribunaux de châtellenie*, pp. 81–6.

accepting Ganshof's thesis, supported by his various studies,[1] that wherever seignorial justice, that is, public jurisdiction unconcerned with feudal relationships, is being exercised in a lord's court, something like the history of the county of Mâcon has been repeated. As the freemen are more depressed by economic forces, the social level of the descendants of the *scabini* will tend to rise. But the fact that the judgments are found by knights does not make the procedure feudal. So long as the law is a customary law you must have custodians of that law. If the rights of status are to be upheld, the men who know the rights of their own class must find the judgments for that class, and the *assise de chevaliers* must co-operate with the royal *bailli*. But in the *pays de droit écrit* the practice will die out earlier than in that of *droit coutumier*; and as royal justice and the new science of law develops the amateur judge grows more afraid of the penalties of wrong judgment, so that by the fourteenth century the *hommes jugeurs* are very ready to surrender the dangerous function of judgment-finding even in northern France.[2]

III

We are now in a position to compare the process of transition from communal to seignorial jurisdiction in the two countries.

The significant period in the process of transition is the tenth and eleventh centuries. Under the shocks of invasion in both countries the royal authority became dismembered. The kings, unable to do the work of government, were forced to surrender or make over the rights and obligations of police, defence, and justice to the local officials, already hereditary and fast being transformed into great feudatories. These in their turn, in France at least, had to submit to the usurpation of local governmental functions by their subordinates and dependents.

In England the Danish invasions had a different sequel. The process of recovery by the royal authority had two great stages; the first when Alfred's grandson, having completed the conquest of the Danelaw, imposed the West Saxon system of administration on the

[1] In addition to those cited above, see paper in *Mélanges d'histoire offerts à H. Pirenne* (Brussels, 1926), I. 161 ff.

[2] Waquet, *Bailliage de Vermandois*, p. 59. Compare the description of the professionalization of the *assises* in Dupont-Ferrier, *Les officiers royaux des bailliages* (Paris, 1902), pp. 328 ff.

whole of England, defining the boundaries of the shires and creating or adapting the hundreds as units for police and for taxation;[1] the second when William the Conqueror introduced the Norman feudal system into England and at the same time taught the English sheriff that he must be as obedient to his king as the Norman vicomte was to his duke. The first stage made the shire and the hundred court ubiquitous in England; the second, by subordinating them to royal purposes, preserved their existence to posterity.

The shire-moots, as we have seen, retained their public character in a feudalized England. It is possible that the shire-moot of Cheshire, but for the extinction of the male line, might have become the great franchise court of the earls of Chester, comparable to the count of Flanders' court of the *châtellenie* de Bruges,[2] but when the crown recovers it in the thirteenth century it is in full possession of its popular traditions, so that even when the royal justiciar sits in the sheriff's place the suitors 'teach and instruct him' as to the customary procedure of the shire.[3] Again, in Durham, which remained a palatinate to the close of the middle ages, the shire-moot retained its communal character in spite of the bishop's privileges; and the sheriff continued to function alongside his seneschal.[4] In the other counties, even in Westmorland and Worcestershire, with their hereditary sheriffs, the shire court remained both popular and royal; the place where royal acts were proclaimed, royal inquests held and royal justices might on occasion sit, but where the men of the shire made and recorded the judgments for which they were held legally and financially responsible. William the Conqueror's use of the shire courts to establish the rights of his Norman tenants in chief[5] early set the tradition which was followed by his son Henry I and his great-grandson Henry II; the counties and hundreds were to be held as they were in the time of King Edward, and on account of royal needs—*propter mea dominica necessaria*—and no otherwise.[6] The sheriff was limited on the two sides by the custom of the shire and by the authority of the king, and the earl was out of the picture. He and the other great magnates ceased to attend the shire court, and it

---

[1] W. J. Corbett, in *Camb. Medieval Hist.* III. 366–7.
[2] Ganshof, *Tribunaux de châtellenie*, p. 82, n. 5.
[3] *Eng. Hist. Rev.* 1927, p. 119.
[4] G. T. Lapsley, *County Palatine of Durham*, pp. 106–14, 126.
[5] M. M. Bigelow, *Placita Anglo-Normannica*, pp. 4, 7, 20, 22, 34–8.
[6] Stubbs, *Select Charters* (9th ed. Oxford, 1913), p. 122.

became the field of action of the sub-vassals, the knights of the shire, the country gentlemen whom Bracton called the *busones*,[1] the fore-runners of the Edwardian members of parliament.

The story of the hundred courts is different. Not only were a large number of hundreds in private hands by the twelfth century, but it seems probable that the delegation of hundredal jurisdiction to a subject is as old as the hundred itself. Leaving on one side the tradition that Offa had bestowed the hundred of Cashio on the abbey of St Albans, there are a number of West Saxon bishoprics and religious houses in Wiltshire, Hampshire, Somerset, Dorset, and Devon who traced their tenure of private hundreds to the gift of Edward the Elder, Edred and Edwy.[2] The extension of the hundredal system beyond the original West Saxon kingdom is marked by Edgar's grants to Ely and Peterborough in the east and to Worcester in the west,[3] where the triple hundred of Oswaldslaw, built up out of the scattered lands of the church of Worcester, may well have been created when Worcestershire was first divided into twelve hundreds. In Cnut's reign comes the first clear case of the grant of hundreds to the laity, when the eight and a half hundreds of Bedricsworth, later the liberty of St Edmund, were assigned to his wife Emma as her dower.[4] Edward the Confessor granted hundreds in Norfolk, Suffolk, Berkshire, Essex, Surrey, and Lincolnshire to various religious houses,[5] and Domesday Book gives further evidence of hundreds held both by laity and clergy in Nottinghamshire, Gloucestershire, and other counties.[6] To sum up, one can say that in 1066 there were private hundreds in twenty counties of England, and that

---

[1] *De Legibus Anglie*, ed. Woodbine, II. 327.

[2] In Wiltshire: Chalk (Wilton), Wherwelsdon (Romsey), Bradford (Shaftesbury), Downton (Winchester Old Minster); in Hampshire: Micheldever (Winchester New Minster); in Somerset: Taunton (Old Minster) and Twelve Hides (Glastonbury); in Devon: Crediton (Bishop of Sherborne); in Cornwall: Pawton (Bishop of Sherborne).

[3] W. de Gray Birch, *Cartularium Saxonicum*, nos. 1130, 1267, 1135.

[4] *Eng. Hist. Rev.* 1909, pp. 417–23.

[5] In Norfolk, Clackclose (Ramsey); in Suffolk, the eight and a half hundreds (Bury St Edmunds); in Berkshire, Hornmere (Abingdon); in Essex, Waltham (Waltham Cross), Winstree (St Ouen); in Surrey, Godley (Chertsey); in Wiltshire, the three hundreds of Malmesbury; in Lincolnshire, Well (St Mary of Stow).

[6] Fishborough, Pershore, and Westminster in Worcestershire; Clavering and Rochfort in Essex; Tunstead, Hersham, Mitford, Guiltcross and Shropham in Norfolk; Hoxne in Suffolk; Newark in Nottinghamshire; Wargrave in Berkshire; Deerhurst in Gloucestershire; Pider in Cornwall, etc.

there is strong presumption of the existence of at least a hundred and thirty private hundreds by 1086.

In some of these hundreds, such as Taunton, held by Winchester, or the two hundreds of the Isle held by Ely, it is possible that the crown had surrendered most of its rights—fiscal, administrative, and judicial. But even over the most highly privileged franchise the crown never abandoned all its control, and the hundred, constituting, as it did, a police unit concerned with the taking and punishing of thieves, was seldom completely withdrawn from the sheriff's supervision. All through the Middle Ages the national police and military system turned on the hundredal organization;[1] and as royal justice tightened its hold on crime and the pleas of the crown really became the crown's concern once more, the lords of hundreds found themselves being transformed into the king's justiciars, as Edward I's lawyers called them.[2] The murdrum fine, the sheriff's tourn, the jury of presentment, the *posse hundredi* of the assize of arms all linked up the private hundred with the crown, and preserved its ancient customary organization. The suitors of the hundred, like those of the shire court, were the judges, and shared the responsibility of the president, whether he were the king's bailiff, or the earl's, or the abbot's.

So far as can be seen then the English communal courts never became completely feudalized. Where a lord, like the abbot of St Albans or of Ramsey, was lord both of a hundred and of an honour, the courts of the hundred and of the honour might be held at the same place and on the same day, but they did not merge. Only in the few instances where the lord of the hundred held all the soil of the hundred did the territorial and the governmental rights of the lord apparently become blended. The hundred court preserved its identity, and outlived the court of the honour, if not of the manor.

The hundred, as a district, did not always remain intact. A large number of lords who had been granted exemption from suit of shire and hundred, withdrew their men to a court of their own exercising hundredal jurisdiction. In some counties, Dorset, for instance, the liberties appear to take almost as much space in the map as the hundreds. But the insistence on the theory that all such franchisal or seignorial jurisdiction was held by royal grant, a theory, if Galbraith is right,[3] as old as the reign of Edward the Confessor, prepared the

---

[1] Cam, *The Hundred and the Hundred Rolls*, pp. 188–94.
[2] See below, p. 65.   [3] *Eng. Hist. Rev.* 1920, p. 382.

way for the insistence on the responsibility of the franchise holder to the king, and the extension to the liberties of the machinery of royal police and justice enforced through the lords, who thus became in a sense the king's officials.[1]

In France also the great abbeys could produce their charters, and the great feudatories, as Lot has shown,[2] in most cases derived their authority from a Carolingian grant; but the lesser men, like the count of Mâcon, seem to have annexed or maintained their powers undisturbed, and in practice the doctrine of responsibility so closely bound up with English feudalism is seldom enforcible in France outside the royal demesne. William the Conqueror himself seems as completely lord over his Norman courts of justice as over his English ones.

IV

Why did the communal courts of the two countries have so different a fate? The question cannot be answered summarily or finally. A few suggestions may, however, be hazarded.

In the first place, the influence of the Northmen in England revivified those communal traditions of the country which the Anglo-Saxons and Jutes had brought with them originally. The Danes, who contributed to the English language the word *law*, undoubtedly fortified the democratic institution of the land, above all that obstinate maintenance of custom as law which characterizes the medieval and modern Englishman. The institution of *lawmen* or *judices* is, as we have seen, characteristic of the shires of the Danelaw, but it does not appear to have diminished the sense of responsibility of the ordinary freeman of those parts, who seem both more numerous and more active than those of the south.

In the second place, the substitution by Charles the Great of the attendance of official *scabini* for that of the ordinary freemen of the *mallus* and *centena* must have helped to diminish the sense of responsibility of the *boni homines*, even in those sessions which they were bound to attend. On the other hand, the great variation of the number of *scabini* whose presence is recorded at different pleas suggests that they themselves were not as faithful to their duties as they should have been.

[1] See below, pp. 184, 202 ff.   [2] *Fidèles ou Vassaux?* (Paris, 1904).

It is possible that the practice in England, first noted by Maitland, of attaching the duty of suit to shire and hundred to specific holdings of land[1] helped to keep the institution of judgment by the suitors alive and working. The practice had certainly begun before the Norman Conquest. Edward the Confessor granted sixty-four sokemen or suitors along with the hundred court of Clackclose to Ramsey Abbey.[2] The hundred court was known as the sokemanmoot,[3] and the records show how the individual responsibility for rendering 'common suit' was insisted on at the opening of every session of a hundred court. The obligation was enforced by law, on behalf both of the crown and of private lords of hundreds: suits might not be 'withdrawn' without warrant.

In the third place, the fact that the feudal system was transferred to England already fully formed helped to prevent the merger of the two kinds of tribunal. The honorial courts, so valuable, as Stenton has shown, in building up Anglo-Norman and Angevin land law in England in the first century after the Conquest, did their work alongside the older communal courts, but they did not absorb them. The hundred might be held appendent to a manor, it might descend by the rules of feudal law, it might even be held 'for a knight's fee'; but the suitors of the hundred had a function and a duty that did not depend on their personal or tenurial relationship to the lord of the hundred. As in Germany, the *Landsgericht* and the *Lehngericht* remained distinct. On the other hand, the fact that feudalism was applied to the whole of England at one stroke made possible the application of the principle of responsibility that it enshrines to those lords who held public functions by royal grant. The Quo Warranto policy is implicit in the grants of William the Conqueror.

But possibly the most important of all the causes for the contrast is the strength of the English monarchy. Ganshof attributes to the strength of the counts of Flanders the preservation of the older judicial institutions of the country.[4] The investigations of Halphen and Ganshof into jurisdiction in Anjou and Burgundy[5] in the

[1] Pollock and Maitland, *History of English Law*, 1. 540 ff.; D. C. Douglas, *Medieval East Anglia*, pp. 146 ff.

[2] *Historia Rameseiensis* [R.S.], pp. 160, 202.

[3] *Rot. Hund.* II. 143, compared with 151 and 195, proves that *sockemanmot* is the court of Babergh hundred.

[4] *Tribunaux de châtellenie*, p. 84; cf. Nowé, *Les baillis comtaux de Flandre*, p. 369.

[5] *Revue historique*, LXXVII (1901), 279–307; CXXXV (1920), 198–218.

eleventh century make it clear that strong executive power was the main desideratum; that men would not seek justice in courts where there was no security of execution of judgment. In England the determination of Edmund, Athelstan and Edgar to enforce peace expressed itself in the hundredal system; and the Norman monarchy, by making the sheriff the chief military and police agent of the crown in the shire, and by associating the hundred with police measures like murdrum and frankpledge, prepared the way for the policy of the Angevin kings which worked the communal traditions of shire and hundred into the new bureaucracy. The juries of Henry II and the tax-assessing knights of Henry III not only paved the way for the shire representatives of Edward I, they assured to the ancient Anglo-Saxon system of shire and hundred a permanence which is unique in European history, and thus blended Teutonic and Roman elements into that characteristic hardy hybrid which we call the English constitution.

V

Manerium cum Hundredo: *the Hundred and the Hundredal Manor* [1]

In the thirteenth century, and indeed to a much later date, it was not uncommon for lordship of a hundred to be associated with a particular manor. The fact is familiar to many local historians, but it is doubtful if any attempt has hitherto been made to correlate local studies and to examine either the geographical distribution of this practice or its antiquity. The results of such an investigation are of interest both in themselves and for the support they appear to lend to suggestions put forward by various scholars as to the origin of the administrative district known, at least from the tenth century, by the name of *hundred* in southern and western England. No attempt is here made to put forward a theory that will cover the whole of England; no one formula can account for a Kentish hundred of two vills, a Norfolk hundred of twenty vills, and a Worcestershire hundred consisting of eighteen detached pieces of territory. Nevertheless, the hundredal manor presents features suggesting a remote antiquity, and the evidence of twelfth-century conditions may be found on investigation to throw light on governmental arrangements as old or older than the time of Alfred the Great.

The Quo Warranto inquiries of Edward I's reign form a good starting-point for a survey of the history of the hundredal manor. Again and again, in the eyres of 1281 and onwards, issue is joined between the king's counsel and the claimants of liberties as to whether a hundred can be held as the appurtenance of a manor. In 1281, for instance, Theobald Bussel claims a moiety of the hundred of Teignbridge, Devon, under a charter of Henry III granting the manor of Teignbridge with its appurtenances. To this William of Giselham replies, for the crown: 'Hundredum nunquam ad aliquod manerium pertinet nec eidem est annexum, immo specialiter pertinet ad coronam domini regis.' [2] In 1284 Fulk fitz Warine claims the hundreds of

[1] Read at the International Congress of Historical Sciences at Oslo, 1928. Reprinted from *The English Historical Review*, July 1932.

[2] *Plac. Quo War.* p. 165.

Ganfield and Wantage (Berks.), by a charter which grants the manor of Wantage with all its liberties and appurtenances. William of Giselham says that this charter is not sufficient warrant for the holding of these hundreds. 'In predicta carta nulla fit mencio specialis de predictis hundredis que non pertinent ad aliquod manerium.'[1] In the case of Wargrave hundred (Berks.) the manor and hundred are conterminous, and the bishop of Winchester claims the hundred as pertaining to the manor, in which King Edward himself has quit-claimed all rights to him. Again William of Giselham rebuts the argument: 'Rex non potest ab accione sua excludi per cartam aliquam, quoad hundreda petenda, nisi in eisdem cartis de eodem hundredo mencio fiat specialis.'[2] Again, in 1287, Thomas of Berkeley claims the hundred of Berkeley (Gloucs.) under a charter of Henry II granting the manor with all its liberties and dependencies, asserting that the said hundred was at the time of the feoffment one of the appurtenances of the manor of Berkeley. William Inge, for the king, rejoins: 'Officium hundredarii est quasi quaedam iusticiaria spectans mere ad coronam regis et non ad aliquod tenementum', and as the king's predecessors granted nothing belonging to the hundred in express words he claims judgment for the king.[3]

Now this doctrine put forward by the king's counsel in these trials—the judgment of the king's justices has not been traced in any of the cases cited[4]—is entirely in accordance with the policy, and, one might say, the political theory of Edward I; the same theory that Bracton had enunciated, that all judicial functions could only be exercised as delegated by the king, and that an explicit grant of such iusticiariae was needed to give a title.[5] But, historically speaking, the evidence goes to show not only that hundreds had long been and still were being granted as appurtenant to manors, but that grants of manors cum pertinentiis had been held and in some cases were still being held to involve the grant of hundredal jurisdiction beyond the manor itself.

Besides the Quo Warranto pleas a few parallel examples from the reigns of Edward and his son may be noted. In 1313 and again in 1325 the jurors of a post-mortem inquest present that the manor of Yardley Hastings includes the hundreds of Wymersley and Ham-

---

[1] Plac. Quo War. p. 82.   [2] Ibid. p. 81.   [3] Ibid. p. 256.
[4] The fact that the claimants or their heirs are holding the hundreds in 1316 does not prove that they won their cases, as Edward undoubtedly restored forfeited liberties for payment.   [5] Bracton, ff. 107–8.

fordshoe (Northants.).[1] In 1313 Coleridge hundred (Devon) is
asserted, in a lawsuit, to be appendent to the manor of Stokenham.[2]
In 1303 a special inquest finds that the holder of Ermington manor
has held the foreign hundred[3] of Ermington (Devon) since the
Conquest.[4] In 1285 the hundred jurors in the eyre of Oxford find
that the holder of Bloxham manor holds the hundred also;[5] and the
jurors in the Essex eyre find that the half-hundred of Harlow goes
with the vill and manor of Hatfield.[6] In 1281 an entry on the Patent
Roll alludes to the hundreds of Bullingdon and Northgate as being
'members' of the manor of Headington,[7] and an extent of that
manor in 1282 explains the omission of the hundred of Northgate
by the fact that it is temporarily sub-let to a separate holder.[8] The
jurors of the Hundred Rolls inquest of 1274 say that one part of
Felborough hundred (Kent) is annexed to the manor of Chilham, and
the other two parts to the manors of Chartham and Godmersham.[9]

It would be easy to multiply examples; we can safely say that even
contemporary evidence indicates, in some cases, official acquiescence
in the theory denied by Inge and Giselham. Turning to the reign of
Henry III, we find a long list of grants of manors with hundreds on
the charter rolls. In 1252 the king grants the manor and hundred of
Burne (Eastbourne, Sussex) to Peter of Savoy;[10] in 1246 the manor
and hundred of Knowlton, Dorset, to Nicholas de Molis;[11] in 1230
the hundred of Winterstoke, annexed to the manor of Cheddar,
Somerset, to the bishop of Bath;[12] in 1229 the manor and hundred of
Braunton (Devon), to the abbot and monks of Cleeve;[13] in 1227 the
hundreds of North and South Erpingham, annexed to the manor of
Aylsham, Norfolk, to Hubert de Burgh;[14] in 1221 the manor and
hundred of Godalming, Surrey, to the bishop of Salisbury,[15] and so
on. In 1247 Henry granted the manor of Cheltenham (Gloucs.) with
its hundred to the monks of Fécamp,[16] and a special inquest, held
probably at this time, found that in the time of King John, when

[1] Inq. Post Mortem, v. 231; VI. 388.
[2] Yearbooks of Edward II (Selden Soc.), XV. 218–24; cf. also VIII. 191, for the
hundred of Faversham, Kent.
[3] For meaning of term see below, pp. 70 ff.   [4] Cal. Misc. Inq. no. 1914.
[5] Ass. R. 705, m. 20 (P.R.O.).   [6] Ass. R. 242, m. 92 d.
[7] P.R.C. Edw. I, 1272–81, p. 440.   [8] Cal. Misc. Inq. no. 1253.
[9] Rot. Hund. I. 210.   [10] Cal. Charter Rolls, I. 412.
[11] Ibid. p. 291.   [12] Ibid. p. 118.
[13] Ibid. p. 98.   [14] Ibid. p. 25.
[15] Rot. Lit. Claus. I. 455.   [16] Cal. Charter Rolls, I. 321–2.

Ralph de Monford held it, 'the hundred belonged to the manor'.[1] It is said in 1224 that the hundred of Spelhoe (Northants) has always been held with the manor of Kingsthorpe, now farmed by the men of that town.[2] An even more explicit statement is found in an Essex fine of 1242. William de la Dune and Margery his wife make over to William Gifford two carucates of land at Bures (Bowers Gifford) with its appurtenances, except the hundred of Barstable, which is of the appurtenances of the said land, but is retained for Gundreda, the daughter of Margery.[3]

The reigns of John and Richard supply a further series of grants of manors with hundreds. Richard granted the royal manor of Sadberge (Northumberland), with its wapentake, to the bishop of Durham.[4] John confirmed to the knights of the Temple his father's grant of the manor of Strood and the hundred of Shamwell (Kent), 'which they hold because it pertains to Strood'.[5] He likewise grants the manor of North Curry (Somerset) with the hundred pertaining to it to the church of Wells;[6] and the manor of Corby (Northants) with the hundred and all its other appurtenances to Henry de Braybrok.[7] Equally significant is the grant of the manor of Axminster (Devon) with all its appurtenances *except* the hundred to William Briwere in 1204,[8] followed by the second grant to him in 1215 of the manor *with* the hundred.[9] Of another hundred held by William Briwere, Andersfield (Somerset), we are told in 1219 that it was a member of Somerton, a demesne manor of the king, and had been granted to William by King John.[10]

We are now reaching the position at which it seems possible to say that the grant of a manor 'cum pertinentiis' or 'cum omnibus liber-

[1] *Cal. Misc. Inq.* no. 423.   [2] *Rot. Lit. Claus.* I. 609.
[3] Kirk, *Essex Fines*, p. 143. There are special features of interest in the history of this manor and hundred. In 1086 Grim the reeve held two hides of land at Bura—one hide of the sheriff (*D.B.* II. 98). These may be the two carucates of 1242. The manor and hundred had been granted to Gundreda's ancestors by Henry I, and the manor and hundred were again held together by Robert, son to her and William Gifford. He finally quit-claimed the bailiwick of the hundred to the king in 1281, and was declared free of the ancient farm due in the exchequer for the said bailiwick, *especially in the manor of Bures*, which manor he retained (*P.R.C.* Edw. I, 1272–81, p. 453 (1281)).
[4] *Reg. Pal. Dunelm.* [R.S.], I. lxix. Sadberge is now in the county of Durham, Houghton le Skerne parish.   [5] *Rot. Cart.* p. 3.   [6] *Ibid.* p. 158.
[7] *Ibid.* p. 187; cf. *Bracton's Notebook*, case 1236, which mentions the grant by John of the manor of Higham Ferrers with the 1½ hundreds and other appurtenances.
[8] *Ibid.* p. 139.   [9] *Ibid.* p. 217.   [10] *Book of Fees*, I. 261.

tatibus et liberis consuetudinibus' may very likely involve the grant
of a hundred, even though the fact is not expressly stated. The history
of a few typical hundreds gives good warrant for this generalization.
In 1231 a jury found that Thomas Basset's tenure of the hundreds of
Bullingdon and Northgate (Oxfordshire) was warranted by a
charter of King John, which granted the whole manor of Headington
with its appurtenances and made no mention of a hundred court.[1]
In 1194 Richard I granted the manors of Kerswell and Diptford in
Devon, with their appurtenances and liberties, to Henry fitz Count,[2]
who was holding the hundreds of Heytor and Stanborough annexed
to these manors in 1212.[3] On the charter roll of 1203 is entered a
statement of the marriage portion of Alice de Bethune, daughter and
heiress of Baldwin de Bethune, and first wife of William Marshal,
junior. It includes the manors of Brabourne (Kent), Foulsham
(Norfolk), Luton (Beds.), Wantage (Berks.),[4] and Norton (Northants).[5] No mention is made of the hundreds, but at a later date
William Marshal or his heirs or assigns are found holding Bircholt
hundred in Kent as an appurtenance of Brabourne,[6] Eynsford hundred as appurtenant to Foulsham,[7] Flitt hundred as appurtenant to
Luton,[8] Wantage and Ganfield hundreds as appurtenant to Wantage,[9]
and Norton hundred as appurtenant to Norton.[10] Family descents,
in the same way, enable us to identify the 'hundred of Aure', granted
to Richard Marshal in 1233,[11] with the hundred of Blideslow (Gloucs.),
held by the lords of Awre manor.[12] Similarly the hundred annexed
to Bedwyn and Westcumbe[13] can be identified as Kinwaston hundred,
in the hands of the Marshals from the time of Henry I downwards.[14]

---

[1] *Bracton's Notebook*, case 513.

[2] Round, *Ancient Charters*, p. 102. Mr Turner points out that this grant, convey-
ing the two hundreds as appendent to the manors which alone are named, is not
unique (*Trans. R. Hist. S.* (n.s.), XII. 137).   [3] *Book of Fees*, I. 97; cf. 1426.

[4] For the grant of the manor of Wantage see Cart. Ant. Ee. 27. The writer in
Vict. Co. Hist. Berkshire, IV. 267, 501, points out that in Shrivenham, Wantage and
Ganfield hundreds the grant of the manor was an adequate title to the tenure of the
hundred.   [5] *Rot. Cart.* pp. 112–13.   [6] Ass. R. 362, m. 11.

[7] Lord Treas. Remembr., Misc. Roll 5/67 (P.R.O.); *Rot. Hund.* I. 488, 524.

[8] *Bracton's Notebook*, case 102; C.R.C. p. 518 (1231).

[9] *Pipe Roll*, 1242, p. 61; *Plac. Quo War.* p. 81.

[10] Ass. R. 615, m. 2.   [11] *Cal. Charter Rolls*, I. 174.

[12] *Rot. Hund.* I. 176.   [13] *Rot. Cart.* p. 47.

[14] A charter of William Marshal senior refers to the grant of Henry I: 'hundredi
mei de Kyneuuarestone que pertinet ad manerium de Weycumbe, et omnes con-
suetudines que ad hundredum illum pertinent secundum quod carta Regis Henrici

So Henry II grants the hundred of Newbottlegrove (Northants), as an appurtenance of Upton Manor;[1] the manor of Sutton (Northants) with its hundred,[2] and the manor of Earsham (Norfolk) with its half-hundred.[3] So Stephen grants Witham manor (Essex) with its half-hundred,[4] and Wargrave (Berks.) and East Meon (Hants.) with their hundreds.[5] So Henry I grants Frome (Som.),[6] Reading (Berks.), and Leominster (Herefordshire),[7] with their hundreds.

Another fact that emerges as we go backwards is that the manors to which hundreds are attached are very frequently ancient demesne manors. In some cases the manor with its hundred has escheated to the crown and been granted out again, but in a good many cases it is clear that the manor has been in the hands of the kings since 1066, and has been farmed by royal officials till granted out with the hundred. To take only a few of those mentioned above, Bedwyn, Kingsthorpe, Axminster, Luton, Reading, Wantage, Upton, Sutton, Somerton, Kerswell and Foulsham were all in the hands of William the Conqueror as royal manors.

The *Dialogus de Scaccario*, it will be remembered, refers to the association of hundredal jurisdiction with the grant of a royal manor.,

If the king bestows an estate on anyone together with the hundred or the pleas arising there, that estate is said to be granted 'blanch'; and if he keeps for himself the hundred by which the farm is said to be blanched, and gives the estate without naming the hundred or calling it 'blanch', it is said to be given 'by tale'.[8]

If the Pipe Rolls are examined, it seems clear that a grant of lands 'blanch' recorded under the heading *Terrae Datae* does not always involve the grant of the court of the whole administrative hundred in which they lie. In Oxfordshire, for instance, in 1161, Hugo de Plugenoi has £42. 10s. 0d. blanch in Headington,[9] and this almost

patris Imperatricis testatur' (B.M. Add. MS. 29436, fo. 39). The Pipe Roll of 1155 allows for blanched lands of the Marshals in Westcumb (p. 57) and that of 1242, at the same amount, for blanched lands in Westcumb and Bedewind (p. 166). In 1281 the hundred is called the hundred of Bedewynd, and is held by the Marshals' heir (*Plac. Quo War.* p. 809).

[1] *Rot. Hund.* II. 9; *Pipe Roll*, 15 Hen. II, p. 72.
[2] *Pipe Roll*, 2 Hen. II, p. 40.   [3] *Rot. Hund.* I. 466.
[4] Dugdale, *Monasticon*, VI. 821.
[5] Brit. Mus., Add. MS. 15350, fo. 4.   [6] *Ass. R.* 759, m. 37.
[7] Cart. Ant. X. 22 (9) (P.R.O.); B.M. Add. Charters 19575.
[8] *De Scaccario*, II. 5 (Oxford ed. p. 126).
[9] Stubbs, *Select Charters* (9th ed.), p. 159.

certainly includes the hundred courts of Bullingdon and Northgate which, as we have seen, were appendent to that manor;[1] but on the other hand the abbess of Godstow has 100s. blanch in Headington, and Henry of Oxford 50s. blanch there also. These two cases must be explained by the second alternative of the *Dialogus*: the holders of these lands had the pleas that arose in the hundred court as far as their own lands and tenants were concerned; they had hundredal jurisdiction over their own lands, and exemption from attendance at the hundred court, and probably also from the fiscal obligations that went with such attendance.[2] Such a jurisdiction is, as will be shown, sometimes described as 'a hundred', but it is easy, as a rule, to distinguish such a hundred geographically from the jurisdiction that extends over the whole administrative hundred. Thus, though the evidence of the Pipe Rolls needs careful checking, a reference to *terrae datae blancae* is often a valuable clue to the lordship of a private hundred at a given date. The terminology of the exchequer seems to be echoed in the Norfolk Hundred Rolls of 1275, where the *firmae albae* of six hundreds are mentioned,[3] the rate having been fixed in two cases under Henry I, in four under Henry II. The blanch farm occurs in two other instances from Norfolk,[4] but the only example of it that has been noted outside Norfolk is that of Bosham, Sussex.[5]

The association of the grant of a hundred with that of a royal manor has thus been carried back to the reign of Henry I, and shown to be recognized as a familiar practice by the exchequer. Further evidence is contributed by another technical term already cited, namely, the foreign hundred: *hundredum forinsecum, hundredum extrinsecum,* or *uthundredum.* Though the term was in use from the twelfth to the seventeenth century, and is familiar to the historians of

[1] Reference is made in 1231 to the time when Hugh de Plugeneye held the manor and hundreds (*Bracton's Notebook,* case 513).

[2] Ellesmere manor in Shropshire is thus granted *cum hundredo,* at a farm of £20 a year, in 1253 (*P.R.C.* Hen. III, 1247–58, p. 214), and in 1255 the jurors of Pimhill hundred say that by loss of suit from Ellesmere for the last two years the king has lost 20s. a year, that is, a shilling in the pound, the amount which, according to the *Dialogus,* 'blanches the farm' of a manor (*Rot. Hund.* II. 76).

[3] Shropham and Guiltcross, *Rot. Hund.* I. 468; Diss and Earsham, *ibid.* p. 466; Tunstead, *ibid.* p. 507; Freebridge, *ibid.* p. 461. These blanch farms are clearly distinguished from the farm payable by the acting bailiff to the lord of the hundred.

[4] Aylsham manor, 1227 (*Cal. Charter Rolls,* I. 25). Launditch and S. Greenhoe hundreds, 1305 (*Inq. Post Mortem,* IV. 208).

[5] *Rot. Cart.* p. 47 (1200).

the south-western counties, it is doubtful if its significance has been generally recognized. Mr Reichel has discussed its use in Devonshire,[1] but there are serious objections to the account which he, following Eyton,[2] gives of the historical origin of the Devon and Somerset hundreds, and the interpretation of the facts suggested here differs in some respects from his, and is based on a wider range of examples.

The term *hundredum forinsecum* is always found in connection with, and generally in contrast to, some other unit. It is very occasionally used to describe the royal as distinguished from the private hundred;[3] it is sometimes used to describe that part of a hundred which lies outside the liberty of a borough.[4] But it is most frequently used in contrast with the *hundredum intrinsecum* or *in-hundred*. In 1212 in a Hampshire case on the rolls of the king's court the verdict or witness first of the forinsec and then of the intrinsec hundred of Alton is given.[5] In 1236 the intrinsec and extrinsec hundreds of Andover give one joint verdict.[6] In 1280 the jurors of the eyre of Dorset say that the prior of Christchurch has two-thirds of the manor of Piddleton with a free intrinsec court, by the gift of William de Vernon, former earl of Devon, and one-third of the same manor with the forinsec hundred by the gift of William de Montacute in the time of Henry III.[7] In some eighteenth-century transcripts from a Newnham cartulary are found lists of the hamlets and tithings composing the inland and outland hundreds of Axminster.[8] We have also lists of the members of the inhundred and the outhundred of Sherborne respectively.[9] An inquest in Tendring hundred in 1308 is made by twelve 'forinsec' jurors of the hundred supplemented by eight jurors of the vill of Manningtree.[10] The most significant example, however, is that of Reading hundred. In 1125 Henry I granted the hundred of

[1] *Trans. Devon Assoc.* XXXIII. 566-9.
[2] See J. H. Round in *Vict. Co. Hist., Somerset*, I. 395.
[3] *Rot. Hund.* II. 238.
[4] E.g. Bideford and the foreign hundred of Shebbeare (Ass. R. 176, m. 38; Melksham, Lord Treas. Remembr., Misc. Roll 6/13). Cf. 'the foreign' of Biggleswade, Wotton, Colchester, Dodbroke (*Vict. Co. Hist., Beds.*, II. 212; *Gloucs. Notes and Queries*, IV. 27; Webb, *Manor and Borough*, p. 51, n. 2; *Yearbooks of Edward II* (Selden Soc.), XV. 219).
[5] *Select Pleas of the Crown* (Selden Soc.), pp. 64-5.
[6] *Book of Fees*, p. 1865.
[7] Ass. R. 204, m. 31.   [8] B.M. Add. MS. 28649, p. 492.
[9] Hutchins, *History of Dorset* (1774), II. 332.
[10] See below, p. 168.

Reading to Reading Abbey.[1] In 1208[2] John granted to the abbey 'id quod eis defuit de hundredo suo de Reding, scilicet totum forinsecum hundredum', to hold freely, with all the liberties which Henry I had granted. A Reading cartulary[3] gives a transcript from the records of a Berkshire eyre of 1218[4] under the heading 'de forinseco hundredo in manum regis aliquando dimisso et iterum reddito et in rotulo scaccarii notato'. The jurors of 1218 found that the abbot and monks of Reading were fully seised of the foreign hundred of Reading, of which they had all assizes and pleas of the crown and all sorts of liberties, as in their demesne lands.

For this hundred, with all these liberties, was given them by the founder at the first foundation of the church, as the charter of foundation and the charters of other kings of England seen and read (in the eyre) testify, and they always held it in peace until the war between King Stephen and King Henry. Then a certain abbot of the house of his own accord surrendered it. But later King John gave them back the hundred with the said liberties by the charter seen and read (in the eyre). So when a dispute arose before the justices of novel disseisin soon after, as to the liberties belonging to the said hundred, judgment was given for the abbot and convent at the exchequer, before Peter, bishop of Winchester, and others, and the barons of the exchequer, to the effect that the abbot and monks of Reading ought to have their court of the foreign hundred and of all assizes and recognitions and pleas of the crown and all liberties belonging to the king...and the king commanded that no sheriff should interfere in the said matters after the said liberty was restored to them as aforesaid.

If from this narrative of surrender and restitution we go back to the original grant of Henry I, we find that by it the abbey is granted jurisdiction in criminal matters 'quantum ad regiam pertinet potestatem' both in the manor of Reading and in its dependencies (*appendiciis*), with the right to suit of court from the lands lying round Reading.

[1] *Eng. Hist. Rev.* 1924, pp. 79–80. See also Cart. Ant. X. 22 (9).

[2] *Rot. Cart.* p. 175; *Monasticon*, IV. 44 (Harl. MS. 1708, fo. 32b). Cf. *Red Book of the Exchequer*, p. 760, which refers to the Pipe Roll of 10 John, under Berkshire 'ubi Abbas de Redinges finem fecit pro lx m. pro habendis pertinentiis ad hundredum suum'.

[3] Harl. MS. 1708, fo. 4.

[4] The date is fixed by the reference to Richard le Poer, bishop of Salisbury 1217–28, as the chief justice in eyre.. Cf. the commission on the Patent Roll for 1218 (*P.R.C.* Hen. III, 1216–25, p. 207).

Veniant que ad hundreda de Redinga et de Leomenestria[1] homines cir-
cumiacentium maneriorum secundum consuetudinem temporum prece-
dentium.

From these passages it becomes clear that the grant of a foreign
hundred meant the transfer of royal rights of jurisdiction and to
suit of court over a tract of land not, as a rule, held in demesne. It
would seem that, when the church of Reading surrendered its
'foreign' jurisdiction, it still retained hundredal jurisdiction over the
lands of the church, that is, the manor of Reading itself. If the foreign
hundred was 'what was lacking' in 1208 to make up the whole
hundred of Reading, we may fairly suppose that the ancient demesne
manor of Reading was a part of it, even its natural nucleus, since
territorially the foreign hundred lay round it, and the men of those
lands were anciently accustomed to come to the hundred courts of
Reading. It seems, therefore, that we might safely call the demesne
jurisdiction retained by the abbey under Henry II the 'intrinsec
hundred' of Reading.

This interpretation of the word 'foreign' is entirely consistent with
its use in manorial diction, where the foreign service is the public or
national service as distinct from the personal and seignorial.[2] The
outland and inland hundreds correspond to the *utware* and *inware*.[3]
In Piddleton hundred, where the manor was before 1066 a 'comital
vill'[4] with the third penny of the shire annexed to it,[5] the 'foreign'
rights seem to have passed from the king to the earl, and to have been
at his disposal.[6] Another case that brings out this contrast of the in-
hundred and out-hundred is printed in the *Placita de quo Warranto*.[7]
In the eyre of Wiltshire of 1281 William of Giselham, for the king,
claims the half-hundred of Roborough from the bishop of Salisbury.
The bishop comes and says he claims no hundred at Roborough. He
holds a court every three weeks, in which pleas which pertain to the

---

[1] The foreign hundred of Leominster, in Herefordshire, was also held by Reading
Abbey. Cowell's *Interpreter* (1708), *s.v. Foreigne*, speaks of the 'Foreigne of Lem-
ster' as 'within the jurisdiction of the Mannor, but not within the liberty of the
Bayliff of the Burrough'.

[2] Bracton, fo. 36, 'servitia quae dicuntur forinseca...pertinent ad dominum
regem et non ad capitalem dominum'.

[3] Vinogradoff, *English Society in the Eleventh Century*, pp. 194–5. Cf. also the use
of *inland* and *sokeland* pointed out by Mr W. H. Stevenson, *Eng. Hist. Rev.* 1912,
p. 24, n. 174.   [4] *Instituta Cnuti*, III. 55.   [5] D.B. I. 75.

[6] The origin of the Montacute rights in the hundred, traceable in 1189 (Madox,
Exchequer, p. 336), is not, however, clear.   [7] p. 804.

hundred are held, but only for his own men, under a charter of Henry III which freed his men from suit of shire and hundred, and his land from the entrance of sheriffs and their bailiffs. William of Giselham rejoins that the bishop holds a hundred at Roborough, 'et placitat ibi omnia placita quae pertinent ad hundredum, tam de hominibus forinsecis quam de hominibus suis propriis'. The jurors find that the bishop holds a free court in his manor of Roborough, and holds pleas there for his own men under the charter which exempts them from suit of shire and hundred, but, as he says, has nothing in that manor belonging to the hundred. He has, that is, an intrinsec, not a forinsec, hundred there. The inquest post-mortem of the earl of Lincoln, again, in 1311 finds that the pleas and per-quisites of the hundred of Badbury belong to the manor of Kingston, and are worth so much; those of the 'intrinsec court' of Kingston are worth so much.[1]

The very existence of the terms in-hundred and out-hundred implies the relation of the hundred to a particular manor. The fact that the royal rights over a hundred should need to be distinguished from the lord's rights in his manor indicates a close connection between hundred and manor. A number of instances suggest that the foreign hundred, though separable from the manor, might naturally be expected to go with it. In 1274 the manor of Black Torrington, Devon, was held by Roger de la Zouche and the foreign hundred by Thomas de Winford; but Thomas holds it by charter from a former lord of the manor, and pays rent for it to Roger.[2] Some time before 1257 Richard of Cornwall granted the manor of Bensington to the men of the manor with all rents and customs, excepting the foreign hundreds and the vill of Henley.[3] These are the same four and a half hundreds which belonged to Bensington in 1086. In 1327 a subsidy roll defines the limits of the intrinsec and extrinsec hundreds of Shrivenham, Berkshire, and it appears that the intrinsec hundred is identical with the manor of Shrivenham, the grant of which in 1218 had conveyed the hundred with it.[4] The modern names of the hundreds of Bath Forum,[5] Wells Forum,[6] and Beaminster Forum (Dorset) point in the same direction. In 1235

---

[1] Chanc. Inq., Edw. II, 22/21 (P.R.O.).   [2] Rot. Hund. I. 64.
[3] M. T. Pearman, History of Manor of Bensington, p. 30.
[4] Vict. Co. Hist., Berkshire, IV. 501. Note also Rot. Hund. I. 13: 'Valet totum manerium (Shrivenham) sine hundredo' £40.
[5] 'Bath forinsecum' in 1280.   [6] 'Forinsecum de Wel' in 1280.

Robert de Blakeford and Avice his wife are granted all that her ancestors held in the manor of Braunton, Devon, saving the out-hundred,[1] which in 1219 was in the hands of the king, administered by the sheriff,[2] and in 1229 was granted by the king to Cleeve Abbey.[3] In the case of Ermington hundred, Devon, we are told in 1303 that the tenure of the manor, with the foreign hundred, goes back to the Conquest.[4] The Hundred Rolls say that Henry I had given the manor to Matilda Peverel, ancestress of the later lords of the hundred.[5] Domesday tells us that the king holds Ermentone and the customs of the hundred belong to this manor.[6] In this one case at least, then, the foreign hundred is carried back to 1086.

The instances of *hundredum forinsecum* cited above are confined to the old West Saxon kingdom.[7] The evidence of Domesday, which we now have to examine as a whole, indicates a more widespread association of the hundred with a particular manor. Much of the ground has already been traversed by Maitland[8] and by other scholars, but no general survey of the evidence seems to have been attempted hitherto.

In an appreciable number of cases the association of hundred and manor recorded in the thirteenth century can be traced continuously back to Domesday. In the thirteenth century sixteen of the thirty-one hundreds of Norfolk are clearly associated with manors; of these ten are stated to be so linked in Domesday.[9] Clackclose hundred was held with Wimbotsham,[10] the soke of Diss and Earsham hundreds was appurtenant to their manors,[11] Guiltcross was held with the manor of Kenninghall,[12] Mitford was attached to East Dereham,[13] North Greenhoe to Wighton,[14] Shropham to Old Buckenham.[15] It would appear that the three hundreds of Happing, East Flegg and

[1] *Cal. of Charter Rolls*, I. 211.
[2] *Book of Fees*, I. 265.
[3] *Cal. of Charter Rolls*, I. 98.
[4] *Cal. Misc. Inq.* I. 520 (no. 1914).
[5] *Rot. Hund.* I. 69.
[6] *D.B.* I. 100b.
[7] But cf. 'Borgha forinseca' in Kent (*Plac. Quo War.* p. 350).
[8] *Domesday Book and Beyond*, p. 92.
[9] E.g. *D.B.* II. 113b: 'Soca et sacha de Grenehou hundret pertinet ad Wistune manerium Regis quicunque ibi teneat.' *Ibid.* II. 114: 'H. de Dice...appendet ad Dice in Sutfulc, et ibi appropriatur tota soca et saca istius dimidii hundredi, praeter....'
[10] *D.B.* II. 215b. Compare charter of William I confirming the grant of 'Wyne-bodesham cum hundredo et dimidio infra Bichamsdich' (*Historia Rameseiensis* [R.S.], p. 202.
[11] *D.B.* II. 114, 139b.
[12] *Ibid.* p. 128.
[13] *Ibid.* p. 214.
[14] *Ibid.* p. 113b.
[15] *Ibid.* p. 127.

West Flegg were appendent to Yarmouth,[1] and, though this is less explicit, that the soke of Forehoe lay in Hingham,[2] that of Eynsford in Foulsham,[3] and that of Wayland in Saham.[4] Later tradition carried the association of Launditch and South Greenhoe hundreds with Mileham manor to the time of William the Conqueror,[5] and Blomefield says that the fee of the hundred of Humbleyard belonged to the manor of Hethersett before the forfeiture of Earl Ralph.[6] It is thus quite likely that Domesday's account is not exhaustive, but it seems also highly probable that the greater fullness of its second volume has preserved for us details which have been crowded out of the first.

In Oxfordshire the account, though more comprehensive, is less particular. Seven royal manors are mentioned,[7] to each of which two or more hundreds are annexed, but in no case are the hundreds named. Later evidence enables us to equate the four and a half hundreds annexed to Bensington manor with the four and a half hundreds of Chiltern; the two hundreds of Headington with Bullingdon and Northgate; the two and a half hundreds of Kirtlington with the later Ploughley hundred; the three hundreds of Upton with Wootton[8] hundred; the three hundreds of Shipton with Chadlington hundred; the two of Bampton with Bampton hundred and the two of Bloxham and Adderbury with Bloxham hundred. It does not seem too much to infer with Professor Chadwick[9] that the three remaining hundreds of Banbury, Thame and Dorchester were annexed to the three manors of that name held by the bishop of Lincoln.[10]

The most complete and explicit statements, however, are found along the borderlands of the west. All the six hundreds in the land between Mersey and Ribble—the later Lancashire—are annexed to

[1] 'Gernemua valuit cum duabus partibus soche de tribus hundredis xviii lib. ad numerum' (D.B. II. 118).

[2] Ibid. p. 227.   [3] Ibid. p. 262b.   [4] Ibid. p. 110.

[5] Rot. Hund. I. 434; Inq. Post Mortem, IV. 208.

[6] F. Blomefield, Hist. of Norfolk (2nd ed.) v. I. I can find no evidence in support of this statement.   [7] D.B. I. 154b. See below, p. 110.

[8] 'The three hundreds of Wootton' are mentioned in the Pipe Roll of 1172.

[9] Anglo-Saxon Institutions, p. 254.

[10] D.B. I. 155. It should be noted that the hidage of the bishop's manors is almost exactly 300 hides. In 1279 the bishop of Lincoln is said to hold the hundred of Thame 'with the manor' (Rot. Hund. II. 820). In 1285 he claims the hundred of Dorchester by virtue of his tenure of the manor from time immemorial (Plac. Quo War. p. 664).

royal manors in Domesday.[1] In Cheshire the third penny of the hundred is in two instances annexed to a manor,[2] but for the other ten hundreds no such statement is made. In Salop ten of the fifteen Domesday hundreds are annexed to manors, formerly held by Edward the Confessor, held in 1086 by Earl Roger.[3] In Hereford-shire, again, the association is only mentioned in the case of five out of the nineteen Domesday hundreds; the third penny of two hundreds had been annexed to the manor of Burghill, that of three hundreds to the manor of Cowarne, both formerly held by Earl Harold, but the connection no longer obtained in 1086.[4] For Worcestershire there is no such statement; the seven private hundreds mentioned in Domesday were apparently made up of the estates of their lords, and of the remaining five hundreds still in the sheriff's control, only one, Clent, bears the name of a royal manor. In Gloucestershire the existence of the hundredal manor has been assumed or accepted by the local Domesday historian, Canon C. S. Taylor,[5] though the actual Domesday evidence is slight. He quotes the account of the three hundreds annexed to the royal manor of Winchcombe and the other two annexed to Longborough;[6] points out that the manor and the hundred were conterminous in the cases of Tidenham and Berkeley, and the hundred tenurially homogeneous in the case of Tewkesbury, Deerhurst and Bernintreu (the later Henbury); and draws up a list of royal manors to which, as he believes, hundreds were appendent, a list based, in fact, on later evidence.[7]

It is on later evidence that we are forced more and more to rely as we come to the counties of the south-west. Domesday evidence of the sort available for Shropshire or Norfolk is lacking; only

---

[1] *D.B.* I. 269b-70: 'Totum manerium cum hundredo reddat'...'Ad hoc manerium uel hundredum pertinent....' See W. Farrer, 'Notes on Domesday Survey between Ribble and Mersey' (*Trans. of Lancashire and Cheshire Ant. Soc.* vol. XVI). Amounderness was also annexed to Preston (*ibid.* XVIII. 25).

[2] *Ibid.* p. 263b. Macclesfield and Frodsham manors.

[3] *Ibid.* p. 253–253b: e.g. 'Odenet. Rex E. tenuit. Modo reddit viii lib. cum hundredo quod ad manerium pertinet. Membrefelde Rex E. tenuit. Huic manerio pertinet totum Alnodistreu hundredum. ij den. erant regis E. et tertius comitis.'

[4] *Ibid.* p. 186; cf. *Vict. Co. Hist., Herefordshire,* I. 301, 337.

[5] *Analysis of Gloucestershire Domesday* (Bristol and Gloucestershire Arch. Soc.).

[6] *D.B.* I. 162b, 163.

[7] He does not examine the history of either the seven hundreds depending on Cirencester or the seven hundreds of Grumbalds Ash. See below, p. 95 f.

sporadically does a definite statement associating a hundred with a manor occur. Yet when the later evidence is considered, and when the incomplete and even contradictory character of the records for 1084–86 is remembered, we do not seem to be going too far in **inferring an organization of hundreds attached to manors as complete in 1086 as that in Lancashire or Oxfordshire.** In the case of Devon and Somerset, as in Gloucestershire, local historians have drawn the inference as confidently as Eyton in Salop or Blomefield in Norfolk.[1] The facts that have cumulatively brought conviction to the writer are the very frequent identity of the name of a hundred with that of a royal or comital manor;[2] the descent of the later holder of a hundred from the Domesday tenant of a manor;[3] the descent, at a later date, of manor and hundred in the same hands;[4] the statement of later holders that their title to both manor and hundred goes back to the Conquest[5]—this, it may be admitted, is not conclusive evidence to the fact, but, for what it is worth, it occurs in Devonshire in 1238, forty years before the Statute of Gloucester—and, in some cases, the existence of alternative names for the same hundred.[6] Thus Heytor and Stanborough hundreds (Devon), known to be annexed to King's Kerswell and Diptford manors from 1194 on, are called Cerseuuilla and Dipeforde hundreds in Domesday, and Abdick and Bulston hundreds, Somerset, annexed to Curry Rivel from 1155 on,[7] are called Couri. If this kind of evidence is admitted, it affects some twenty-six of the forty Somersetshire hundreds and twenty-nine of the thirty-three Devonshire hundreds of Domesday. In a very few cases an explicit statement is made by Domesday. As we have seen, the customs of the hundred pertain to Ermington manor;[8] the third

[1] For Somerset see Eyton, *Domesday Studies, Somerset*, I. 74, 92; II. 1. His views are endorsed by Dr Round (*Vict. Co. Hist., Somerset*, I. 395). See also *Somerset Record Society*, III. x–xi. For Devon see O. J. Reichel, *Transactions of Devonshire Association*, XXVIII. 395. 'The king's crown lands did not pay geld...the manors gave their names to the hundreds in which they lay, and probably formed the centres round which the hundreds were grouped.' See vols. XXVI–LIV (Index vol. LXX) for studies of the Devonshire hundreds.

[2] E.g. in Devon, Plympton, Tawton, Tiverton (royal); Winkley, Wonford (comital); in Somerset, Bruton, Cannington, North Petherton (royal).

[3] E.g. in Devon, Ottery, Crediton; in Somerset, Taunton, Wells.

[4] E.g. Axminster, Black Torrington, Fremington (Devon).

[5] Ass. R. 174, mm. 32d, 34, 40 (Printed *Book of Fees*, pp. 1369–72).

[6] E.g. Hayridge=Silverton (Devon); Horethorne=Meleborne (Somerset).

[7] *Pipe Roll*, 2 Hen. II, p. 30.

[8] *D.B.* I. 100b.

penny of Teignbridge hundred belongs to Moreton Hampstead;[1] the third penny of Bampton, Braunton, and Northmolton hundreds is annexed to Molland Botreaux.[2] The above instances are in Devon; Taunton appears to be the only manor in Somerset to which the customs of the hundred are said to be annexed.[3]

In Devonshire and Somerset the association of the hundred with a hundredal manor is the easier to trace because so large a proportion of the hundreds in these two counties have come into private hands by the thirteenth century. In Cornwall, where most of the county has been, from the eighth century onwards, an appanage of the royal family,[4] evidence of this kind is not at first sight obvious. Closer investigation, however, provides good ground for believing in the existence of the hundredal manor here also in the eleventh century. Domesday itself gives the names of no Cornish hundreds, and the list in the Exon Domesday[5] consists of the names of manors, some royal, like Wineton and Conarton; some comital, like Stratton, Fawiton, and Tybesta; and some ecclesiastical, like Pawton. These have been identified by Polwhele[6] with the later hundreds, and in most cases the boundaries have not been greatly altered. Other Cornish antiquarians have adduced evidence of a connection between these manors and the bailiwick of the hundreds in which they lay which is highly suggestive and of remarkable interest as an archaic survival into the eighteenth century of eleventh-century or possibly even ninth-century arrangements. William Hals, who died in 1742, writes that the manor of Conar or Conarton 'claims by prescription royalties and jurisdiction over the whole hundred of Penwith',[7] and the steward or judge of both manorial and hundredal courts, commonly the same person, is appointed by the lord of the manor, Sir John Arundel of Penwarne, descendant of the Pincerna to whom Henry II confirmed the grant of both hundred and manor.[8] The manor of Tybesta carried with it, when Hals wrote, the jurisdiction of the hundred of Powder and had the same steward;[9] the lord of the manor of Trenay Fawiton nominated the bailiff for the hundred of West and paid his salary in 1824.[10] In Kerrier the hundredal manor

[1] D.B. I. 101.   [2] Ibid.
[3] Ibid. p. 87b. For a discussion of the meaning of these phrases see Eng. Hist. Rev. 1920, p. 78 ff.; 1924, p. 166.   [4] Corbett, in Camb. Medieval Hist. III. 344.
[5] fo. 63b.   [6] Polwhele, History of Cornwall, II. 34.
[7] Hals, Parochial History of Cornwall, II. 145.
[8] Polwhele, op. cit. II. 33; J. P. Yeatman, The House of Arundel, pp. 233–4.
[9] Hals, op. cit. I. 253.   [10] Hitchins, History of Cornwall, II. 512.

was in Hals's time Mawnan (or Penwarne);[1] in the Exon Domesday the manor named is Winnentone, the later Gunwallo.[2] Stratton, a royal manor mentioned in Alfred's will,[3] was given by William I to the count of Mortain;[4] it was almost certainly the manor to which Triggshire, later the three hundreds of Stratton, Lesnewth, and Trigg, was annexed. Pawton, the manor given to the bishop of Exeter by Egbert in 825 with other lands making up a tenth part of Cornwall,[5] was presumably the head of another hundred which, with the lands of St Petrock, made up the modern Pydershire.[6] Thus there seems good ground for saying that the Cornish 'shires', if Welsh in origin,[7] were before the Norman conquest administered in connection with manors or *tuns*.[8]

When we pass eastwards to Dorset, Wiltshire and Hampshire, the phenomena are very similar to those we have noticed in Somerset and Devon. In Dorset the Domesday evidence does not go very far. Seven of the hundreds bear the name of royal manors.[9] Glastonbury, Shaftesbury and Salisbury are holding manors identical in name with hundreds of which these churches are known to have been the lords at a later date.[10] There is later evidence for the holding together of other manors and hundreds,[11] but it is less complete and less useful than that in Somerset or Devon, partly because a larger number of hundreds are retained in the king's hands, partly because there has been a drastic rearrangement of the hundreds after 1086 which makes it more difficult to reconstruct Domesday conditions.[12] The Wiltshire Domesday associates two hundreds with Malmesbury: these are

[1] Hals, *op. cit.* III. 74.   [2] *Ibid.* p. 128.

[3] 'Streatnet on Triconshire', Corbett, *Camb. Medieval Hist.* III. 345.

[4] *D.B.* I. 121 b.   [5] Corbett, *Camb. Medieval Hist.* III. 344.

[6] In 1742 Rialton manor, held by St Petrock in 1086, claimed jurisdiction over the whole hundred of Pyder (Hals, *op. cit.* I. 209). It is possible that there was then a St Petrock's hundred centred in Rialton (in St Columb Minor). Canon T. Taylor, however, has shown that Rielton hundred in Domesday is the modern East, centred in the comitalman or of Risleston (Rillaton in Linkinhorne), *Vict. Co. Hist.*, *Cornwall*, II. 61. See also O. S. Anderson, *The English Hundred Names*, III. 151–5.

[7] Corbett, *Camb. Medieval Hist.* III. 345.

[8] *Vict. Co. Hist.*, *Cornwall*, II. 54 (Part 8, *The Cornwall Domesday*).

[9] Bere, Albretesberga, Knowlton, Gillingham, Pimperne, Winfrith, Dorchester.

[10] Buckland and Newton (Glastonbury); Beaminster and Yetminster (Sarum); Handley (Shaftesbury).

[11] See Hutchins, *History of Dorset*, I. 206, 470; III. 1, 47.

[12] See Eyton, *A Key to Domesday*.

probably the two held with the town by the abbey after the Conquest.[1] Seven of the Domesday hundreds bear the name of royal manors;[2] five of them are named after ecclesiastical manors whose holders were later lords of the hundreds also.[3] In the thirteenth century eighteen of the twenty-eight hundreds were held with manors, and in some cases at least the tenure is traceable back to 1154.[4]

In the Hampshire Domesday, Winchester is immemorial lord of the manors which gave their names to that church's hundreds as known later;[5] the soke of two hundreds is annexed to the manor of King's Somborne,[6] and the third penny of six hundreds belongs to the manor of Wallop.[7] In the thirteenth century twenty-eight of the thirty-eight hundreds of Hampshire were annexed to manors, ten of which were ancient demesne.[8]

Without going into the history of every county in such detail as this, it is possible to survey cursorily the rest of the field. In Sussex five ecclesiastical manors have hundredal associations.[9] Only two royal manors are traceable in Domesday, both giving their names to hundreds,[10] but the manors of Brede and Eastbourne, to which the hundreds of Gostrow and Eastbourne were later annexed, had been royal vills at an earlier date.[11] Other hundreds bear the names of comital manors.[12] The Kent Domesday supplies the interesting instance of the twenty-two and a half hundreds attached to the manor of Wye, to which we shall return later,[13] besides several hundreds that take their name from royal vills.[14] In the thirteenth century

[1] D.B. 1. 64b: 'The pleas of Cicemantone and Sutlesberg hundreds belong to the farm of Malmesbury.' Later Chedglow and Startley. See O. S. Anderson, The English Hundred-Names: The South Western Counties (1939), pp. 158–9.
[2] Amesbury, Bradford, Calne, Chippenham, Melksham, Warminster, Westbury.
[3] Chalk, Damerham, Downton, Potterne, and Cannings.
[4] Heytesbury, Highworth, Kinwaston, Melksham, Mere. See Pipe Roll.
[5] Bishop's Waltham, Crondall, Fareham, Overton. Winchester also held Crawley and Chilcomb, to which Budlesgate and Fawley hundreds were annexed. Hyde Abbey held Micheldever.
[6] D.B. 1. 39b.   [7] Ibid. p. 38b.
[8] Ancient Demesne Manors with hundreds attached in private hands: Alton, Andover, Barton Stacey, Basingstoke, East Meon, Hurstbourne (Pastrow), Kingsclere, King's Sombourne, Twynham (Christchurch), and Odiham. In royal hands: Broughton (Thorngate), Selborne, and Meonstoke. For other hundreds see Vict. Co. Hist., Hampshire. For the six hundreds appendent to Basingstoke, see ibid. IV. 129.
[9] Malling, Hamfelde, Steyning, Bury, Bexhill.
[10] Bosham, Rotherfield.   [11] Rameslie, Burn (D.B. 1. 17, 20b).
[12] Poynings, Singleton.   [13] See below, pp. 88, 101–3.
[14] Faversham, Middleton or Milton, Eastry, Sturry, Barham, Hoo.

many Kentish hundreds are appurtenant to manors. In Surrey the Domesday names of the hundreds suggest dependence on manors,[1] and there are a few later instances of association. In Berkshire, Domesday gives no such explicit evidence as in Oxfordshire, but eleven of the twenty-two hundreds bear the names of royal manors.[2]

North of the Thames, in Essex, there is only one clear statement in Domesday that a hundred is annexed to a manor,[3] though it seems highly probable in some other cases.[4] Two other hundreds bear the names of royal manors,[5] and eight are found attached to manors in the thirteenth century.[6]

In Suffolk two hundreds are definitely described in 1086 as being annexed to manors,[7] and there is a strong presumption in the case of fifteen others.[8] Seven of the Northamptonshire hundreds bear the names of royal manors in Domesday,[9] eight hundreds are traditionally annexed to Oundle,[10] and of the twenty-one hundreds appendent to manors in the thirteenth century, the tenure and descent make it highly probable that the association of several goes back to 1086.[11] One of the seven Nottinghamshire hundreds is annexed to a manor in Domesday:[12] one such hundred is later traceable in Bedfordshire,[13] and one in Hertfordshire.[14] There is no other trace at any date in these counties, or in Huntingdonshire or Cambridgeshire, with the

---

[1] Effingham, Farnham, Godalming, Kingston, Reigate, Wallington, Woking.

[2] Thatcham, Blewbury, Wantage, Bray, Bucklebury, 'Nachededorne', Kintbury, Lambourne, Shrivenham, Sutton, Reading. The royal manors of Cookham, Wargrave, Compton, and Faringdon gave their names to post-Domesday hundreds.   [3] Witham; D.B. II. 2.

[4] Clavering, Rochford (Reyley), Winstree (W. Mersea).

[5] Lexden, Maldon.

[6] Barstable (Bures), Harlow (Hatfield), Ongar, Waltham, Rochford, Witham, Havering, and Clavering.

[7] Sanford to Bergholt, Blything to Blythburgh (D.B. II. 282, 287, 312).

[8] Biscopes Hundret, later Hoxne, is probably annexed to the bishop of Thetford's manor of Hoxne, 'the seat of the bishopric of Suffolk' (D.B. II. 379). Edward the Confessor gave the soke of the eight and a half hundreds that 'lie into Thinghowe' to St Edmund's Abbey (Eng. Hist. Rev. 1909, p. 418; Kemble, Codex Diplomaticus aevi Sax. 1342); and Ely claimed the soke of the 'five hundreds in Wicklaw', i.e. Plumesgate, Loes, Wilford, Carlford, and Colneis by Edgar's grant, as well as Thredling, 'the trilling of Winstou' (Liber Eliensis, pp. 111, 169, 258).

[9] Corby, Fawsley, Rothwell, Sutton, Towcester, Stoke, Norton.

[10] Monasticon, I. 382: 'Undale cum...Eahtahundred.' See below, p. 100 f.

[11] E.g. Higham Ferrers, Hamfordshoe, Wymersley.

[12] Newark (D.B. I. 283 b).   [13] Flitt.   [14] Hitchin.

possible exception of the two hundreds of Ely.[1] In Yorkshire, according to Mr Farrer,[2] the association of hundred and manor is not traceable in Domesday, though in the thirteenth century Allertonshire, Richmondshire, Howdenshire, Pickering, and possibly Claro seem to be so held. In Derbyshire, Wirksworth and Scarsdale emerge in the twelfth century as hundredal manors.[3] In the Domesday of Warwickshire two hundreds bear the name of royal manors;[4] two or possibly three such hundreds are to be found in the Buckinghamshire Domesday;[5] in neither county is any later evidence traceable. With the possible exception of the wapentakes of Well, Bolingbroke and Horncastle,[6] Lincolnshire shows no trace of the system, and Leicestershire and Middlesex are without a sign of it.

The accompanying map gives a bird's-eye view of the distribution of the system, as shown by the evidence set forth above. It will be seen that it is pretty general in all the counties south of the Thames, being most strongly marked in the south-west and least perceptible in Sussex; that it is sharply marked on the western borders and in East Anglia, well established in Essex and Northamptonshire; only post-Conquest in Yorkshire, and hardly discernible in the typical Danelaw counties and in Cambridgeshire, Huntingdonshire, Hertfordshire, Bedfordshire, Buckinghamshire and Middlesex.

If these facts stood alone it might be suggested that the system of associating hundreds with particular manors was introduced, as a system, by William the Conqueror. A good deal of the Domesday evidence is so worded that it might only apply to the time of King William and not to that of King Edward. It is only in combination with other and earlier evidence that it becomes so suggestive as to warrant arguing from it into pre-Conquest history. The theory

---

[1] *Liber Eliensis*, p. 111; *D.B.* 1. 191 b. Two Cambridgeshire hundreds bear the name of royal manors, but when these are granted out, the hundreds remain in royal hands.   [2] *Vict. Co. Hist., Yorkshire*, II. 150.

[3] *Rot. Cart.* p. 108; cf. Stenton, in *Oxford Studies*, II. 72 ff.

[4] Coleshill, Stoneleigh.

[5] Aylesbury, Risborough, Brill (?).

[6] 'The wapentake of Well represents the Domesday soke of Stow' (F. M. Stenton, in *Danelaw Charters*, p. cix). Well wapentake is called Stow wapentake in the Pipe Roll for 1153 and 1156. It was held by the church of Lincoln before and after the Conquest (*D.B.* 1. 376; H. W. C. Davis, *Regesta*, no. 333). For the sokes of Bolingbroke and Horncastle see F. M. Stenton, in *Oxford Studies*, II. 44; he considers, however, that the soke in Lincolnshire, Nottinghamshire, and Leicestershire is of later origin than the wapentake and usually originated in private arrangements and not in a royal grant (*ibid.* pp. 45–6).

outlined below can only be tentatively advanced, but does not seem too extravagant to be considered.

The term *hundred*, as used for a territorial division, is not traceable in England before the tenth century.[1] Whether or not its use be attributed to Danish influence, there seems to be a general consensus of opinion that the thing itself, the administrative district regulated by the laws of Edward the Elder and his successors, is of West Saxon origin. Mr Corbett's interpretation of the administrative history of the tenth century as an extension to the Danelaw of West Saxon local governmental arrangements by the division of the East and Midlands into shires and hundreds (or wapentakes)[2] holds the field at present. The investigations of Professor Stenton,[3] Dr Douglas,[4] and Mr Jolliffe,[5] whilst helping to demonstrate the diversities of local practice, have not yet fully cleared up the administrative systems of the Danelaw, East Anglia, Northumbria, Kent and Sussex before the West Saxon ascendancy was established.

If the administrative unit known in the tenth century as the hundred originated in Wessex, what was its origin? The fact that in many instances a hundred is assessed at a hundred hides does not prove that the district was created for the purpose of taxation; there are many instances up and down England where it is clear that the assessment was imposed upon a district already in existence.[6] The suggestion that the earliest form of the West Saxon hundred is a district dependent upon a king's *tun*, administered by the royal reeve who had charge of the *tun*, was worked out in detail by Professor Chadwick[7] in 1905 and has been supported since that date by other scholars. Professor Chadwick adduced the seven Oxfordshire hundredal manors of Domesday, and also Dorchester (Oxon.), Wye (Kent), and Micheldever (Hants.) in support of his theory. Professor Tait, writing of the Lancashire hundredal manors of Domesday, suggested that this organization 'may throw some light on the origin of the hundred system'.[8] Professor Stenton, in his essay on the early

---

[1] Liebermann, *Gesetze der Angelsachsen*, II. ii, 516.
[2] *Camb. Medieval Hist.* III. 366–7.
[3] *Danelaw Charters*; *Oxford Studies in Social and Legal History*, II.
[4] *Oxford Studies in Social and Legal History*, IX.
[5] *Eng. Hist. Rev.* 1926, pp. 1–42; 1929, pp. 612–18; 1930, pp. 427–35.
[6] For instance, the 'seven hundreds of Cirencester' consisted of eight units but was assessed at 700 hides.
[7] *Anglo-Saxon Institutions*, pp. 233–7, 249–58.
[8] *Vict. Co. Hist.*, Lancashire, II. 179 (1908), n. 29.

history of the abbey of Abingdon, suggested that Hormer hundred in Berkshire was originally the hundred hides attached to the royal manor of Abingdon, the royal rights over which were granted to the abbey by Eadred, lost later in the anti-monastic reaction, and granted to the church a second time by Edward the Confessor. He gave reasons for thinking that such a grant would not have stood alone. 'Many facts combine to indicate that in the tenth century local divisions regarded each as a hundred hides were being annexed to royal estates.'[1] The hundred of Bath Forum appears to derive from the hundred hides adjacent to the city of Bath,[2] the hundred of Micheldever from the hundred hides belonging to that royal vill,[3] the hundreds of Fawley and Budlesgate from the hundred hides that lay round Winchester.[4] Chalk[5] and Downton[6] in Wiltshire are also the subject of royal grants mentioning the hundred hides that go with the *tun* in question.[7] Evidence of this kind is only available where the king's *tun* has passed out of the king's hands, and even then the document is generally lost and the grant has to be reconstructed from later evidence. But it is highly significant that, of the sixty royal *tuns* mentioned in the will of Alfred the Great, twenty-nine can be identified as giving their names to hundreds, or as having hundreds dependent on them in the thirteenth century.[8] The same is true of ten out of the twelve royal vills mentioned in Eadred's will (c. 955).[9] Local investigation in detail, moreover, tends to produce so strong a presumption that the local antiquary takes for granted far more than the general historian of institutions has consciously accepted.

Professor Chadwick's suggestion that the association of king's *tun* and hundred was not merely fiscal but administrative and judicial is

[1] *Early history of Abingdon*, p. 47.

[2] Kemble, *Cod. Dipl.* no. 12: 'Centum manentes qui adiacent civitati quae vocatur Hat Bathu' (c. 950).

[3] *Liber Monasterii de Hyda* [R.S.], p. 85: 'Quendam fundum quem indigenae Myceldefer appellant centum cassatorum quantitatem continentem' (c. 901).

[4] Kemble, *Cod. Dipl.* nos. 342, 642.   [5] *Monasticon*, II. 322.

[6] Kemble, *Cod. Dipl.* no. 342.

[7] For Crediton, see *Crawford Charters*, pp. 1, 43.

[8] Stratton, Hartland, Carhampton, Cheddar, Chewton, Cannington, Bedwyn, Hurstbourne, Sutton, Alton, Meon, Amesbury, Sturminster, Yeovil, Crewkerne, Axmouth, Milborne, Exminster, Lifton, Wellow, Kingsclere, Candover, Chippenham, Crondall, Godalming, Steyning, Rotherfield, Lambourne, Wantage (Harmer, *Eng. Hist. Documents*, pp. 95–9).

[9] Downton, Damerham, Calne, Wherwell, Andover, Kingsclere, Thatcham, Bradford, Amesbury, Wantage (Harmer, *op. cit.* pp. 119–20).

further supported by the investigations of Miss Demarest and Dr Stephenson.[1] The customs of the hundred, including both the fixed rent charges and the profits of justice arising from all the vills of a pre-Conquest hundred, are linked up with the tenure of a particular manor in Wessex, Lancashire and East Anglia.

Mr Jolliffe's researches raise a further issue. He has shown that in those parts of the old Northumbrian kingdom where Danish influences did not submerge older institutions a system obtained by which wide districts were administered from central estates in which 'we are puzzled to draw the line between public and private rights'.[2] These districts, known in Yorkshire, Northumberland, Westmorland, Lancashire and Cheshire as *shires*, took their name from a central vill and were, it would seem, administered by officials whose tenure of office was not yet hereditary in the eleventh century. The Northumbrian *drengs* or stewards for the administration of these shires bear the closest resemblance to the king's reeves or *horderes* as we meet them in the south-west of England before the Norman Conquest or the hereditary hundred bailiffs who appear so frequently in Somerset, Devon and Cornwall in the thirteenth century.[3] Many of the shires of the north disappeared in the later readjustments for military purposes which created the wards of Cumberland, Westmorland, Durham and Northumberland; in Lancashire they were known concurrently as shires, wapentakes and hundreds throughout the Middle Ages, and Howdenshire and Richmondshire survive to this day in local speech in Yorkshire.[4] A similar usage is to be found in Cornwall, where the hundreds retained the name of shire to a very late date, and have a longer history, it would seem, than any others in the island. Stratton in Triggshire is mentioned by that name in Alfred's will; it was the comital manor upon which Triggshire was dependent in 1086; the hundred courts were still held there in 1333. Of the other six hundredal manors mentioned in 1086 three, as we have seen, still carried with them in 1742 the jurisdiction of the hundred in which they lay, and as late as 1824 the lord of the manor of Trenay Fawiton nominated the bailiff of West Wivelshire, known in 1086 as the hundred of Fawitone.[5] Both Mr Corbett, writing of

---

[1] *Eng. Hist. Rev.* 1918, pp. 62–72; 1920, pp. 78–89; 1923, pp. 161–70; 1924, pp. 161–74; 1927, pp. 161–79.   [2] *Ibid.* 1926, p. 2.

[3] Cam, *The Hundred and the Hundred Rolls*, p. 145.

[4] For modern usage see *Vict. Co. Hist.*, *Lancashire*, I. 271; Bateson, *Hist. o, Northumberland*, I. 2.   [5] Hitchins, *History of Cornwall* (1824), II. 512.

Cornwall,[1] and Mr Jolliffe, writing of Northumbria,[2] have suggested that Celtic influences may have moulded the local governmental forms; that both the boundaries and the administration of the shires may be continuous from the time when they were under British rule. If there is foundation for this hypothesis, it would go to support the evidence of the early charters that the system of administrative districts centring in royal vills was not, as Professor Stenton's phraseology might suggest, a tenth-century innovation.

In yet another field the evidence seems to point to the antiquity of the practice. Mr Jolliffe has shown that both in Sussex and in Kent the fiscal evidence of Domesday appears to ignore the hundred as a unit. The tiny hundreds of these counties have long been a stumbling-block in the way of any general theory as to the origin of the hundred. In Sussex later administrative history reinforces Mr Jolliffe's conclusions as to the predominance of the rape in local government,[3] and, as we have seen, the evidence of the association of hundred and manor there is slight and late. Yet Sussex was part of the West Saxon kingdom before the time of Alfred. In Kent another kind of evidence is traceable. Mr Jolliffe, following in the footsteps of Henry Adams and Professor Chadwick, has traced the Kentish lathes backward to districts, ever smaller and more numerous, which are to be identified with the *regiones* of the early charters, and which he describes as districts '"lying into a *kinges tun*" for purposes of justice, administration, and the payment of royal tribute'.[4]

If Mr Jolliffe's views be accepted, we should see in the West Saxon system of administrative units centring in royal vills a parallel with the institutions both of Northumbria and Kent and a possible common descent from Celtic governmental arrangements. Leaving such far-off conjectures, an attempt may be made to sum up the conclusions suggested by the facts here presented.

The accompanying map gives the result of combining, though not, it is hoped, confounding, the evidence of Domesday, of the earlier charters, of hundredal nomenclature,[5] and post-Domesday tradition

[1] *Camb. Medieval Hist.* III. 345. See also O. S. Anderson, *op. cit.* III. 151 ff.
[2] *Eng. Hist. Rev.* 1926, pp. 25, 40 f.
[3] *Ibid.* 1930, pp. 434 f. But see *Sussex Archaeological Collections*, LXX. ii, 20–29.
[4] *Ibid.* 1929, p. 618.
[5] For a detailed investigation of this, see O. S. Anderson, *The English Hundred Names* (Lund, 1934, 1939). Whilst it is broadly true to say that hundreds named after natural features—hills, trees, fords, and the like—are commoner outside the old West Saxon kingdom, such evidence can only be negative, since the meeting-

and practice. It shows the association of hundred and manor to be ubiquitous in Lancashire, Shropshire, Cornwall, Devon and Oxfordshire, the rule in Somerset and Berkshire, and very general in Gloucestershire, Wiltshire, Dorset, Hampshire and Surrey. In every county mentioned there is evidence going back to Domesday and beyond, and we seem to see the relics of a general system of government by royal reeves of *manungs* or *stirs* dependent on king's *tuns*.

The later and scantier evidence in Sussex and Kent seems to point to a different history, and suggests a system of administration by larger units—rapes in Sussex, lathes in Kent, organized very probably round royal vills in the first place but not in hundredal units, though in Kent the hundred of Milton may well be a survival of the early Kentish fiscal and administrative districts, and the 'twenty-two and a half hundreds of Wye' mentioned in Domesday undoubtedly formed such a district, the disintegration of which was not complete before the twelfth century.[1]

In Lancashire, Cheshire, Shropshire, Herefordshire and Cornwall the general prevalence of the manorial centre of government in Domesday Book suggests that the lands most lately conquered from the Welsh had been kept most completely under royal control and that thus the original system, whether Celtic or West Saxon, had been less modified by 1066. In Cheshire and Herefordshire the hundredal manor is comital, not royal, and the evidence is not complete. In Worcestershire,[2] and to some extent in Gloucestershire,[3] administrative arrangements have been moulded or distorted by ecclesiastical commitments, yet even here there are traces of the manorial nucleus of the hundred.

In the three eastern counties the hundredal manor was certainly established by 1086, and probably by 1066, but the organization bears a different aspect. The hundreds themselves are larger, framed on more convenient lines for the administrator, and in very few cases do they bear the name of a royal manor, or indeed of any manor. Too much stress must not be laid on this, as the name of a hundred is often changed without any accompanying administrative or geographical alteration, but it does seem to be true that in the east the hundred more often takes its name from the mootstow than

place of a court need not be identical with its administrative centre, and may indeed be situated within the bounds of a hundredal vill.

[1] See below, pp. 101–3.   [2] Fishborough (Evesham), Oswaldslaw, Pershore.
[3] E.g. Westminster and Deerhurst hundreds.

from the manor in which its soke lies. It seems as if here the manorial organization had been imposed upon pre-existing districts, a theory which may be supported by the number of double or 'one and a half' hundreds to be found here. Though double or half-hundreds may occasionally indicate the fusion of two or the division of one, in many cases the terminology undoubtedly is due to the imposition of two hundred, or a hundred and fifty, or fifty hides upon a district, and shows that assessment came after organization and did not determine it.[1] The evidence, then, all goes to support Mr Corbett's theory of the extension of the West Saxon hundredal system[2] to East Anglia in the time of Athelstan or Edmund, and suggests the imposition of a royal administrative system upon districts of possibly communal origin.

In Buckinghamshire, Bedfordshire, Hertfordshire, Middlesex, Cambridgeshire and Huntingdonshire the scantiness of evidence pointing to hundredal manors may partly be due to the preponderance of royal over private hundreds after the Norman Conquest. When the governmental profits were all retained by the crown, the practical motive for keeping up the association of manor and hundred would disappear, especially after 1240, when the royal manors were removed from the sheriff's charge.[3] But it is also noticeable that the nomenclature of the hundreds points, as in East Anglia, to the mootstow rather than the manor as the original centre of the hundred,[4] and it seems a fair inference that the history of the Middle Anglian block[5] approximates administratively to that of East Anglia.

Northamptonshire, however, like Oxfordshire, detaches itself from the rest of this block. Both in nomenclature and in organization the association of hundred and manor is clearly marked, and in the case of Spelhoe hundred we have one of the rare instances of the letting of a royal hundred to the men of a royal manor.[6] Whatever may be the historical explanation of this divergence, Northamptonshire is a perplexing county in more ways than one.[7]

[1] The eight and a half hundreds of Bedricsworth (St Edmund's) and the five and a half hundreds of Wicklaw (St Etheldreda's) may be instances of such assessment. For the widespread existence of such larger units see below, pp. 91–106.

[2] The small Danish hundreds of Yorkshire, Lincolnshire, and East Anglia are another story.   [3] M. H. Mills, *Trans. R. Hist. S.* 1927, p. 123.

[4] E.g. see *Place-Names Survey for Bedfordshire.*

[5] Cf. Corbett, in *Camb. Medieval Hist.* III. 367.

[6] Kingsthorpe; see Rot. Claus. 8 Hen. III, m. 4; cf. Basingstoke (Hants.) and Kingston (Surrey).   [7] Cf. Mawer, in *Camb. Medieval Hist.* III. 337.

In the five counties of the Danelaw, as we have seen, it is the soke rather than the wapentake which is dependent on the manor, and only in a few instances do soke and wapentake coincide.[1] In Yorkshire, apart from the traces of the shire-system[2] pointed out by Mr Jolliffe, the association of wapentake and manor is completely lacking.[3] It would seem as if Danish habits, either social or administrative, were strongly resistant to the system.

In the theory repudiated by Edward I's lawyers, that the tenure of a manor might carry with it rights over a hundred, we seem, then, to see the last traces of a system of administration going back to the ninth century or even earlier, whereby the unit of local government was a district centring in a royal *tun* and administered by a royal reeve; a district rated, it may be, at a hundred hides, but older than the territorial hundred so called, and very possibly described in the laws by the vague name of *manung*—jurisdiction. Such a district would be emphatically an administrative district, organized from above, with a royal rather than a popular basis.[4] Indigenous in Wessex, akin to the systems of Northumbria, Kent and Sussex, the organization was, it is suggested, extended to the Mercian and East Anglian kingdoms, probably in connection with those fiscal and administrative innovations assigned by Mr Corbett to the reign of Athelstan. Most applicable along the western frontiers, it proved quite inapplicable in the wapentake districts of the Danelaw, and was superimposed on the existing local divisions, whether East Anglian or Danish in character, of Guthrum's kingdom. Hardly before the thirteenth century could even the appearance of uniformity be imposed upon an administrative system of such varying origins.

4 [For valuable evidence of the existence of local divisions with moots as early as the seventh century, sometimes with boundaries identical with those of the later hundred, which indicate, in the author's view, the popular origin of the pre-hundredal unit, see O. S. Anderson, *English Hundred Names*, III (Lund, 1939), pp. 209-17.]

VI

Early groups of Hundreds[1]

In the eyre held at Northampton in 1329–30, the justices had occasion twice to call in question the method of hundredal administration. To them, one may suppose, a hundred was primarily a unit responsible for providing a presenting jury; a unit which was therefore fair game for penalization if it made any mistake in the half-forgotten, obsolescent technique of the general eyre. For each hundred represented by a jury, the justices laid down, there must be a distinct bailiff, either ignoring or genuinely ignorant of the fact that in the past it had been very common for one man's name to appear on the *Calendarium* of the eyre roll as chief bailiff of two or more hundreds. When only one bailiff appeared for Emmeline Longsword's two hundreds of Sutton and Abbotstowe the justices accepted her plea that these two hundreds were in fact one.[2] They had been held together unbrokenly since the twelfth century; they had for all practical purposes become one hundred, and only the names survived to recall the period of their distinct organization. The same plea could not be put forward in the case of the eight hundreds of Peterborough, for which the abbot of Peterborough presented only two bailiffs. The justice enquired for which two hundreds the bailiffs were acting, and said that the king would provide bailiffs for the other six. To avert the confiscation of his liberty the abbot changed his ground, and with the leave of the court presented a bailiff for each hundred, and the new men were sworn in to do the work of the eyre.[3]

The historian, approaching the question from another position than Justice Scrope's, sees in these two instances traces of two different kinds of grouping: one due to administrative exigencies, the other traditional, going back in all probability to an arrangement older than the hundredal system itself. It is with these archaic units that this essay is mainly concerned, but the later groups are also worthy of notice, all the more as it is not always clear whether in a given case the whole district or its component parts is the older, and

---

[1] Reprinted from *Historical Essays in Honour of James Tait*, Manchester, 1933.
[2] *Plac. Quo War.* p. 557.   [3] B.M. Add. MS. 24063, f. 3.

arrangements apparently made for administrative convenience may in fact be survivals from another period.

The practice of grouping two or more hundreds under one bailiff, leading in many cases to their permanent merger, is most readily traceable in the case of royal hundreds. The sixteen hundreds of Cambridgeshire outside the isle of Ely were in the Middle Ages administered in six compact groups,[1] and a study of the boundaries of Papworth, Stow and Chesterton hundreds, the last of which is in three discrete portions, lying between the other two, strongly suggests that they must have been so administered from their formation, though for some unknown reason their fiscal assessment[2] was thus awkwardly distributed. The sharing of bailiffs did not in Cambridgeshire lead to fusion: in Buckinghamshire, where the eighteen hundreds were, probably already in 1086,[3] organized in groups of three, fifteen had merged into five large hundreds by the close of the Middle Ages, and only the three Chiltern hundreds of Parliamentary fame retained their separate identity. In some counties there are traces of resistance to this process of merger where it involved the disturbance of established habits. In Wiltshire in 1274 the suitors of Stodfold hundred protested against being compelled to attend courts held 'three leagues outside the hundred', whilst the suitors of Swanborough complained of having to go to a site in Stodfold hundred.[4] Swanborough, Stodfold and Roborough hundreds, administered by one bailiff in 1255, were in process of becoming the one hundred of Swanborough. The same was happening to the group Blakingrove, Kingsbridge and Thornhill hundreds in the same county, now Kingsbridge hundred, and to various Berkshire groups, now represented by Faircross, Ock, Morton and Shrivenham hundreds. Shrivenham, like Sutton, represents the merger of two private hundreds, and the same complaint from the suitors of having to go outside their own hundreds is recorded by the jurors of 1274.[5] Instances of such amalgamation, only possible when the hundreds concerned have one lord, are to be found in Bedfordshire,[6] Derbyshire,[7] Gloucestershire,[8] Lincolnshire[9]

---

[1] Ass. R. 82, 83, 86, 95.
[2] Round, *Feudal England*, pp. 44–54.
[3] Morley Davies, *Home Counties Magazine*, VI. 134 ff.
[4] *Rot. Hund.* II. 274, 275.   [5] *Ibid.* I. 15.
[6] Manhead and Stanbridge; Willey and Botlowe.
[7] Repton and Gresley; Morleyston and Litchurch.
[8] Kiftsgate, Holford and Gretestan.
[9] Boothby and Graffo; Bradley and Haverstoe.

and Suffolk.[1] Instances of the sharing of one bailiff by two or more hundreds, which, like the administration of two shires by one sheriff, is the normal practice without leading to a merger, may be found in almost every county.

These groups are clearly the product of administrative exigencies in the twelfth and thirteenth centuries. There are, however, other instances of the association of hundreds which appear to derive from an earlier period and older problems. There is, in the first place, the *sipesocn* of Warwickshire. According to the *Leges Henrici*, 'Comitatus in centurias et sipesocnas distinguntur',[2] but the only counties in which such districts are actually mentioned are Worcestershire and Warwickshire. The famous *Altitonantis* charter, a twelfth-century version of a tenth-century grant, represents Edgar as declaring that the three hundreds of Oswaldslaw should constitute a *naucupletionem*, *scypfylleð* or *scypsocne*,[3] and the Warwickshire Pipe Rolls of 16 and of 21 Henry II use the term *sibbesoka* and *sipesocha* as equivalent to *hundred* in the case of Knightlow, Kineton and Hemlingford hundreds.[4] Knightlow is made up of three Domesday hundreds, Meretone, Bomelau and Stanlei. Of these Meretone and Stanlei pay each its own murder fine in 1175, as does Brinklow hundred, which seems to correspond geographically with Bomelau, and Stanley or Stoneleigh retained enough individuality to make a separate presentment in the Hundred Roll inquests of 1279.[5] Kineton is made up of four Domesday hundreds, one of which, Tremelau, pays a murder fine in John's reign.[6] In the fourteenth century some of these Domesday hundreds were still known under the name of leets.[7]

The grouping of these Warwickshire hundreds, which became permanent, is ostensibly explained in the Worcester charter. Three hundreds together had to provide a ship's complement. It is possible that an entry in the Anglo-Saxon Chronicle for the year 1008 refers to this system or its extension.[8] Liebermann suggests that for a sixty-oared ship every five hides found one man.[9] In any case, there is a

---

[1] Bosmere and Cleydon; Blackburne and Bradwell!

[2] *Leges Henrici*, 6, 1b.   [3] 3 Birch, *Cartularium Saxonicum*, 1135.

[4] *Pipe Rolls* of 21 Hen. II, p. 94; 26 Hen. II, pp. 90, 91. Cited in Dugdale's *Warwickshire*. I owe these references to the kindness of Mr O. S. Anderson.

[5] Exchequer Book 15, fo. 6.   [6] Pipe Rolls 5 John.

[7] Dugdale, *Warwickshire* (1765 ed.), p. 2. Leta de Merton, de Stanlei, de Brynklow.   [8] Plummer, *Saxon Chronicle*, II. 185.

[9] *Gesetze der Angelsachsen*, II. ii, 638. Cf. Archbishop Aelfric's will, where armour for sixty men is bequeathed, with a ship. Whitelock, *Anglo-Saxon Wills*, p. 52.

clear analogy with the *skiplag* of Sweden, the *skipreið* of Norway and the *skipæn* of Denmark. The obligation of these districts to supply ships is described in laws of the thirteenth century,[1] but the system is held to have originated in the Viking age, and in the case of Norway the sagas ascribe it to Hakon the Good, a contemporary of Edgar's.[2] If the *sipesocn* in England is due to Danish influence it is interesting that it is only noted outside the Danelaw proper.[3] Von Schwerin has suggested that Norway borrowed the system from England,[4] but it seems on the whole more likely that England took a leaf out of the enemy's book.

Another purpose for which hundreds might be associated is also mentioned in the *Leges Henrici* and confirmed elsewhere. If for want of suitors or for any other reason a hundred court could not deal adequately with a case, it might be transferred to a joint session of two, three, or more hundreds, which could apparently revise the judgment of a single hundred.[5] The *Liber Eliensis* records meetings of three, six and eight hundreds in the time of Edgar,[6] Peterborough records mention meetings of two, three and eight hundreds,[7] the Ramsey chronicles enroll a command from William II to hold a joint session of three and a half hundreds,[8] and report a case held before nine Norfolk hundreds under Henry I.[9] Similar joint sessions are recorded in Somerset in 1122,[10] in Gloucestershire in 1183,[11] and in Berkshire in 1230.[12]

The practice of holding joint sessions of hundreds is explained on rational grounds, as we have seen, by the compiler of the *Leges Henrici*, but in one or two of the instances just cited another explanation suggests itself, namely that the court is really the court of a district that existed before the hundred had become the general

---

[1] E.g. *Upplands Law*, King's Section x. I have to thank Miss Dorothy Whitelock for this information. Tunberg, *Till Svearikets äldsta historia* (1930), gives the best and latest account of the *skiplag*.

[2] Tunberg, *Studier rörande Skandinaviens äldsta politiska indelning*, pp. 60 ff.

[3] The same applies to the Buckinghamshire triple hundreds, if they are connected with ship duty.   [4] Liebermann, *ut supra*.

[5] *Leges Henrici*, 7, 5; 31, 1.   [6] *Liber Eliensis*, I. 11, 14, 35, 59.

[7] Birch, *Cart. Sax.* 1130; *Harvard Law Review*, xx. 552.

[8] *Hist. Ram.* [R.S.], p. 214. The hundreds were probably Freebridge ($1\frac{1}{2}$) and Smethdon, which included the Domesday hundred of Docking. Freebridge and Smethdon shared one bailiff throughout the thirteenth century.

[9] *Cart. Ram.* [R.S.], I. 148; *Hist. Ram.* pp. 266–8.

[10] Palgrave, *Anglo-Saxon Commonwealth*, II. 250.

[11] Round, *Ancient Charters*, p. 81.   [12] *Bracton's Notebook*, case 469.

administrative unit. The existence of such districts was suggested long ago by Henry Adams; it is proposed here to indicate as fully as possible such evidence for it as administrative survivals can give.

The adjoining counties of Oxfordshire and Gloucestershire may be first examined. The evidence of Domesday for Oxfordshire is well known; Maitland and Professor Chadwick have described the division of the county into seven groups of hundreds dependent upon royal manors, and it only remains to add that these districts retained their administrative integrity throughout the Middle Ages whether in royal or in private hands.[1]

The Gloucestershire evidence is more scattered, and for that reason perhaps more striking. Four if not six well-marked groups can be traced, but their antiquity is a matter of inference rather than statement. The 'calendar' of the eyre roll of 1248[2] reveals the fact that hundreds held by different lords were at that time grouped for administrative purposes under one common bailiff and that these groups of hundreds formed admirable administrative units from the geographical point of view. One of these groups, the so-called seven hundreds of Cirencester, subsisted into modern times. The district comprised eight hundreds in Domesday,[3] with a total assessment, according to Canon Taylor's calculations, of 705 hides, and as early as 1221 consisted of only five administrative hundreds.[4] The 'seven hundreds' were granted in 1189 to the abbot and convent of Cirencester as 'our whole manor of Cirencester with the seven hundreds pertaining to the said manor and its farm' at a rent of £30 in the exchequer.[5] As the Canons of Cirencester are credited with £29 blanch in Cirencester on the Pipe Roll of 1155, however, it is not

---

[1] The groups are (a) the three hundreds of Shipton=Chadlington hundred; (b) the two hundreds of Bampton=Bampton hundred; (c) the two hundreds of Bloxham=Bloxham hundred; (d) the two hundreds of Upton=Wootton hundred; (e) the two and a half hundreds of Kirtlington=Ploughley hundred; (f) the two hundreds of Headington=Bullingdon and Northgate (or Soterlawa) hundreds; (g) the four and a half hundreds of Bensington=Lewknor, Ewelme, Pyrton, Langtree and Binfield hundreds. The bishop of Lincoln's three scattered hundreds appear to have been cut out of the original grouping and made an episcopal franchise like Oswaldslaw before 1066. See below, p. 110 for map.

[2] Ass. R. 274, m. 10.

[3] Bradalei, Wacrescumbe, Bristoldesberge, Begeberie, Cirecestre, Gersdon, Raspiet, Langetreu.

[4] Ass. R. 271. Printed by Maitland, *Pleas of the Crown for the County of Gloucester.*

[5] *Monasticon,* VI. 178; *Cal. Charter Rolls,* I. 145.

improbable that Richard I's charter only confirms an existing arrangement.[1] Be that as it may, a petition of 1403 declares that 'the said
seven hundreds are but as one hundred, and time out of memory
have been used as one, before the making of the deed' (of 1189).[2]
Less familiar to the Gloucestershire man than the seven hundreds
of Cirencester are the seven hundreds of Grumbalds Ash, mentioned
in a deed of 1183, when a grant to Pershore Abbey was witnessed by
the 'knights and free tenants of the seven hundreds of Grumbalds
Ash'.[3] The eyre roll of 1248 shows that in that year there was one
chief bailiff for the hundreds of Grumbalds Ash, Aggemed, Swines-
heved, Langely, Pucklechurch, Thornbury and Bernintre, and this
in spite of the fact that some of these hundreds were in royal and
some in private hands.[4] There are traces of the same arrangement
on the eyre roll of 1221,[5] though it does not contain a calendar of
officials. The hundred rolls of 1275 speak of a bailiff of Grumbalds
Ash who has the entry into several other hundreds for making the
king's summons.[6] Examination of geographical details enables us to
identify them with a group of Domesday hundreds[7] in the south-west
corner of the county which royal grants and administrative readjustments were to transform into a maze of intertwining boundaries on
the modern map, but which, taken as a whole, form a compact district of which Bristol may well have been the original administrative
centre.[8] By 1287 each of the three private hundreds has its own
bailiff,[9] and the bailiff appointed by the sheriff has only the four royal
hundreds in his keeping. The disintegration of the district may well

[1] The Pipe Roll of 1242 has the same formula as that of 1155, but adds a reference to the seven hundreds, p. 247.

[2] C. S. Taylor, *Analysis of Gloucester Domesday*, p. 122. Canon Taylor suggests
that we have here the survival of 'a shire, like Winchcombeshire'.

[3] J. H. Round, *Ancient Charters*, p. 81.

[4] Ass. R. 274, m. 10.

[5] *Ibid.* 271, m. 12. 'Agg. in Grum.' 'Pukelecherche-Grumb.' 'Langley
Oliveslane de Grumb.'

[6] *Rot. Hund.* I. 168. Petrus de Chavent (1270–73) tradidit ad firmam hundredum
de Grumboldesasse Philippo Bacun cum ingressu ad sumonitiones domini Regis
faciendas in hundreda sc. Agemed Enderinton Button Swynesheved Wynterburn
Langleye. (Some of these are manors.)

[7] Edredestane, Grimboldestou, Bachestanes, Langelei, Sineshevdes, Pulcecerce,
Bernintreu.

[8] The inclusion of Bristol might bring the assessment nearer to 700 hides; the
hidage of the seven small hundreds named is only 352 in all.

[9] Ass. R. 278, m. 78. Note the royal prohibition against royal hundred bailiffs
being stewards of local lords. *Plac. Quo War.* p. 265.

have begun long before the Conquest with the grant of Henbury to the bishop of Worcester in Offa's reign.[1]

North of the Grumbalds Ash hundreds, the private hundred of Berkeley and the royal hundred of Whitstone share one bailiff in 1248. In 1086 Berkeley was still a royal hundred and Whitstone consisted of the two hundreds of Blachelau and Witestan, so that we may here have three Domesday hundreds dependent on the royal manor of Berkeley. Similarly Deerhurst, Tewkesbury and Tibaldstone, held by three different lords in 1248, had one head bailiff and form, taken together, a fairly compact unit of government. In the north-east of the county, the tract represented to-day by the great hundred of Kiftsgate consisted in 1248 of three royal hundreds, Kiftsgate, Holeford and Greteston, and in 1086 of six hundreds, concerning which Domesday makes the definite statement that three hundreds are annexed to the royal manor of Longborough, and three to Winchcombe.[2] Canon Taylor believed that the three hundreds of Longborough were Cheftisihat, Celflede and Wideles, and those of Winchcombe, Winchcombe, Holeford and Gratestones.[3] In this case, however, there is a definite statement as to dates which may seem to cast doubt on the antiquity of these groups. According to Domesday, these hundreds have been annexed to the manors in question, since 1066, by the sheriff.[4] On the other hand, a charter of 803 alludes to Wincelcumbscira,[5] and Heming says that the *vice comitatus de Wincelcumb* was added to Gloucestershire in the time of Cnut by Eadric Streona.[6] It seems possible that Domesday is merely describing one of a series of readjustments, and that the six hundreds annexed to the two royal manors formerly made one whole district with Winchcombe for its centre, possibly with the addition of the hundreds of Cheltenham and Slaughter,[7] which had been granted to a foreign monastery by 1248.

We have thus traced back to the twelfth century certainly, and to the ninth possibly, districts in Gloucestershire which bear a striking

[1] Heming, *Cart.* I. 10.   [2] *D.B.* I. 163, 162b.
[3] *Analysis of Gloucester Domesday*, pp. 31–2.
[4] T.R.E. reddebat de hoc manerio (Langeberge) quod exibat ad firmam. Modo reddit xv lib. cum ii hundredis quo ibi vicecomes appropriavit. (fo. 163) Burgus de W. reddebat T.R.E. vi lib. de firma; postea xx lib. cum toto hundredo; modo, adjunctis tribus hundredis, xxviii lib. (fo. 162b).
[5] Birch, *Cart. Sax.* 309.   [6] Heming, *Cart.* I. 280.
[7] In 803 Cheltenham, apparently, lay in *Wincelcumbscira*. [For all this, see H. P. R. Finberg, *Early Charters of the West Midlands* (1961), pp. 228–35.]

resemblance to those existing in the neighbouring county of Oxfordshire in 1086; which, like them, leave unequivocal traces on the medieval administration of the county. Though no other shire affords so many instances of groups that look like archaic survivals, there are, besides the customary groupings of medieval administration, at least two other groups that suggest a pre-Conquest origin.

The first of these is found in Berkshire. The seven hundreds of Cookham and Bray seem to be first mentioned in the Pipe Roll of 1190,[1] and in 1220, the knights and free tenants of the seven hundreds of Windsor are asserting the special privileges of the district against the sheriff and the tax collector.[2] In 1251 they are described as the seven hundreds of Cookham and Bray,[3] and by that name they continue to have some sort of administrative unity down to the close of the Middle Ages.[4] In the various references to the seven hundreds upon the rolls of the exchequer and chancery[5] no list of names is given, but the eyre rolls again supply us with working details, and reveal a unity of administrative command which the diversity of lordships would not lead us to expect. In 1241[6] there is one sworn serjeant or head bailiff for the five royal hundreds of Bray, Beynhurst, Charlton, Cookham and Ripplesmere, the town of Windsor, the bishop of Salisbury's hundred of Sonning and the bishop of Winchester's hundred of Wargrave.[7] Two of the units which compose this group are, however, comparatively young; the hundred jurors of 1274 report that the private hundreds of Wargrave and Sonning have been recently 'withdrawn' from the king's hundreds of Charlton and Bray,[8] and in 1086 Cookham was still in Beynhurst, so that the district contained only four Domesday hundreds. It is for this reason probably that the grouping has been regarded as a post-Conquest arrangement,[9] but the remarkable geographical compactness

[1] *Pipe Roll*, p. 14.
[2] *Royal Letters* [R.S.], I. 162–3.
[3] *P.R.C.* p. 110.
[4] *Vict. Co. Hist.*, Berkshire, III. 117, 237.
[5] Ass. R. 37, m. 33 (1241); Mem. R.L.T.R. 32, m. 7d (1257); *P.R.C.* pp. 315–16 (1269); *ibid.* p. 684 (1272).
[6] Ass. R. 37, m. 27.

[7] The other Berkshire groups revealed by the eyre rolls are homogeneous in tenure; the three hundreds of Faircross (Gossetfield, Rogeburugh and Borghildebury); the two hundreds of Wantage (Ganfield and Wantage); Ock and Sutton; Morton and Slotford; Kentbury and Eagle; Shrivenham and Ildeslaw. Here again the resemblance to Oxfordshire suggests a similar antiquity in the arrangement, but there has been more geographical re-arrangement since 1086.

[8] *Rot. Hund.* I. 9, 15. The cession of these two private hundreds is at least as old as Stephen's reign.
[9] *Vict. Co. Hist.*, Berkshire, III. 137.

of the district, together with its claim to special privileges, strongly suggests a pre-Conquest district similar to the four and a half hundreds of Bensington just across the river in Oxfordshire. If so, the seven hundreds of Windsor may possibly, like those of Cirencester, derive from an early assessment of 700 hides, and the 'Bensington land' of 996[1] would be matched by the 'province of Sonning' of 666.[2]

Another administrative group revealed by thirteenth-century records directly adjoins the seven hundreds of Windsor, namely the six hundreds of Basingstoke. The Pipe Rolls show the sheriff of Hampshire accounting, down to 1207, for the farm of six hundreds dependent on the royal manor of Basingstoke.[3] Round has argued that the amount of the farm points to a pre-Conquest origin for this group,[4] which preserved its integrity down to 1225, having been farmed for two short intervals by the men of Basingstoke. Only one list of the hundreds appears to be known; that of the inquest of June 1274,[5] which names Basingstoke, Bermondspit, Chutely, Holdshot, Odington and Overton. The list presents some difficulties. Overton hundred was held by the bishop of Winchester, and as with the other hundreds held by him in Hampshire, no grant is extant, and the tenure seems to be immemorial. The manor had been his since 904. Geographically speaking, as well as tenurially, the royal hundred of Odiam would round off the group far more neatly. On the other hand, Odington hundred had disappeared from the administrative map long before 1274; it does not figure on any of the thirteenth-century eyre rolls. It had been absorbed partly into the new hundred of Odiam, and partly into Bermondspit. Odiam also included the Domesday hundred of Edefele. One is strongly tempted to correct the unsupported statement of the jurors of 1274 by substituting Edefele for Overton. If, on the other hand, the tradition they preserve is correct, it points to an origin at least as old as the ninth century for the group. After Basingstoke hundred had been detached from it, the other five hundreds were still farmed jointly for some time, and in 1256 Bermondspit, Chutely and Holdshot were administered by one bailiff.[6]

---

[1] Kemble, *Cod. Dipl.* no. 1292.
[2] Birch, *Cart. Sax.* 34; cf. Brownbill in *Notes & Queries*, XII. vii, 401.
[3] Baigent and Millard, *History of Basingstoke*, pp. 362 f.
[4] *Vict. Co. Hist.*, *Hampshire*, I. 402.
[5] *Rot. Hund.* II. 21. See *Oxford Studies in Legal History*, VI. i, 123.
[6] Ass. R. 778, m. 55.

Another Hampshire group of six hundreds mentioned by Domesday, the six hundreds dependent on Wallop[1] in Brocton, later Thorngate, hundred, are not named in 1086 nor mentioned elsewhere. The two hundreds of Somborne[2] apparently made up the present hundred of King's Somborne. Other Domesday groups are the three hundreds of Malmesbury in Wiltshire,[3] the three hundreds of Molland in Devon,[4] the two hundreds of Burghill and the three hundreds of Cowarne in Herefordshire,[5] and the three hundreds of Yarmouth in Norfolk.[6] Of these the three hundreds of Malmesbury retain their unity as an ecclesiastical franchise, and the three hundreds of Happing, East Flegg and West Flegg, which are almost certainly those annexed to Yarmouth in 1086, remain an administrative unit under one bailiff, down to the end of the Middle Ages.

The surest preservative of these ancient complexes was ecclesiastical lordship, and, apart from the Cirencester group, the outstanding examples are the great monastic franchises of the east. Whilst the three hundreds of Oswaldslaw are obviously an accumulation of estates that has been transformed by special grant into an administrative entity, the eight and a half hundreds of St Edmund are known to have existed as royal dower lands before they were bestowed on the church. The district, which to this day persists as a local government unit, has a history older than the religious house which administered it till the dissolution of the monasteries. Bury St Edmunds, the old Bedricsworth which was a royal vill in the ninth century[7] and had a mint in the tenth,[8] is the natural administrative centre for the eight and a half hundreds which met at Thingoe,[9] the moothill just outside the town, and it is not likely that the district was created for the benefit of Emma, though it is first mentioned in connection with her.[10] Bede's *regio* of Ely,[11] formerly held to have been Etheldreda's dower, can no longer be identified with Domesday's two hundreds of the Isle, but from Edgar's days these were held by the abbey as one unit.[12] Bede also mentions[13] 'the province

---

[1] *D.B.* I. 38b.
[2] *Ibid.* p. 39b.
[3] *Ibid.* p. 64b. Malmesbury, Cicemantone and Sutlesberg (see above, p. 81).
[4] *Ibid.* p. 101. Bampton, Braunton and North Molton.
[5] *Ibid.* p. 186.
[6] *Ibid.* II. 118.
[7] *Memorials of St Edmund's* [R.S.], I. 19.
[8] *Eng. Hist. Rev.* 1896, p. 761.
[9] Kemble, *Cod. Dipl.* no. 1342.
[10] *Eng. Hist. Rev.* 1909, p. 418 f.
[11] *Hist. Eccl.* IV. 19.
[12] [E. Miller, *Abbey and Bishopric of Ely* (1951), pp. 10–15, 31.]
[13] *Hist Eccl.* v. 19.

of Oundle', where Wilfrid died in 709: the first reference, it would seem, to the district which in a diminished form survives to-day as the Soke of Peterborough, and which in 1329 was administered by two hundred bailiffs only, though it called itself 'Eight hundred'.[1]

Three of the four great East Anglian franchises owed their existence traditionally to Edgar. He had granted the eight hundreds of Oundle to Medeshamstede,[2] 'confirming their ancient privileges', and he had bestowed on Ely not only the two hundreds in the marshes which in 1086 met at Wichford,[3] but also the five and a half hundreds of Wicklaw or Sudborn,[4] the district of which Woodbridge is to-day the administrative centre. Wicklaw has been identified by Mr Redstone of Woodbridge as a hill in the parish of Hacheston, though this identification is not certain. The five and a half hundreds of Wicklaw, like the eight and a half of Bury, appear to represent hidation rather than division; there are no other halves corresponding to the half hundred of Parham, later absorbed into Plomsgate, or to the half hundred of Corsford, unlike the twin half hundreds of Mutford and Lothingland in the same county. This is the more significant as the Trilling or Thredling of Winstow which was added to the Wicklaw group is clearly the third part of Cleydon hundred, which was represented in the eyres by eight jurors while Thredling had four.[5] The two districts appear to be older than their hundredal organization.

One other great group of hundreds held by a religious house in the eleventh century, but dissipated later, leads us to fresh ground. According to Domesday Book William I had bestowed on his new foundation of Battle Abbey the manor of Wye with the sake and soke and royal forfeitures of twenty-two hundreds which belonged to it.[6] No complete list of these hundreds exists; but it is difficult to avoid the conclusion that they are identical with the district called Wiwaralest—the region dependent on the royal estate of Wye, references to which are found from the eighth century onwards,[7] and which

[1] In 1329 the eight hundreds were made up of the vills of Peterborough and Thingden (Finedon) and the hundreds of Nassoburgh, Pullbrook, Navesford, Huxloe, North Navislund and South Navislund. *Plac. Quo War.* p. 553.

[2] Birch, *Cart. Sax.* 1130. See also *Monasticon,* I. 390.

[3] *Inquisitio Eliensis,* p. 100. [4] *Liber Eliensis,* II. 5, 41.

[5] Hundredum de Thredling est tercia pars hundredi de Cleydon et respondit cum aliis ita quod sunt xii in numero in universo. Ass. R. 818, m. 49.

[6] *D.B.* I. 11b; cf. *Monasticon,* I. 319.

[7] Chadwick, *Anglo-Saxon Institutions,* p. 249; *Eng. Hist. Rev.* 1929, p. 617.

later came to be called the lathe of Scrawinhope or Scray. The Battle Custumals, about 1230, state that this lathe then contained sixteen hundreds,[1] several of which are not mentioned in Domesday; but the hundreds of Kent are very small and there were certainly more ways than one of reckoning them up.[2] However this may be, the Battle Abbey records assert that twenty-two and a half hundreds owed suit to Wye, and that the Conqueror granted the abbey his own share of the profits of justice throughout those hundreds, that is, two-thirds of all pleas and forfeitures, the remaining third being the earl's portion.[3] But the unit, as a district fiscally or judicially dependent on Wye, had begun to disintegrate before the beginning of the thirteenth century. The *Chronicon de Bello*, written apparently about 1176, represents the jurisdiction as still wholly in the hands of the abbey;[4] the Custumals, some fifty years later, say that though all but three of the hundreds in the lathe of Scrawinhope belong to the summons of the abbey, the abbot has the two pennies of the pleas only in eight, namely in Longbridge and the seven hundreds of the Weald. In the other five hundreds the abbot has the suit but not the profits of justice, 'since these have their own pits (*fossas*)'.[5] In 1259 the abbot of Battle complains before Hugh Bigod that he no longer receives the two pennies of the pleas of the seven Wealden hundreds, which had been withdrawn since the time when William of Casingham became their bailiff.[6] Thus in 1275 all that is left to the abbey is the

---

[1] *Battle Abbey Custumals* (Camden Soc.), p. 126.
[2] The custumals appear to count three vills in Felborough hundred as hundreds of themselves—Chartham, Godmersham and Chilham. If this reckoning is used the number would be made up as follows:

    (*a*) The seven hundreds of the Weald;
    (*b*) Faversham, Tenham, Bocton ('not of our summons' in 1230);
    (*c*) Bircholt, Chart, Felborough, Chartham, Godmersham, Chilham, Calehill, Longbridge, Newenden, Wye, Middleton, Marden.

    According to Mr Jolliffe (*Eng. Hist. Rev.* 1929, p. 617), Faversham had been absorbed into Wiwaralest by 1086, but Middleton or Milton was still a distinct half-lest, though it was later absorbed into Scray.

[3] *Chron. de Bello*, p. 29.   [4] *Ibid.*

[5] *Custumals, ut supra*. The association of the profits of justice with the apparatus for ordeals is interesting, and may be compared with the later association of the right to enforce the assize of bread and ale with the possession of pillory and tumbril.

[6] Ass. R. 362, m. 11. Only three of the Wealden hundreds are named in Domesday, but the abbot asserts that William I bestowed them on the abbey. They are mentioned in the *Leges Henrici*, 48, 2. William of Casingham was bailiff for 40 years: c. 1216–56. *Rot. Hund.* I. 217.

two hundreds of Longbridge and Wye,[1] which they are still holding in 1316. But the lathe of Scray remains an administrative unit, though no longer dependent on the manor of Wye; like the other lathes it has one chief bailiff,[2] and its court is still meeting regularly in 1275.[3]

The antiquity of the lathes or lests of Kent may be taken as established after the work of Professor Chadwick, Mr Jolliffe and Miss Neilson,[4] and with their antiquity their origin as *regiones* dependent on royal vills. It follows that the hundredal organization of the county is of more recent origin, and the Wye evidence is of value as illustrating the process of disintegration of the archaic provinces under the two forces of administrative centralization and proprietary rights. The national system of finance, police and justice required the hundred and the hundred jury, and an alien pattern was imposed on the villages of Kent. Royal grants created a host of other beneficiaries —the archbishop, the prior of Christchurch, the prior of Faversham and so on—and the judicial and fiscal unity of the lest disappeared, though administrative custom preserved its memory.

It is clear by now that tenurial unity gave these pre-hundredal districts their best chance of survival. Generally this was best secured by ecclesiastical lordship, but there was one other force which might guard them from disintegration. Its effects are most clearly seen in Sussex. There has been much dispute as to the antiquity of the Sussex rapes, Mr Salzman[5] maintaining that they are later, Professor Tait[6] and Mr Jolliffe[7] that they are earlier than 1066. Mr Salzman shows that the boundaries of the rape of Bramber, which cut both hundreds and deaneries in half, point to a late origin, and argues that in early days the county was divided into two great sections comparable to East and West Kent, and that the creation of the rapes was the work of the Conqueror, was due to military considerations, and took place between 1066–75, with a later readjustment between 1075–86 when the rape of Bramber was created.

In the *Victoria County History* Mr Salzman maintained that both name and district were introduced by William I; in 1931 he admits

---

[1] *Rot. Hund.* I. 211.   [2] *Ibid.* pp. 200, 201, 204, 206, 211.
[3] *Ibid.* pp. 206, 217. 'Secta lesti.'
[4] *Anglo-Saxon Institutions*, p. 250; *Eng. Hist. Rev.* 1929, pp. 612 ff.; *Vict. Co. Hist.*, *Kent*, III. 177 ff.
[5] *Vict. Co. Hist.*, *Sussex*, I. 351 ff.; *Sussex Arch. Coll.* LXXII. 20–9.
[6] *Place-Names of Sussex*, p. 8.   [7] *Eng. Hist. Rev.* 1930, p. 434.

that the name may be primitive.[1] It is possible to find an explanation that will cover the facts ascertained both by him and by Mr Jolliffe. If the early districts of Sussex were called rapes, statistics do not compel us to reduce their number to two. The subdivisions in which the county was organized for fiscal and military purposes before the Norman Conquest may well have been called rapes. The evidence for the post-Conquest creation of the rape of Bramber is very strong; but it does not prove either that all the rapes as we know them were the creation of the Conqueror, or that the rape system in Sussex is later than the hundred system. We are still free to accept the evidence for the primitive division of Sussex into districts far larger than hundreds, organized for purposes both of taxation and of justice, the general pattern of which was preserved after the Conquest by tenurial unity due to military considerations. Sussex was a highly vulnerable county; and the policy of making one magnate responsible for each main port, castle and line of communication by giving him the administrative lordship of the block of territory surrounding them explains itself if the map is studied. Geographical facts, such as the points at which the rivers cut the chalk hills, must have determined the early divisions of the county no less than they determined the location of the Norman castles. In the same way, military considerations dictated the retention of a single lordship for each of the aggregates of hundreds which made up the rapes; only in Chichester was this policy abandoned. The twelve hundreds of Lewes or the thirteen hundreds of Hastings formed as permanent medieval units as the eight and a half of Bury St Edmunds. And to this stricter tenurial unity corresponded a more effective administrative unity than that of the Kentish lests. The court of the rape, called also the court of the ledh, lathe or lest from the twelfth to the sixteenth century,[2] met every three weeks, and did the work done by the three-weekly hundred court elsewhere, whilst it was only the six-monthly lawdays that 'were held in the hundred courts.[3] The bailiffs of the

---

[1] *Sussex Arch. Coll.* LXXII. 28–9.

[2] Charter of 1176. Hec conventio facta est in curia comitis coram le ledh... Testibus his...cum multis aliis de hundredis et del ledh. *Hist. Man. Comm., Delisle and Dudley MSS.* pp. 34–5. See also p. 49. In 1335 the tenants of the rape of Hastings owed suit to the court of the barony called the Lathe every three weeks. C. Dawson, *History of Hastings Castle*, p. 167. I owe these references to the goodness of the late Professor Levett. For the three-weekly court of Pevensey, see Jacob, *Baronial Reform and Rebellion*, p. 363.

[3] B.M. Add. Rolls 31516–32400.

rapes were the chief administrative officials under the sheriff of Surrey and Sussex, doing the work that in the larger hundreds of other counties was done by the hundred bailiffs.[1]

One other primitive unit appears to lie behind the Yorkshire group of five wapentakes[2] that centred in Richmond in the thirteenth century; the northern shire.[3] It seems certain that Richmondshire is a pre-Conquest unit, and it may well be that other earlier districts may lie concealed under the later administrative divisions of Northumbria; but on the knowledge so far available, the palimpsest resulting from the superposition of Norman, Danish and Anglian on Celtic arrangements is exceedingly difficult to read.

Few facts that were not already known have been adduced above, but it is hoped that the value of thirteenth-century administrative records in throwing light on earlier systems has been indicated. The calendars of the eyre rolls may still have clues to afford for tracing or confirming the existence of units like the seven hundreds of Grumbalds Ash or the seven hundreds of Windsor.

[1] Dawson, *Hastings Castle, passim.* For the rape in Sussex and the lathe in Kent, see also J. E. A. Jolliffe, *Pre-feudal England.*
[2] Halikeld, East Hang, West Hang, East Gilling, West Gilling.
[3] See Jolliffe, in *Eng. Hist. Rev.* 1926, p. 1.

APPENDIX

Groups of hundreds associated into one centre

County	Centre	No.	Earliest reference	Date
Berks	Windsor or Cookham and Bray	7	[Birch, *Cart. Sax.* 34] Pipe Roll	[666] 1190
Bucks	Aylesbury	8	*D.B.* I. 143 b	1086
Cambs	Ely	2	[Bede] Birch, *Cart. Sax.* 1267	[750] 970
Devon	Molland	3	*D.B.* I. 101	1086
Gloucs	Cirencester	7	*Cal. Ch. R.* I. 145	1189
	Grumbalds Ash	7	*Ancient Charters*, p. 81	1183
	Longborough	3	*D.B.* I. 163	1086
	Winchcombe	3	[Birch, *Cart. Sax.* 309] *D.B.* I. 162 b	[803] ,,
Hants	Basingstoke	6	Pipe Roll	1207
	Wallop	6	*D.B.* I. 38 b	1086
	Somborne	2	*D.B.* I. 39 b	,,
Hereford	Burghill	2	*D.B.* I. 186	,,
	Cowarne	3	—	,,
Kent	Cranbrook (Weald)	7	*Leges Henrici*, 48, 2	c. 1110
	Wye	22½	*D.B.* I. 11 b	1086
Norfolk	Yarmouth	3	*D.B.* II. 118	
Northants	Oundle	8	[Bede] *Monasticon*, I. 390	[732] 1146
Oxon	Bampton	2	*D.B.* I. 154 b	1086
	Bensington	4½	,, [Kemble, *Cod. Dipl.* 1292]	[996] ,,
	Bloxham	2	*D.B.* I. 154 b	,,
	Headington	2	,,	,,
	Kirtlington	2½	,,	,,
	Shipton	3	,,	,,
	Upton	3	,,	,,
Suffolk	Bedricsworth or Bury St Edmunds	8½	Kemble, *Cod. Dipl.* 1342	1043–44
	Wicklaw or Sudborn	5½	*Liber Eliensis*, II. c. 5, Birch, *Cart. Sax.* 1267	970
Wilts	Malmesbury	3	*D.B.* I. 64 b	1086
Worcs	Oswaldslaw	3	Birch, *Cart. Sax.* 1135	964 (?)
Yorks	Richmond	5	Pipe Roll	1242

VII

The Hundred outside the North Gate of Oxford[1]

The controversies as to the origin of hundreds are ancient and familiar. The ambiguities in the use of the term, at the period when the hundred was a well established and indispensable governmental district, that is, from the eleventh to the sixteenth century, are less familiar. It is possible to distinguish at least four different senses in which the word is used during this period.

The best known and the most important is the administrative hundred of royal government. The district that paid the murdrum fine, furnished a jury of presentment for the eyre, contributed its quota of primitively equipped soldiers to the *posse comitatus*, figured with its neighbours in the sheriff's accounts as making up the items of the farm of the shire, and sent its residents twice a year to the sheriff's tourn held at its traditional meeting-place, can be located on the map as early as 1086 in some counties (though not in Oxfordshire), and in most cases before 1200; and the boundaries traceable by that date are in most cases not materially modified after that date. Whether in private hands or under the sheriff's subordinates, this hundred can be confidently handled, for the king's government had fixed the pattern, and the uniform action of the central administration standardized its character.

Outside this official list of hundreds the ambiguities begin. Liebermann[2] says that in the eleventh century the word may be used to denote any public tribunal, and possibly private jurisdictions also. Long after that date the word is being used for at least two types of court, distinct from that of the governmental unit, whilst another district besides the one the sheriff handles is still alive in the twelfth century.

[1] Reprinted from *Oxoniensia*, vol. I, 1936. I have to acknowledge my debt to the kind help and criticism of Dr Salter, Professor Tait, Mrs Lobel and Miss E. Evans of Somerville College. Miss Evans' essay on the Manor of Headington, in the *Report of the Oxfordshire Archaeological Society* for 1928, contains the fullest account so far of Northgate Hundred. The two sketch-maps have been re-drawn by Mr H. S. Harrison, A.R.I.B.A.

[2] *Gesetze der Angelsachsen*, II. ii, 519.

This areal hundred has been examined by Mr Douglas and need not detain us long. It is the little hundred of East Anglia, Lincolnshire and Yorkshire, assessed at 12 carucates to the geld, the forerunner of the later leet, and serving both judicial and fiscal purposes in the twelfth century.[1]

A second usage is more indeterminate. *Hundredum* is used of the court of a lord, manorial or feudal, sometimes, but not always, exercising a jurisdiction equivalent to that of the public hundred. In the Kent returns of 1275 the jurors say that the abbot of St Augustine has a *halimot* at Langport in the suburb of Canterbury, and *in the same hundred* he appoints a borsholder and receives the presentments of the pleas of the crown.[2] In 1238 the abbot of Tavistock arrested two men in 'his hundred of Warrington'—a manor in Black Torrington hundred, and 'the whole hundred' came in force to Tavistock to get the men released.[3] A series of emancipations of serfs recorded in the Exeter Book are said to have been made by the witness of 'all the hundreds' of Cowick, Topsham, Alphington and Holecombe respectively,[4] all manors in Wonford or Exminster hundreds. I have shown elsewhere how widespread is the use of the expression *in-hundred* or *intrinsec hundred* for the court of the capital manor in contrast to the *out-hundred* or *foreign hundred* which is the court of the public administrative hundred.[5] Men are described, again, as owing suit or custom to their lord's manorial court 'at the hundreds of Martinmas and Hokeday'.[6] In Oxfordshire the bailiff of the earl of Cornwall is accused of withdrawing men from the court of Wootton hundred to 'his hundred of Yarnton'[7] and in Gloucestershire the steward of the honour of Wallingford holds a 'hundred' at Cherrington in Longtree hundred.[8] In 1481 Crowland and Peterborough Abbeys came to an agreement about 'another court or Hundred, called Rennyng Courte, the whiche in the foresaid Marisse hath been accustomed to be holdyn'.[9]

There are also larger units than the single manor for which courts exist which are described as hundreds, though not recognized as

[1] See D. C. Douglas, *Medieval East Anglia*, pp. 55–6; F. M. Stenton, *Danelaw Charters*, pp. 93–4. *Domesday Book*, I. 293 (Rutland), 361 (Lincs.), 375 (Yorks.).
[2] *Rot. Hund.* I. 203.   [3] *Ass. R.* 174, m. 40d; cf. *Feudal Aids*, I. 327.
[4] Between 1100 and 1140; Thorpe, *Diplomatarium*, pp. 632, 634, 639, 645.
[5] See above, pp. 70–5.
[6] *Somerset Record Society*, II. 56, 64, 93.
[7] *Rot. Hund.* II. 865.   [8] *Gloucester Cartulary* [R.S.], III. 250, 258 (1376).
[9] *Monasticon*, I. 398–9.

administrative hundreds in the official lists, such as the hundreds of Ellesmere in Shropshire or Tickhill, Nottinghamshire.[1] A late attempt to create such a liberty is described by John Smyth of Berkeley, who writes of the 'pretended hundred of Wotton' set up by the countess of Warwick within Berkeley hundred in 1591.[2]

A third well-established meaning is the court of a borough, and the term is so used from the twelfth to the eighteenth century, at Bristol, Cardiff, Dover and all the Cinque Ports, Swansea, Haverford West, Dublin, Cork, Waterford, Kilkenny, Tewkesbury, Chichester, Preston, Whitby and other boroughs.[3] The word is used of a court, and not of a district, and, although some of these boroughs are assessed as a hundred, more often they are not.

On the other hand, the word hundred is sometimes used of a district surrounding the town, which may be called the forinsec hundred or foreign of the town. Examples of this type of urban or suburban hundred are the hundreds of Sandwich, of Leominster and of Colchester.

It is with this last type that the hundred outside the north gate of Oxford seems at first sight to present the closest analogy. Its nomenclature and its position on the map appear to suggest an outgrowth from the city. But if we start not from the modern but from the medieval end, the character of this hundred wears a very different look, and we find ourselves compelled to begin our narrative not with the borough of Oxford but with the rural manor of Headington.

The Domesday survey of Oxfordshire is so imperfectly rubricated that no map of hundredal boundaries can be based on it. We hear of nineteen hundreds, but only three are named.[4] Instead, there is a list of eight royal manors, on each of which two or more hundreds are dependent.[5] Later evidence, however, makes it safe to identify the two hundreds of Bampton with the modern Bampton hundred, the four and a half of Bensington with the five Chiltern hundreds, those dependent on Bloxham and Adderbury with Bloxham hundred, the two and a half of Kirtlington with Ploughley hundred, the three of Shipton with Chadlington hundred, and the three of Upton with Wootton hundred. The two hundreds dependent upon Headington are to-day represented by Bullingdon and Northgate hundreds.

---

[1] *Rot. Hund.* II. 76, 318.   [2] John Smyth, *Lives of the Berkeleys*, II. 318–19.
[3] M. Bateson, *Borough Customs*, II. cxlv *et passim*.
[4] Lewknor, Piriton and Bensington (=Ewelme). It is doubtful if the *Prima* and *Secunda Gadre* of D.B. I. 159a are hundred names at all.   [5] D.B. I. 154b.

All of these hundreds are mentioned in the Pipe Rolls of 1188–93 with the exception of Northgate hundred, and with the addition of Dorchester and Thame, two of the three hundreds held by the bishop

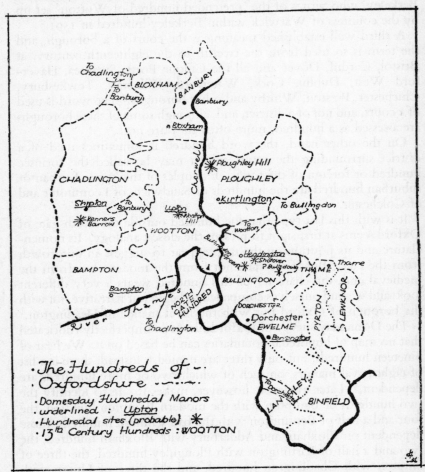

Map 4. Sketch-map of Oxfordshire showing the Hundredal boundaries.
Scale about 8 miles to 1 inch.

of Lincoln. One of the three hundreds of Chadlington is given the name of Keneswardeberga, which may be confidently identified with Kenner's Barrow, the seventeenth-century name of what is now called Shipton Barrow, an interesting and typical hundred site on the hill above Shipton.[1] The two hundreds of Headington are called Buledon and Soterlawa in 1189, Bulesdon and Schotelawa in 1193. The last, it seems highly probable, took its name from a *law* or burial mound on Shotover,[2] where in the seventeenth century two little barrows were still to be seen on the left side of the road coming from Oxford. If so, it is rather unlikely that the other hundred assembled at the traditional site, Bullingdon Green, where the Roman road from Alchester to Dorchester and beyond passes the south-west side of Shotover.[3] Several records of the court of the hundred of Bullingdon describe it as meeting at Wheatley, the earliest statement occurring in the Oseney Cartulary, for a court held in 1223,[4] and the latest in the court rolls, now in the Bodleian Library, for the years 1595–1614.[5] Wheatley in the east of the modern hundred and Shotover in the west balance admirably, as the natural centres for the two hundreds of Headington, and it is tempting to identify the Bulesdon of 1193[6] with the modern Bullsdown, a hill above Wheatley which possesses many of the features of the primitive mootstow, with its commanding outlook and its proximity to an early settlement and ancient trackway. On the other hand, the 'sheepfold of Cowley', where the hundred of Bolendona was held on 10 February 1240,[7] may have been on Bullingdon Green.

The grouping of the hundreds mentioned in Domesday becomes, save in the case of the four and a half Chiltern hundreds, a permanent amalgamation. Where in other counties there was a long-standing tradition of two or three hundreds, and protests at the abandonment of old hundred sites, or representation in the eyre of the double hundred by a jury of twenty-four, in Oxfordshire, Wootton, Chadlington and the others seem to have been regarded as ordinary single

---

[1] R. Plot, *Natural Hist. of Oxfordshire* (1705), p. 333.

[2] [For a correction of these erroneous conjectures, see *The Place-Names of Oxfordshire*, Part I (1953), pp. 159–60, where Shotteslawe (12th c.) is located near Fritwell.]

[3] Plot, *op. cit.* p. 343; R. Hussey, *Roman Road from Allchester to Dorchester*, p. 13.

[4] *Oseney Cart.* (O.H.S.), IV. 345.   [5] MS. Rolls Oxon. 117.

[6] Cf. also the form Bolesdene in 1259, in *Snappe's Formulary* (O.H.S.), p. 282.

[7] *Oseney Cart.* IV. 344. If Bullsdown was the original site, Bullingdon Green might have acquired its name as a result of Bolendon hundred sometimes meeting there, but this is not very probable.

hundreds for administrative purposes.[1] No more is heard of Keneswardeberga hundred or Soterlawa hundred after the reign of Richard I. On the other hand, the official records begin to refer to a new hundred—the hundred outside the north gate of Oxford. They first mention it in the eyre of 1247, when it is alluded to as 'the liberty outside the north gate', 'the hundred outside the north gate', and 'the suburb of Oxford outside the north gate'.[2] The rolls of 1241 had enrolled the presentments of a jury for 'the suburb of Oxford';[3] in 1261 the same area is described as 'the foreign hundred outside the north gate', 'Oxford outside the wall', and, again, 'the suburb of Oxford'.[4] This recurrent use of the expression *suburb* suggests that the hundred is an outgrowth of Oxford. It may be so in fact, but it is not in law.

Outside the eyre rolls, the first mention of the hundred outside the north gate seems to occur in a charter of c. 1140 enrolled in the cartulary of St Frideswide, whereby Maud the Empress confirms to the canons of St Frideswide all the land which Alan the Rosemonger held in the parish of St Mary Magdalen, and all the other land which the canons have within the hundred outside the north gate of Oxford.[5] Whether this can be accepted as evidence for Stephen's reign or no, it was about 1142 that the empress conferred the manor of Headington on Hugh de Pluggenait, who appears in the first Pipe Roll of Henry II as holding the manor blanched, that is, with the hundredal soke.

In 1231 a jury found that both when the crown held the manor, and when it was in the hands of Hugh de Plugeneye and later, it carried with it the tenure of the hundred of Bolendon 'and a certain other hundred'.[6] From the Pipe Rolls of 1190–91 we should expect the other hundred to be Soterlawa. But at least as early as 1163 Hugh de Pluggenait makes a grant of land 'coram hundredo extra portam del North'.[7] From Stephen's reign till 1281 the manor of Headington was held by a subject along with the soke of two hundreds, and whenever these two hundreds are named, they are the hundreds of Bullingdon and Northgate.

---

[1] Dr Salter points out that their hidation still corresponds to the Domesday numbering.   [2] Ass. R. 700, 13 d, 11 d, 12 d.

[3] *Ibid.* 697, m. 26 d.   [4] *Ibid.* 701, m. 29 d, 30 d, 31.

[5] *Cart. St Frid.* (O.H.S.), II. 23.   [6] *Bracton's Notebook*, case 513.

[7] *Oseney Cart.* (O.H.S.), II. 195. The deed survives in the original. Dr Salter inclines to the earlier date—1155.

The descent of the manor and hundreds has been traced by Miss Evans. Hugh de Pluggenait's son held it for a short time only; it was then granted by John in 1203 [1] to Thomas Basset and held successively by him and his daughter Philippa, countess of Warwick, who died in 1265, when her three nieces inherited as co-heiresses. Hugh de Plessis, the husband of Isabella, the youngest niece, bought out the other two, and held it till his wife's death, in 1280, when he sold the manor and the two hundreds to the crown. When in 1282 the manor was valued, the hundred of Bullingdon, worth £6. 9s. 1d., was still held with it, but the hundred of Northgate was held separately at a rent of £20 a year, by Henry Dymmok.[2] But the traditional association of Northgate hundred with Headington manor was not forgotten; though temporarily detached it was still a 'member' of the manor, and in 1317 it was again held with Bullingdon hundred by the lord of Headington.[3] Held successively by the D'Amorys and the Willicotes, the manor and the two hundreds were sold to John Brome in 1482, and the final severance only came when in 1592 George Brome sold 'the liberty of Northgate Hundred' to the mayor and corporation of Oxford for £180.[4]

The evidence for the association of the suburb north of the town wall with Headington manor is early and constant. The lands given by the king to Godstow 'in the village of Walton' always figure in the Pipe Rolls as *in Hedendona*.[5] The meadow held by Oseney is 'beyond the water...nigh to the Burgeys' medes of Oxenford which are of the fee of Hedyndon'. These are the strips in the meadow of Bolestake, held by Oseney of Eynsham Abbey, which paid a quitrent to the chief lord of Headington.[6] In 1261 a man arrested outside the north gate is imprisoned in the gaol of Philippa, countess of Warwick, and William le Yreis or de Hibernia who answers for his chattels, is described both as bailiff of Northgate hundred and bailiff of Philippa,

[1] *Rot. Cart.* p. 109. The hundreds are not named in this grant, but the case of 1231 indicates that they were covered by the grant of the appurtenances of the manor, and the jurors of 1279 say precisely that John granted the manor with the hundreds of Bullingdon and Northgate. *Rot. Hund.* II. 305.

[2] Evans, 'Manor of Headington', *Rept. Oxfordshire Arch. Soc. for* 1928, p. 215.

[3] *Fine Roll Calendar*, p. 336.

[4] Evans, *op. cit.* pp. 173–6; White Kennett, *Par. Antiq.* II. 155, 157, 234; *Oxford City Properties* (O.H.S.), p. 254.

[5] Dr Salter kindly pointed this out to me.

[6] *English Register of Oseney*, pp. 52, 54 (translating document of circa 1180).

countess of Warwick.[1] Most significant of all, perhaps, is the inquest *ad quod damnum* of 1284–85 into the tenure of three holdings on the site where Balliol Hall was to stand. Two of the three tenants owed mowing services at Headington, as well as carrying services at Northam, and three-weekly suit to the hundred of Northgate.[2] In 1556 the mayor alleged that Walton Farm was 'within the hundred of Bullington, otherwise called the hundred without the North gate'.[3]

What evidence is there as to the geographical extent of the hundred of Northgate? The records of royal administration supply the most trustworthy evidence on the whole, as they imply a financial responsibility. The eyre rolls and the coroners' rolls must be considered first. The pleas of the crown presented by the juries for Northgate hundred arise from happenings in the parishes of St Mary Magdalen and St Giles. Other places involved are Stockwell Street, Walton, Broken Heys, Holywell and St Cross, Bradmore, the field called Northam, and Beaumont Fields.

The survey of 1279 recorded in the Hundred Rolls[4] includes in the hundred 123 acres in Walton Field, two carucates in Holywell, one carucate and twenty-four acres near Brummans Well, eighty-two and a half acres of meadow land 'behind Osney', sixteen and a half acres in Bissopeseite, and meadows or crofts of unspecified areas called Gybberys, Honifurlong, Thistledene, Lenart hill, Northeye, Langeneye, Denescroft and Buricroft,[5] besides Horsemongere Street (Broad Street) and the king's way outside the north gate (St Giles's). The limit of the hundred to the north can be determined by the eyre rolls for 1247 and 1261; Godstow, Cutslow, Watereaton and Wolvercote[6] are all in Wootton hundred. The northern boundary would seem to correspond with that of the city of Oxford on the hundred map of 1834.

---

[1] Ass. R. 701, m. 30d; *Medieval Archives of City of Oxford* (O.H.S.), pp. 312, 313, 314.   [2] *Oxford Deeds of Balliol College* (O.H.S.), pp. 12–13.

[3] W. H. Turner, *Records of the City of Oxford*, p. 254.

[4] *Rot. Hund.* II. 805–11.

[5] Dr Salter tells me that Bishopseyt, the late Burgessmead, was east of Port Meadow, that Langney is now united with Binsey, and that Buricroft is probably the same as Denescroft, which is the site to-day of the Radcliffe Infirmary and Observatory. The other meadows were probably between the Banbury Road and the Cherwell, near Northam.

[6] Ass. R. 700, m. 8 d; 701, mm. 21 d, 22. See also Coroners' Roll 129 (1341–47), where Wolvercote is described as in Wootton hundred.

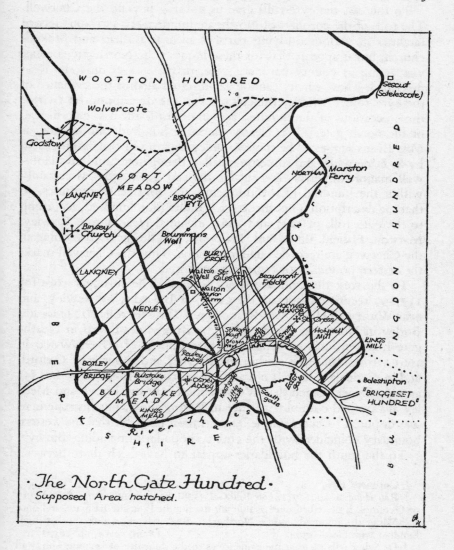

Map 5. Sketch-map showing the probable area of the
North Gate Hundred.

Scale about 1¾ inches to 1 mile.

To the east the eyre rolls give us nothing beyond the Cherwell. The rolls of the coroners of Northgate hundred for 1377–99 [1] record fatalities in various outlying parishes such as Elsfield and Stokenchurch, but it appears that for these inquests the Northgate coroner was acting as county coroner, since, in these cases only, he is so described. These entries cannot be admitted against the evidence of the eyre rolls. Another difficulty lies in the description on two or three occasions of the hundred as lying outside the east gate instead of the north gate. [2] It is clearly the same hundred, and cannot, as Miss Evans suggests, [3] be the two hides centring in Boleshipton held by St Frideswide, and sometimes called Bruggesete hundred. Holywell manor, however, lay outside the east gate, and was certainly within the hundred in the thirteenth and fourteenth centuries, so that the description is not incorrect. [4] Bullingdon hundred, according to the eyre rolls of 1247 and 1261, included Headington, Cowley, Marston, Elsfield, Iffley, and 'Petipont', and deaths by drowning in the Cherwell are recorded under its name. Thus the Cherwell marks the eastern boundary of Northgate hundred.

To the west the evidence is not so clear. The coroners' rolls for 1377–99 record fatalities in the castle, at Bulstake, by Rewley, and near Withewell Hill, towards Godstow. [5] The eyre roll of 1247 locates Botley in Northgate hundred. [6] 'The King's mead' was in Northgate hundred, and so apparently was Binsey, of which Wood in 1663 wrote 'Binsey is within the liberties and suburbs of Oxford, and in particular, most, if not all, is in Northgate hundred'. [7] In 1553 an old villager alleged that Wolvercote, Godstow, Binsey and Medley always had common pasture in Portmeadow, but his statement was disputed. [8] On the whole it seems most probable that the western boundary coincided with the county boundary, including Binsey.

To the south the boundaries appear to have been those between

---

[1] Coroners' Roll.

[2] *Rot. Hund.* II. 30 (1274); *Fine Roll Cal.* (1281–82), pp. 148, 167, where Henry of Dymmok is described once as holding the hundred outside Eastgate, and once as holding the hundred outside Northgate. Both references link the 'oriental' hundred with Headington.   [3] Evans, *op. cit.* pp. 165, 173.

[4] Dr Salter tells me that the evidence as to the difficulty of keeping Longwall Street and the road from Eastgate to Pettipont in repair shows that the land between the Eastgate and the Cherwell was not subject to the borough system, but was in the hundred.   [5] Coroners' Roll (1377–99).   [6] Ass. R. 700, m. 12 d.

[7] A. Wood, *City of Oxford* (O.H.S.), I. 320, 458; II. 41.

[8] O. Ogle, *Royal Letters to Oxford*, p. 480.

the parishes of St Cross and St Peter in the east, the north wall of Oxford up to the Castle, which was presumably in the hundred and not in the borough, and the boundaries between St Thomas's parish and Oseney.

The clearest statement as to the extent of the hundred is that made by a jury on April 10, 1419. A dispute had arisen between Oseney Abbey and the town as to the rights of the mayor and bailiffs in North Oseney and South Oseney, and before the commission appointed to investigate the dispute the jury asserted that the town of Oxford had no suburb except that outside the south gate, and that their recent activities in North and South Oseney were usurpations on the king's majesty, since 'the vills of North and South Oseney, the parishes of St Mary Magdalen and St Giles without the north gate, St Thomas's without the west gate, and St George's that is, the whole castle without the west gate, and the hamlets of Walton, Holywell and Binsey and all and every place within those vills, parishes and hamlets are of the body of the county of Oxford and in the lord king's geldable and in the hundred called the hundred without the north gate of Oxford, and are not and never were within the liberty of the said town'.[1] The statement that the land in question is geldable and *de corpore comitatus* is unequivocal evidence that public, and not manorial rights are in question, even whilst the whole setting of the verdict indicates the tendency of the borough to encroach on the hundred.[2]

The administrative and judicial activities of the hundred are attested not only by the periodical references in the eyre rolls, but in the deeds preserved by the various religious houses of Oxford, which have been and are being printed by the Oxford Historical Society. From these can be recovered a list of the bailiffs of the hundred, fairly long if not yet complete, and a picture of some at least of the activities of the hundred court.

The bailiffs whose names occur on the accompanying list generally appear as witnesses to transfers of property. In most cases the bailiff is the only official mentioned,[3] and may well have presided at the

[1] The inquest, transcribed Twyne IV. 15, is printed in full by Dr Salter, *Medieval Oxford*, pp. 154 ff., and I am greatly indebted to him for calling my attention to it and permitting me to quote from it.

[2] The usurpations in question are described as dating from 1403. Cf. below, p. 120.

[3] The steward (*senescallus*) is mentioned several times: e.g. *Cart. St John*, II. 331 (c. 1250); *Balliol Deeds*, 60 (1396), 62 (1422).

court in which the deed was issued; in a few cases, indicated on the list, the mayor and bailiffs of the borough also witnessed the transaction, and therefore presumably attended the court. The references on the eyre rolls indicate that the bailiff, as in other private hundreds, was at once the bailiff of the lord king and of the lord of the manor of Headington, arresting men, accounting for their chattels if they were convicted, answering for the deodand in case of a fatal accident, responsible if prisoners escaped from his custody, and entrusted with the execution of sentence. When Matilda of Northampton, hanged in the eyre of Oxford in 1247, revived in the church of St Mary Magdalen, whither the compassionate had carried her body, it was William le Sauser, bailiff of Northgate hundred, who paid the heavy fine of twenty marks, though the inefficient execution had been the work of his serjeants.[1] Further, the liberty was temporarily taken into the king's hands, and had to be redeemed by Philippa of Warwick. Again, as the lord of Headington had return of writs,[2] the hundred bailiff had all the executive duties involved in that liberty.

The lord of the manor could also, apparently, appoint the coroners of the hundred.[3] Coroners distinct both from those of the hundred and of the county are mentioned for the eyre of 1261,[4] and the roll of the coroners of Northgate survives for 1377–99.[5] They are mentioned as holding an inquest in 1556 when there was a great confusion of claims, Dr Owen, the owner of Godstow and Wolvercote, backing the coroners' rights, and the mayor of Oxford and the bailiff of Northgate hundred opposing them.[6] Deaths in Northgate hundred were, however, the subject of inquiries by borough coroners on several occasions in the later Middle Ages.[7]

The existence of a separate court for the hundred of Northgate is attested both by statements of suits owed to it and by records of the transactions in it. We have already seen that suit was owed to it every three weeks by the occupants of the houses bought by Devorguilla of Balliol in 1284.[8] The prior of Bicester also owed suit to the hundred in 1283,[9] and in the sixteenth century Godstow made a payment to be released from suit to the hundred.[10]

---

[1] Ass. R. 700, m. 12 d.   [2] *Rot. Hund.* II. 35.

[3] Other hundreds which had their own coroners were Lifton hundred, Devon, and Rochford hundred, Essex.

[4] Ass. R. 701, m. 30 d.   [5] Coroners' Roll, 133.

[6] W. H. Turner, *Records of the City of Oxford*, pp. 247–55.

[7] Coroners' Roll, 129.   [8] See above, p. 114.

[9] *Cal. Misc. Inq.* I. 374.   [10] *Monasticon*, IV. 370.

Of transactions in the court of Northgate hundred there is an abundance of evidence.[1] Transfers of land are made *coram hundredo* or *in hundredo* from Hugh de Pluggenait's time onwards.[2] Pleas of land are heard there by the king's writ of right.[3] Conventions are registered there,[4] after the pleading of a royal writ of services. Payments are made there.[5] Royal inquests are taken there.[6] Most interesting activity of all, wills are published,[7] and proved there,[8] in one case, *coram senescallo et sectatoribus hundredi*. There is a reference to criminal proceedings in the hundred in 1261, when the bailiff is penalized for having allowed a man to be accused by *querela* instead of appeal.[9]

It is noteworthy that in a few instances acts done in the hundred are done before the mayor and bailiffs of Oxford as well as the bailiff of the hundred.[10] This opens up the vexed question of the rights of the borough and the university to jurisdiction outside the wall. The situation is perhaps best summed up in Wood's phrase: 'Yet the liberty of the hundred was not so great afterwards that it could exclude the right of the university or city; and it was accounted as a suburb.' As to the university, it seems that its jurisdiction was extra-territorial; clerks were doubtless living outside the wall before the foundation of Balliol, and the Chancellor could claim jurisdiction over them. It was when disputes occurred between clerks and lay-men that trouble arose, as in 1288 when Robert of Welles, bailiff of Northgate hundred, was charged with impleading M.A.s *in curia privata* and stirring up the inhabitants of the suburb to rebel against the ancient liberties of the university.[11] The frontiers of the two jurisdictions were defined in 1356, in an indenture between Sir Richard d'Amory and the Chancellor, Masters and Scholars, which indicates that there had been conflict not only over pleas of contract,

[1] I have to thank Mrs Lobel for most of these references.
[2] *Oseney Cart.* II. 195 (1154–63), 314 (1361); IV. 69 (1195–1205); *Cart. St John*, II. 309 (1230), 258 (1397), 288 (1399), 289 (1413), 314 (1400), 283–4 (1421), 313 (1424); *Balliol Deeds*, 36.
[3] *Cart. St John*, II. 309.   [4] *Ibid.* II. 342.
[5] *Ibid.* II. 299 (1236).
[6] *Ibid.* II. 335 (1393); *Snappe's Formulary*, p. 289 (1286).
[7] *Oseney Cart.* II. 311–15 (1361); *Balliol Deeds*, p. 36.
[8] *Op. cit.* pp. 59–60; *Cart. St John*, II. 287.
[9] Ass. R. 701, m. 30 d.
[10] E.g. *Oseney Cart.* II. 328 (c. 1240); *Med. Arch. Univ.* (O.H.S.), p. 321(1264–65); *Cart. St John*, II. 343 (1276), 322 (1287–88), 324 (1293–94).
[11] *Munimenta Academica* [R.S.], I. 43–5.

but over breaches of the peace[1] and the regulation of the sale of victuals, since the lord of the hundred had the assize of bread and ale and the Chancellor of the University claimed to regulate the prices of victuals to prevent the exploitation of the scholars by the townsmen. The dispute was finally settled before the king's council, by the agreement of both parties.[2]

The relations with the borough implied by the presence of the mayor at the hundred courts probably began similarly, with burgesses acquiring property and even residing in the northern suburb. It is possible that here, as at Northampton,[3] men may have moved out of the borough to escape industrial or mercantile regulation or the payment of borough dues. It was at St Giles' Church that the lesser burgesses met in 1253 to draw up their protest against the oppressions of the town oligarchy, but even there they were disturbed before they could affix their seals.[4] Close relations were inevitable; not only was private property outside the north gate owned by burgesses, but their common pasture, Portmeadow, lay within the hundred. The same man might serve as bailiff of Northgate hundred and as bailiff or mayor of Oxford;[5] John le Sauser's will was proved before the mayor of Oxford, 'according to the custom of the town of Oxford' and before the seneschal and suitors of Northgate hundred 'according to the customs of the said hundred' in January and March respectively of 1340,[6] presumably because he owned property both within and without the wall. A conveyance made in the hundred was recognized and enrolled before the mayor six months later.[7] It is highly probable that the mayor's jurisdiction pursued the burgesses in matters of trade as well as of landed property.[8] References to the ward outside the north gate in 1261[9] and to the

[1] Note ruling of 10 Feb. 1338; Chancellor to have jurisdiction of trespass, felonies reserved (to lord of hundred). *C.R.C.* p. 319.
[2] *Mun. Acad. Oxon.* I. 173–80.   [3] *Vict. Co. Hist., Northamptonshire,* III. 7, 31.
[4] *Cal. Misc. Inq.* I. no. 238; *Snappe's Formulary,* p. 278.
[5] William le Saucer, hundred bailiff 1235–49; mayor of Oxford 1258–59; William de Wodestone, hundred bailiff 1295–96, bailiff of Oxford 1291–92, 1293–94.   [6] *Balliol Deeds,* pp. 59–60.
[7] *Ibid.* p. 38. Mrs Lobel tells me that cases about land in the hundred are frequently found on the Hustings Roll in the fourteenth century.
[8] In 1249 a plea about the sale of a horse was retried in the mayor's court after it had been heard and determined before the steward of Northgate hundred. Twyne, XXIII. 382. In 1293 the mayor successfully claimed jurisdiction in a plea between the Prior of St Frideswide and Richard Aumfrey, and it was removed from the hundred to his court. *Ibid.* XXIII. 330.   [9] Ass. R. 701, m. 30 d.

constables in the north suburb in 1390–94[1] suggest co-operation in the keeping of the peace between the authorities of borough and hundred. In the fifteenth century presentments in the views of frankpledge before the mayor frequently concerned nuisances and purprestures in the hundred.[2] It seems certain that the activities of other borough officials besides coroners extended into the hundred. But it was not until 1592, that, as we have seen, the city purchased from George Brome 'the hundred court, the courts leet, the appointment of officers within the hundred, perquisites of courts, fees, waifs and strays' as well as the quit-rents, the tenements and the waste land within the hundred that belonged to the lord of Headington manor.[3]

It remains to consider the origin of the hundred outside the north gate. It does not seem probable that the two hundreds annexed to the manor of Headington in Domesday Book were divided by the Cherwell. The fact that one of them was still called Soterlawa as late as 1199 strongly suggests that the modern Bullingdon hundred is larger than the Bolenden hundred of the Pipe Rolls. But as early as 1163, as we have seen, one of Hugh de Pluggenait's two hundreds was meeting outside the north gate of Oxford.

It is probable that but for the growth of population north of the city wall, which must have begun well before 1086,[4] the two hundreds of Headington would have become one, like the two of Bampton or the three of Shipton. The suitors of the double hundred would have met at 'Soterlawa' or at 'Bulesdon' very possibly turn and turn about. But the craftsmen and tradesmen round St Mary Magdalen's and St Giles' churches[5] would resent being dragged to Wheatley or Fritwell every three weeks, whilst on the other hand their litigation would make the court far more profitable than that of the ordinary rural hundred, and induce the lord of the hundred to meet his suitors' convenience. Thus the place of meeting might be shifted from Bulesdon to the north gate even before the old name was abandoned. The next step—the re-division of the whole area dependent on Headington into a large rural area east of Cherwell and a small suburban area west of Cherwell, probably took place at some

[1] *Med. Arch. Univ.* II. xix. 56–67, 81, 102.
[2] Dr Salter, *Medieval Oxford*, pp. 146–52, prints Twyne's transcripts from the rolls of the Views.   [3] *Oxford City Properties* (O.H.S.), p. 254.
[4] St Mary Magdalen's church goes back to 1074. James Parker, *Early History of Oxford* (O.H.S.), p. 283.
[5] St Giles' was dedicated in 1138. *Monasticon*, IV. 362.

date between 1190 and 1220. It must have taken place before 1240, when Bolendon hundred sat at Cowley. The change would be due to fiscal and administrative considerations. A bailiff might find his time fully occupied in handling the business of the residents west of Cherwell, whilst the forest of Shotover was better managed independently. From the fiscal point of view, the suburban area was probably more valuable than the rural area as early as 1190. In 1282 the hundred of Bolendon was valued at £6. 9s. 1d. and the hundred outside the north gate was farmed for £20,[1] which undoubtedly left a margin of profit to the farmer.

The fact that the redistribution was accepted and endorsed by the central government, as the roll of the eyre of 1247 shows, might seem to suggest that it had taken place before the hundreds had been granted to Hugh de Pluggenait by the empress. On the other hand, it may have been officially authorized during the period (1200–3) when the manor and hundreds had reverted to the crown before they were granted out again by John. The statement of the jurors of 1231 that Thomas Basset had held the manor 'cum hundredo de Bolendena et *quodam* alio hundredo' almost suggests a consciousness that the other hundred had changed its character if not its name within living memory. It is not likely that the boundaries of Soterlawa hundred or the date of its final disappearance will ever be precisely definable.

If the theory suggested above for the origin of the hundred of Northgate be accepted, its history is, I think, unique among English hundreds.

LIST OF BAILIFFS OF NORTHGATE HUNDRED

F. = Cartulary of St Frideswide
O. = Oseney Cartulary
B. = Balliol Deeds   } Oxford Historical Society
J. = St John Baptist Cartulary
A.R. = Assize Roll

An italicized date indicates an exactly dated document.

Year	Name and description	Reference
? 1190–1200	William, *prepositus de extra Portam del North*	F. II. 27
c. 1230–40	Simon Balehorn, *ballivus: ballivus hundredi extra portam aquilonarem Oxonie*	O. II. 339; J. II. 309, 325
c. 1235–36, 1237, 1238 *1239*, 1240 1242, 1243	William le Saucer, Sauser, Salsarius, *ball. extra portam aq. Ox.: ball. hundredi extra portam aq. Ox.*	J. II. 298, 299, 304, 327, 332, 335 O. II. 259, 260, 263, 269, 270, 292

[1] See above, p. 113.

Year	Name and description	Reference
1245, 1247 1248, 1249	William le Saucer, *ut supra*	*Med. Arch. Univ.* 307, 308, 315, 316, 317 A.R. 697, m. 26 d, 700, m. 12 d, m. 13 d
c. 1240	Simon de Elthrop, *ball. extra portam aq.*	*Med. Arch. Univ.* 317
c. 1240–50	William de Cuteler, *ball. extra portam aq.*	*Med. Arch. Univ.* 309
c. 1250	William de Ybernia, *ball. extra portam aq.*	O. II. 73, 267, 272, 293
1255, 1256	William Hiberniensis, *ball. extra portam aq.*	J. II. 300, 334
1257, 1260	William Ybernicus, *ball. extra portam aq.*	
1261	William le Yreis, *ball. extra portam aq.*	A.R. 701, m. 31
1264, 1265	William le Irreys, *ball. extra portam aq.*	*Med. Arch. Univ.* 312, 313, 314, 321
c. 1260	Richard le Clerk, Clericus } *ballivi* Richard le Messer	A.R. 701, m. 30 d O. II. 272
Aug. 18, 1276	Radulfus de Swereford, *ball. extra portam aq.*	J. II. 343
Mich. 1277–	Henry fil. Milonis, *ball. extra portam borealem*	J. II. 304; B. 20
Mich. 1278–79	*ball. hundredi extra port. bor.*	
1280	Robert de Welles, *ball. hundredi extra port. bor.*	B. 65
May 28, 1281	Henry Dymock (appointed for ten years)	*Fine Roll Cal.* 148
Mich. 1287–88	Philip Mimekan, *ball. de hundredo extra p.b.O.*	J. II. 322
1288 ?	Robert de Welles (deprived by Council)	*Mun. Acad. Oxon.* I. 43–5
Mich. 1293–94	John de Croxford, *ball. extra portam bor. Ox.*	J. II. 324
1295, 1296	William de Wodestone, *ball. hund. extra port. bor. Ox.*	O. II. 285, 309
July 1310 Jan. 1312	John de le Haye, *ball. hund. extra port. bor. Ox.*	O. II. 213, 309
Oct. 1316– Dec. 1317	William de Hakeburne, *ball. hund. extra port. bor. Ox.*	O. II. 301, 310, 321 *Mun. Acad. Oxon.* I. 41
1320	Thomas de Saunforde, *ball. illius hundredi*	B. 65
1332	John (or Josep) de Wodestoke, *ball. illius hundredi*	J. II. 286; B. 221
May 1352	? John de Uppehege, *firmarius Th. de Ferers de hundredo de North*	J. II. 339
1355	Henry le Porter, *ball. hundredi extra port. bor.*	*Med. Arch. Univ.* II. 127
1515	John Royse, *bailiff of the North Gate hundred*	Turner, *Records of the City of Oxford*, p. 14
1535–40	Sir John Brome, *firmarius hundredi de Northegate extra portam borealem.*	*Monasticon,* IV. 370

VIII

Pedigrees of Villeins and Freemen in the Thirteenth Century[1]

It might be supposed that no two aspects of history were more diametrically opposed to each other than the genealogical and the administrative, the one concerned with private, personal, particular affairs, the other with public, impersonal, standardized arrangements. The student of administration often has reason to lament the extent to which genealogical considerations influenced the editors of the earlier volumes of the government's record publications, whose indexes dealt at first solely with personal and local proper names, and only by slow degrees came to include legal, administrative, social and economic categories and reached the perfection of Mr Flower's indexes to the Curia Regis Rolls, but for which this article could never have been written. All the same, if local government is the subject, and the period is feudal, the inquirer is in the thick of a forest of family trees before he can well help it, and they must be dealt with, as far as possible, before the shape of the wood can be seen. To establish a family descent may be the indispensable preliminary for clearing up some legal, political or sociological problem, and the importance of genealogical study, a commonplace to members of this society, forces itself upon the outsider who has previously neglected it.

There are three distinct lines along which the study of local government in the thirteenth century has led the present writer to the investigation of pedigrees. The first is the transmission of public rights of government by the feudal laws of inheritance; the second is the influence of family connections upon political groupings and local political domination; and the third is the relation between legal and social status in the thirteenth-century village as illustrated by the intermarriage of serfs and freemen.

I. In tracing the descent of the lordship of a private hundred some curious facts have emerged. It must be remembered that the hundred was the unit of public government for a number of purposes; it

[1] Read to the Society of Genealogists, 21 January 1933. Reprinted from *The Genealogists' Magazine*, September 1933.

furnished a jury to present offenders before the travelling justices; it was liable for the murder fine; its armed men served both as a police and as a militia unit; the customary revenue for which the sheriff was responsible was collected by hundreds, and its court had a considerable amount of petty civil and criminal jurisdiction. All this held good whether it was a royal hundred with a bailiff appointed by the sheriff, or, as the majority of thirteenth-century hundreds were, a private hundred, whose lord shared the responsibilities and profits of administration with the king. Some of these lords of hundreds held them for a term of years or for life; the majority held them by fee-farm, which meant that unless the lord was an immortal corporation, the right to appoint officials, receive dues, and hold courts descended by the ordinary rules of feudal land-law and could be sublet, assigned as dower and divided among co-heiresses exactly like any other form of real property. Over and over again the answer to the question 'How did so and so come to be lord of such a hundred?' is to be found in a family descent or a family settlement, and not in any direct royal action, the original royal grant to the founder of the family being frequently lost in the mists of antiquity. Numbers of instances of such descents may be found in the *Victoria County History*, where the statement 'the Hundred follows the descent of the manor of so and so' will often be the guide to a long series of transfers along the female line. The Quo Warranto pleas of 1330 for Northamptonshire make a genealogical statement that might be paralleled in many other eyre rolls: 'King John gave the manor and hundred of Corby to a certain Henry of Braybrook, to have and to hold, to him and to his heirs, and from the said Henry they descended to a certain Wischard as his son and heir and from Wischard to a certain Walter as his son and heir and from Walter to Alice and Christian as his daughters and heiresses, and Corby was assigned to Alice as her property, and from Alice it descended to William as her son and heir, and from that William, as son and heir, to the William who now claims it.'[1] Henry of Braybrook's wife also inherited a hundred, as the table on the following page shows, from her mother and her grandmother, which went 'as her purparty' to her great-grand-daughter Christian.

Another incidental result of descent through co-heiresses is illustrated by the descent of Flitt hundred in Bedfordshire. This hundred formed part of the far-flung possessions of the Marshalls upon whom,

[1] *Plac. Quo War.* p. 575.

according to legend, was visited the curse of the conquered Irish, when Eva's five grandsons died in succession childless, and the inheritance was shared among their five sisters. Miss Mills has traced the parcelling out of the old Earl's debt to the exchequer into thirty-fifths among the seven daughters of Sybil Marshall.[1] Sybil received Flitt hundred as part of her share of the Marshall inheritance and the Quo Warranto pleas trace its further history to 1330.

THE LORDS OF WARDEN AND CORBY HUNDREDS, NORTHAMPTONSHIRE

```
          Wido de Rainbudcurt (Lord of Warden, 1086)
                             |
                          Richard
                             |
                  Margaret = Robert Foliot
                             |
                       Richard Foliot
                             |
      Wischard Ledet = Margaret
         † 1221               |
          Christian Ledet = Henry of Braybrook (Lord of CORBY hundred 1212)
            † 1271           |          † 1231
                    Wischard Ledet † 1241
                             |
                     Walter Ledet † 1257
                             |
    † 1316 Alice = William Latimer          John Latimer = Christian
             |                                          |
          William                                    Thomas
             |                            (claims WARDEN hundred in 1330)
          William
   (claims CORBY hundred in 1330)
```

'Sybil died seised, and from her the manor descended to Agnes, Isabel, Joan, Sybil, Maud, Eleanor, and Agatha as her daughters and heiresses, and from Agnes, who died without heirs, her purparty descended to her sisters, so that each had a sixth of the manor.[2] But the hundred descended to Joan, Sybil, Maud and Agatha who held it in common and undivided and died seised of it. And from Joan her purparty descended to John her son and heir and from him to John de Mohun as his son and heir, and John de Mohun enfeoffed Hugh de Mortimer and his wife Elizabeth with his purparty, who now claim. And from Sybil her purparty descended to

[1] *Surrey Record Society*, no. XXI, p. lxv.
[2] Also, as a matter of fact, the hundred, one-sixth of which was held by Isabel's descendants till the line failed.

a certain John as son and heir, and from him to James as son and heir and from James to John de Bohun who now claims. And from Maud her purparty descended to Joan and Cecily as daughters and co-heiresses, and from Joan to Peter as son and heir and from Peter to Roger and from Roger to Henry FitzRoger who now claims and is under age. And from Cecily to John de Beauchamp who now claims. And from Agatha to Henry as son and heir, and from Henry to Hugh de Mortimer who now claims both his own purparty descended from Agatha and the other purparty which John de Mohun inherited from Joan.'[1]

DESCENT OF THE LORDSHIP OF FLITT HUNDRED

Lords of Hundred in Italics

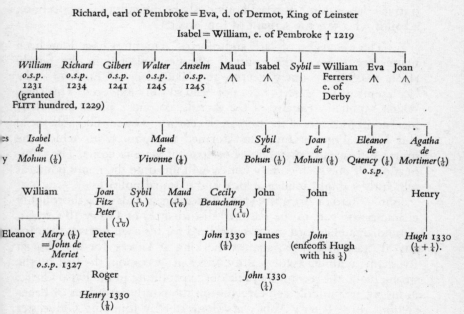

Thus in 1330 the Lordship of Flitt hundred was shared among four lords, in proportions of a half, a quarter, and two eighths.

The remarkable fact is that this should be a workable proposition. The king's lawyers at once asserted that 'hundredum est quoddam grossum et indivisibile', but the precedents were against them, what-

[1] *Plac. Quo War.* p. 54. Various stages are omitted: e.g. in 1300 Sybil de Rochechouard quit-claimed her sixteenth to her sister Cecily Beauchamp.

ever legal theory they might put forward. The king himself held many such fractions of lordships in Kent, for instance. The financial profits of the lordship could be readily shared, but responsibility was less easy to subdivide. Eleven years later, on the occasion of a grand judicial inquiry into official misconduct, the sheriff of Bedfordshire was reprimanded by the justices for supplying an incomplete list of the tenants of Flitt hundred. He said the fault lay with the hundred bailiff, who was responsible not to him but to Hugh Mortimer.[1] Hugh Mortimer did eventually buy out all his co-partners, but it is not clear that he had done so by 1341, and it seems probable that there was a working arrangement between the joint lords, here as elsewhere, whereby one represented the others in public administrative relationship.[2] It would obviously be difficult to bring to book a bailiff who was the servant of four masters.

II. The marriages of earls and of earls' daughters have long been matter for history; the political affinities reflected in the family alliances of the country gentry, the 'Bachelery of England'—the 'vavasours of the shire'—have not been so fully explored. This class, which supplied so many of the sheriffs, coroners, jurors and other local administrators of the thirteenth century, is of considerable social and political importance, and formed the pool from which the fourteenth-century members of parliament were to come. The ramifications of one such county family will illustrate the many points at which they might influence local and national politics.

John Giffard of Brimpsfield in Gloucestershire played a thoroughly characteristic part in the baronial disturbances of Henry III's reign; a minor marcher lord, more concerned for his own interest than for any abstract principles; against the king at Lewes, for the king at Evesham; winning two wealthy wives in succession, the first by the strong hand, the second by judicious expenditure in the Papal Curia; in his soberer middle age carrying on the family traditions of benefactions to St Peter's Abbey at Gloucester by founding Gloucester Hall at Oxford as a hostel for Benedictine monks at the university; leaving to his young son so noble a heritage of wealth and local influence that he was known as 'John the Rich' though, unluckier than his father, he was to suffer a rebel's death after Boroughbridge (1322).

[1] Ass. R. 31, m. 6.
[2] In 1316 John de Meriet, husband of Mary de Mohun, the descendant of the eldest sister, is officially described as Lord of Flitt hundred though in fact he only held one-sixth of it.

John Giffard's descent can be traced from the Domesday magnate, Osbern Giffard, who had lands both in Gloucestershire and Wiltshire.[1] Sir Richard Hoare established his relationship to Walter Giffard, bishop of Bath and Wells, and archbishop of York, 1266–79, whose register reflects his strong family feeling for his married sisters and their children, and to Godfrey Giffard, bishop of Worcester 1268–1302, whose will gives a conspectus of the whole clan.[2]

The political activities and connections of this family ramify widely. John's cousin Hugh was tutor to the sons of Henry III; his sudden death, from apoplexy, in 1246, is described by Matthew Paris. His cousins served the king in Church and State, Walter the archbishop acting as regent on the death of Henry III and Godfrey succeeding his brother as chancellor, and William being sheriff of Norfolk, all of them, apparently, coming out on the winning side at the end of the barons' wars, though Maud Giffard's husband William de Evreux was killed at Evesham fighting against the king.

They were a quarrelsome family; Agatha Giffard had a dispute with her abbess when she was a nun at Elstow, Mabel Giffard, as abbess of Shaftesbury, got into trouble for refusing to pay certain moneys,[3] both the archbishop and the bishop had long disputes with Peckham over the rights of their sees, and John Giffard, having quarrelled with Henry III and Simon de Montfort in turn, was fined three hundred marks in 1271 for the abduction of his wife, Maud Longsword. All his matrimonial adventures gave him trouble. At four years old he was married to Aubrey, one of the Warwickshire Camvilles, but the marriage was, it would seem, never consummated, since the boy would have nothing to say to the girl,[4] and she appears to have entered religion and ended up prioress of Polesworth. In 1271 he carried off by force Maud, daughter of Walter

[1] The accompanying table, based on various original sources, has been corrected in the light of Mr Moriarty's articles, *Genealogists' Magazine*, Sept. 1935, March 1936, and of Mr Watson's article, *Complete Peerage*, v. 639 ff.
[2] The will is summarized by Hoare, *History of Wiltshire*, I. 199.
[3] Power, *Medieval English Nunneries*, p. 464. Juliana Giffard, abbess of Wilton, also got into trouble over a young kinswoman, Alice (William's daughter ?).
[4] *Cal. Misc. Inq.* I. 298 f. John's statement that none of the race of Longsword would stick to a wife married to him in his boyhood is explicable only if (1) the name derived from the Cliffords *or* (2) he thought the name belonged to the *first* line of earls of Salisbury, *or* (3) he had not a correct knowledge of his family tree. See table.

THE GIFFARDS OF BOYTON, WILTSHIRE, AND BRIMPSFIELD, GLOUCESTERSHIRE

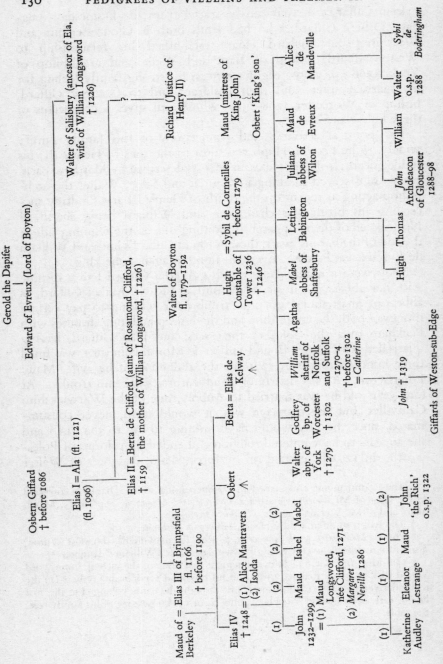

Clifford, widow of William Longsword and cousin of John's marcher comrade-in-arms, Roger Clifford; a great heiress in her own right, augmented by her Longsword dower. Her protest may have been a matter of form, for he made several foundations for their joint spiritual welfare in terms that suggest a happy marriage. Lastly he made interest at the court of Rome, with the help of his cousin Bishop Godfrey, for a dispensation to marry Margaret Neville, his cousin within the fourth degree, though as the Pope declared in 1286 no one could trace the relationship, we can hardly expect to do so to-day. At least £100 was laid out on the expenses of this suit to the Curia. Both lines of the family were involved in the civil wars of Edward II's reign and suffered for it; but whilst Brimpsfield was destroyed and its lord beheaded childless, the bishop's heirs continued lords of Weston-under-Edge down to the reign of James I.

III. The third type of pedigree, that of the medieval villager, has been very little investigated. The unfree peasant would not on the face of it seem likely to preserve such records, but in fact the family trees of a number of villeins have been preserved, and recently made available in the rolls of the king's court, now being published by H.M. Stationery Office. In the reign of King John, when the process of differentiation into the two courts of King's Bench and Common Bench was beginning, there occurred a series of cases in which a man was alleged to be a villein by a litigant who either claimed him as his property or desired to prove that he had no legal standing in the king's court. At a later date the test of villeinage was usually the nature of the services owed and dues paid by the tenant; in these cases, recorded on the rolls for 1205–8, the proof turns on birth—was the tenant's father free or unfree? The method of proof is for either

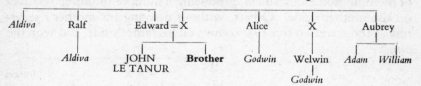

party to produce in court kindred of the man whose status is in dispute. Thus in 1205 John le Tanur complained of assault and imprisonment by the abbot of Waltham, and the abbot alleged that John was his villein purchased by him from Richard FitzAucher, and imprisoned for failure to perform the services due from him, and the abbot produced three cousins on the mother's side and an aunt and a cousin on the father's side, all of whom were villeins, whilst John produced his brother, a free man, and the tenant of his father's holding.[1] John lost his case.

In the same year a Hertfordshire gentleman, Werricus de Marines, claimed Ralf Potter as his villein, alleging that both his father Segar and his brother Geoffrey had died his villeins. He produced Segar's first cousin and great-nephew, and three sons of a cousin of Ralf's mother, all of whom admitted villeinage. Ralf Potter, on the other hand, denied the relevance of the cousin's status, asserted that the great-nephew's relationship was illegitimate, and that the status of his kinsman on the mother's side had no bearing on the case, and produced Thomas and John, freemen, descended on the father's side from his great-grandfather. Werricus denied the relationship of Thomas and John, and a jury was summoned to determine the fact, but as Ralf failed to appear, he lost his case.[2]

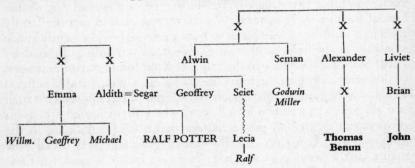

In 1206, a Norfolk gentleman, Roger de Tony, claimed Osbert of Waddington as his villein, producing a number of unfree relatives on the mother's side. Osbert, without denying his mother's servitude, produced two free first cousins on his father's side, and won the case.[3]

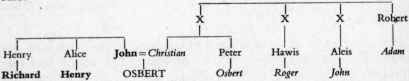

[1] *Curia Regis Rolls*, III. 325. In the tables the admitted villeins are italicized, and the freemen in blacker type.

[2] *Ibid.* IV. 22.   [3] *Ibid.* IV. 128.

In the same year William of St Faith claimed as his villein William son of Simon of Stanford, Suffolk, producing an uncle and two cousins on the father's side who were villeins, and a third witness who proved to be free. This unexpected reinforcement to his side won the case for the other William.[1]

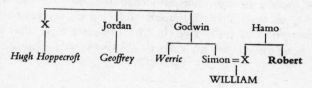

William de Hauterive of Sussex claimed Maud, the daughter of Ernis, producing three alleged cousins on the father's and one on the mother's side. Maud denied their cousinhood and produced three cousins on the father's side, winning her case.[2]

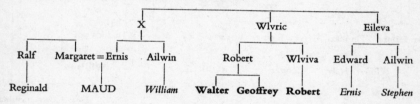

William de Stodham of Bedfordshire refused to receive the homage of Herman son of Ralph on the ground that he was a villein: he produced two cousins on the father's and three on the mother's side who admitted villeinage. Herman denied their kinship, declared his grandfather was wrongly named, and demanded a jury. The result is not recorded.[3]

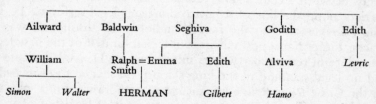

A Cambridgeshire gentleman, Gilbert de Tany, claimed Aubrey of Fulbourn as his villein, producing six cousins on the father's side

---

[1] *Curia Regis Rolls*, IV. 196.   [2] *Ibid*. IV. 234.   [3] *Ibid*. IV. 259.

and an aunt and two cousins on the mother's who owned themselves villeins; Aubrey for his part produced three cousins on the father's side and one on the mother's who were free. The pedigree is exceptionally interesting, going into great details, and there is no dispute as to the facts. It will be seen that Aubrey's grandmother, the wife of Stephen the Lame, was a free woman and that one aunt on the mother's and another on the father's side married free men, so that four of his cousins were undoubtedly free, but by the same rule, that a man's status is determined by his father's, Aubrey was undoubtedly a villein.[1]

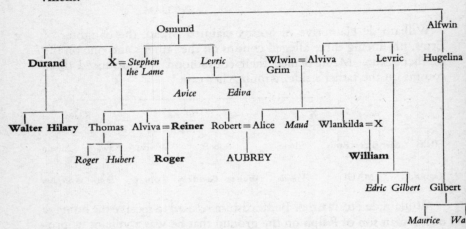

The sociological interest of these cases lies in the evidence they afford that in the life of a village where intermarriage went on so freely between freemen and villeins there can have been no class barriers along the line of legal freedom and legal serfdom. To the king's lawyers and to the feudal landlords the distinction was of practical importance; no villein could avail himself of the new legal procedure in real property cases introduced by Henry II because he had no legal standing in the king's court. In several cases recorded on the *Curia Regis Rolls* a litigant has to withdraw from a plea for that reason. When, however, it was a case not of legal but of social standing, the technical villein may have been a person of dignity and importance in the rural community. In 1195, Maud of Biham com-

[1] *Curia Regis Rolls*, IV. 305.

plained that William de Colevill imprisoned her as his villein when in fact she had been sold by him to a third party. William asserted that he had made good his claim to her before the justices at Leicester. Maud replied that she was not there when he made his claim at Leicester and that he could not prove his case in her absence, and 'as to what the rustics he produced there said about her, she knows nothing'. Maud was able to produce friends of good standing to be her pledges; she carried on a law suit or a series of law suits in the king's court for twelve years, for she was still haggling over her status in 1207, and clearly she had a full sense of the respect due to her and yet she never denied that she was a villein, for all the litigation was on the question *whose* villein she was.[1]

A further illustration of the intermingling of free and unfree blood comes from a Surrey village. The family tree of the Stoughtons of Stoughton as preserved by the seventeenth-century antiquarian, Sir Nicholas Stoughton, shows the son and heir of the lord of the manor marrying a villein's daughter, and his father, Hugh Stoughton, freeing her and all her progeny (sequela) from bondage, in the year 1261.[2]

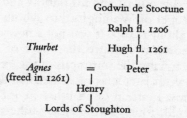

```
                              Godwin de Stoctune
                                     |
                                Ralph fl. 1206
                                     |
              Thurbet             Hugh fl. 1261
                 |                     |
              Agnes        =         Peter
          (freed in 1261)    |
                           Henry
                             |
                   Lords of Stoughton
```

One other point that these cases on the rolls of the king's court bring out is the precision with which family relationships were known. Few of us to-day could write down from memory such a family tree as that which Aubrey of Fulbourn adduced in court; many of us could not produce the written evidence for it. The tenacious memory of the illiterate is proverbial, so that perhaps there is less place for surprise, but it is remarkable that not only the peasant, but the lord's steward was able to supply such a wealth of detail, and we are not surprised that every now and then, as in the case of William of St Faith, someone blundered.

[1] *Curia Regis Rolls*, v. 49, 77.
[2] I owe this reference to the courtesy of the Rev. H. J. Burkitt, who not only called my attention to the passage, but lent me his transcript of B.M. Add. MS. 6174, Sir Nicholas Stoughton's narrative.

IX

The Marshalsy of the Eyre[1]

The office of Marshal of the Eyre is the subject of at least two interesting cases reported in the *Yearbooks of Edward II*.[2] As no account of this Marshalsy appears to exist it seemed worth while to bring together the following particulars, not only for their own sake, but as illustrating the history of a medieval serjeanty. These particulars fall under three heads: the origin and evolution of the office, its tenure and descent, and the functions and activities it involved.

With regard to the first point no exhaustive inquiry is here attempted. The ascertained facts are capable possibly of other interpretations than that which seems most plausible to the writer, namely that the functions of the Marshal of the Eyre were evolved from or were an accretion upon those of the usher of the exchequer. Madox gives an account of this official and his duties[3] and traces the descent of the office from Roger of Wallingford to whom it was granted by Henry II, probably about 1156.[4] It was not a new office at that date[5] when, as Madox shows, it included the duties of supplying wax to the exchequer and carrying the summons of the exchequer about the country. Over 120 years later a far more detailed description is given in the inquisition post-mortem of an usher in 1284.[6] The holder of the office, we are told, found two serjeant-ushers at the king's exchequer, and took for every day the exchequer was open 5*d*. of the king; annual value estimated at £4. 1*s*. 8*d*. He found all the green wax for the seal of the exchequer, and received for each writ sealed one penny; estimated annual value £5. He had the summons and writs of the exchequer carried throughout England, and received threepence for each day of the outward journey; estimated value £1;

---

[1] Reprinted from *The Cambridge Historical Journal*, 1924.
[2] (i) Du Boys *v*. Dagworth. See *Eyre of Kent*, III. 141–2, 212; *Yearbooks of Edward II*, XVI. 208–11 (Selden Soc.). Mr Bolland discusses the matter, *Eyre of Kent*, I. xxvii, 176, 184; *Yearbooks*, XVI. p. xlvii. (ii) Mayor and Aldermen of London *v*. Dagworth. See Harl. MSS. 453, 1062; Egerton MS. 2811.
[3] T. Madox, *Exchequer* (1711), pp. 718–21.
[4] Cartae Antiquae, Roll 9, no. 25. Printed in *Foedera*.
[5] 'Sicut aliquis illud...tenuit tempore Henrici Regis avi mei.' *Ibid*.
[6] *Inq. Post Mortem*, II. 317.

and he had cloth of the exchequer for robes for his messengers once a year. He also found four serjeant-criers in the Common Bench, and received from them yearly for his fee £5. 3s. 4d., also he found one serjeant at the exchequer of the Jews and received from him yearly for his fee £1. 6s. 8d.; and he found in each eyre of the justices two serjeant-criers and ushers; estimated value £25 for each eyre. All the stages of the evolution between 1156 and 1284 are not clear. In 1241 [1] and 1247 [2] the only service mentioned by the hundred jurors in the Oxfordshire eyre is that of keeping the door of the exchequer at Westminster; in 1253 the usher held also a bailiwick in the Common Bench; [3] in 1271 the duties in the Jewish exchequer, the Common Bench and the eyres are also mentioned by the jurors of the inquisition post-mortem, [4] in 1272, as will appear below, the holder of the office claims the fees and perquisites of Marshal of the Eyre *eo nomine*; and in 1285 the Marshalsy of the Eyre is named first by the jurors in the eyre, the holder of the office being described as 'marshal before the justices in eyre throughout England, and before the Justices of the (common) Bench and before the barons of the exchequer'. [5] The fact that activities in four different courts formed part of the same office looks like an instance of that evolution by differentiation of functions which characterizes English institutional history in the twelfth and thirteenth centuries. [6] The close connection of the general eyre and the exchequer is obvious throughout the history of the office; the connection of the Common Bench is less explicable.

[1] Ass. R. 697, m. 6d. [2] Ass. R. 700, m. 1d.

[3] *Close Roll*, 37 Hen. III, m. 5 (C.R.C. p. 394).

[4] *Inq. Post Mortem*, I. 248. 'Half a knight's fee, held by the serjeanty of being grand usher of the king's exchequer, usher of the Jews and crier before the Justices of the Bench and the rest of the justices of eyre for all pleas throughout the realm of England.'

[5] Ass. R. 705, m. 2 (Oxfordshire).

[6] Mr H. G. Richardson, to whose criticisms I am greatly indebted, suggests, however, that the functions of the marshal in the several courts of law may all ultimately derive from the earl marshal, who in 1260 claimed, in effect, the office of marshal in the King's Bench and in the eyre (see *Law Quarterly Review*, April 1923, p. 253, and *Trans. R. Hist. S.* for 1922, p. 61), and was already under Henry II represented in the exchequer by a marshal with functions similar to those of the marshal in other courts at a later date (Madox, *Exchequer*, pp. 33, 726). If so, the office of Marshal of the Eyre would seem to have been conveyed to the usher of the exchequer somewhere between 1260 and 1272. I am not myself satisfied that the claim of 1260 covers eyres *ad omnia placita*, or extends beyond *placita coram rege*, under which heading the special sessions of Hugh le Bigod and Hugh le Despenser 1259–60 might be included.

By tenure, the office was a serjeanty, annexed for a considerable period to a piece of land called Abbesfeld in the parish of Aston Rowant, Oxfordshire.[1] Though the charter of Henry II mentions no land, it seems probable that this connection is ancient. The editors of the *Dialogus de Scaccario* point out that Domesday Book records that land in Aston was held by *ministri Regis*.[2] One of the pieces of land held by the usher in 1279 was called Wygodes land,[3] which suggests a connection with the great Saxon official,[4] though it does not seem possible to supply enough missing links to trace back the descent of this office as far as Dr Round has carried that of the weigher of the exchequer.[5] The warden of the honour of Wallingford was informed in 1242 that military service could not be exacted from the usher's land at Aston, because it was held by the serjeanty of the ushery.[6] The serjeanty is definitely associated with land in Aston in 1241, 1247 and 1285,[7] but in the inquisition post-mortem of 1292 it is mentioned apart from the Oxfordshire lands, under the heading of Essex,[8] and it is separated from the lands for the purpose of assigning dower to the widow.[9] It is clearly rather an asset than a liability on the land. In the vicissitudes of the descent of the office which we shall have to trace the connection with the land becomes completely severed, and in the inquisition post-mortem of 1332 the serjeanty is described under the head of 'Westminster, Middlesex'.[10]

[1] Now in Stokenchurch, Buckinghamshire, where there is a farm bearing the name of Chequers Manor. Kelly, *Directory of Buckinghamshire*, 1923, p. 205. I am obliged to the Rev. H. E. Salter for this fact.

[2] Hughes, Crump and Johnson, *Dialogus de Scaccario*, pp. 23–4.

[3] *Rot. Hund.* II. 782 b. 'Laurentius de Scaccario tenet...de Alano filio Roardi domino de Eston...aliam tenuram que vocatur Wygodesland.'

[4] Freeman, *Norman Conquest*, IV. 728.

[5] *Eng. Hist. Rev.* 1911, 724–6.

[6] Mem. Rolls, L.T.R. 14, m. 4 d.

[7] Ass. R. 697, m. 6 d (Oxfordshire Eyre of 1241). Leukenore, 'De seriantiis dicunt quod Rogerus de Scaccario tenet quandam terram in Eston' per seriantiam ut sit hostiarius ad Scaccarium domini Regis et valet per annum xx s.' Ass. R. 700, m. 1 d (Oxfordshire Eyre of 1247). 'De seriantiis dicunt quod Rogerus de Scaccario tenet xx s. redditus in Aston per seriantiam custodiendi hostium Scaccarii domini Regis apud Westm'.' Ass. R. 705, m. 2 (Oxfordshire Eyre of 1285). 'De seriantiis dicunt quod Laurentius de Scaccario tenuit duas carucatas terre in Abbesfeld in parochia de Aston que valent per annum c s. per seriantiam essendi marescallus coram justitiariis itinerantibus per totam Angliam et coram Justitiariis de Banco et coram Baronibus de Scaccario. Et Symon filius et heres ipsius Laurentii est infra etate et in custodia domini Regis.'   [8] *Inq. Post Mortem*, II. 501.

[9] *C.R.C.* (1292), pp. 220, 229.   [10] *Inq. Post Mortem*, VII. 310.

The history of the descent of the office is seen most clearly from the accompanying table. Madox makes out a good case for its

HISTORY OF THE DESCENT OF THE OFFICE

Roger of Wallingford [granted office ca. 1156;
† 1170? Pipe Roll 16 H. II m. 2 d]

Laurence [under age 1170; first found exercising
= Eleanor   office 1191. Pipe Roll 3 R. I, m. 11]

Laurence de Scaccario
[fines to have office. Pipe Roll
6 John, m. 8; alive 1211. *Red
Book of Exch.* p. 599. †1217? Pipe
Roll 2 H. III, m. 6]

Lora = Roger de Scaccario [under age 1217; holding office 1241.
†1289   Ass. R. 697, m. 6d]
[*Fine Roll Cal.*   †1271 [I.P.M.]
p. 258]

Gunnora = Laurence de Scaccario   A nun of Markyate (I.P.M.
(C.R.C. p. 265)   †1284 [I.P.M.]

Simon (1) = Petronilla = (2) John   Maud   Lora   Beatrice
born 1269   du Boys   born 1251   born 1263   born 1267
o.s.p. October 1291 [*Eyre of Kent*]   †1308   o.s.p. 1325   †before 1313
                                (C.R.C.)   (I.P.M.)   = John Peverel
                                = John de   = (1) Ralph de
                                Dagworth   Leveland †1280
                                †1290   (2) William Peyforer
                                         †before 1313

Alice = John de Dagworth   Hawise = Reginald de Herlizoun   Hamo Peverel
†by 1333   of age Nov. 1297   [L.T.R., M.R. 74, m. 25 d]
        (C.R.C.)
        †27 July 1332 (I.P.M.)

Nicholas de Dagworth   Thomas de Dagworth
   †1351 (I.P.M.)   (captain in French wars)

John de Dagworth = Thomasia
[Makes over office to John Gaunt 1357. Feet of Fines, London]

hereditary transmission from the Roger of Wallingford of 1159 to the Roger de Scaccario with whom, genealogically speaking, we reach daylight in 1241.[1] His son Laurence exercised the office of

[1] The yearbook of the eyre of London of 1321 speaks of a Henry del Escheker who was seised of the serjeanty in the time of King John. B.M. Harl. MS. 1062, fo. 1d. But a consideration of dates will show that there is no room for another

Marshal of the Eyre in the eyre of Cambridge in 1272,[1] and was sheriff of Essex and Hertfordshire from 1275 to 1278. On his death in 1284, leaving a widow, a son under age and three daughters, the escheator was in doubt whether the widow should have assignment of dower on the serjeanty, and apparently she accepted the Essex manor of Twynsted in settlement of all her claims.[2] For the next seven years the serjeanty, with the other possessions of young Simon de Scaccario, was in the king's hands by right of wardship. In February 1291 the king informed the barons of the exchequer that Simon had done homage to him for the serjeanty, and that they were to let him have full seisin of it, with its appurtenances. Simon came before the treasurer and barons and proved his age, and they, having given him seisin, straightway took the office back into the king's hands, because Simon, while he was still the king's ward, had committed the office of the ushery of the exchequer to John de Dymmoke without the king's licence. Simon was fined £40 for the trespass, but John and the other deputy whom he had appointed were allowed to hold the deputyships as granted.[3] Simon only held the office for eight months; in October 1291 he died childless, leaving a widow, Petronilla, and three elder sisters. His lands were ordered to be taken into the king's hands for debts owing to the king,[4] whether the arrears due for his father's term of office as sheriff[5] or for his own fine of £40 or for some other debt does not appear. The serjeanty, with the lands, was committed during pleasure to Guncelin de Badelesmere.[6] The question of the rights of the widow and the sisters of Simon was not a simple one. On 19 February 1292 the barons of the exchequer were instructed to assign to Petronilla dower of a third of the issues of the serjeanty, after deducting reasonable costs and expenses of the ministers serving the office, since the issues were uncertain and division of the serjeanty ought not to be made and had not usually

generation. The Henry de Scaccario who figures in the records is almost certainly the holder of that land in Ellesborough which is now the site of the Prime Minister's Chequers. See *Curia Regis Rolls*, I. 109; *Book of Fees*, p. 252; *Vict. Co. Hist., Buckinghamshire*, II. 333. Compare also *Eng. Hist. Rev.* 1943, p. 10 f.

[1] Ass. R. 85, m. 10. *Vide infra.* Possibly this was the first eyre in which he exercised the serjeanty. The silence of other eyre records does not imply non-exercise.   [2] *Inq. Post Mortem*, II. 319. Cf. *C.R.C.* p. 276 (1284).

[3] Mem. Rolls, L.T.R. 62, m. 10 d. (Two entries.)

[4] *Ibid.* 63, m. 31 d, m. 34.

[5] Laurence was owing nearly £250 in 1279. See *C.R.C.* p. 524; see also *F.R.C.* for 1283, p. 190.   [6] *F.R.C.* p. 301.

been made hitherto.[1] In the assignment of dower recorded on the Close Roll, however, there is no reference to the serjeanty,[2] and it would appear from the law suit of 1312–13 that Petronilla did not secure dower with regard to the Marshalsy of the Eyre. The three married sisters were summoned to appear *coram Rege* on the morrow of the Ascension, i.e. 16 May, to receive their shares of the serjeanty held by Simon in the exchequer, but later it was thought better that the partition should be made in the exchequer, by the judgment (*considerationem*) of the barons of the exchequer, so that justice might be done according to the law and custom of the exchequer.[3] On the appointed day—some date between 3 May and 4 June 1292—the three co-heiresses or their proxies appeared and a partition was made, the detailed record of which I have been unable to trace; in spite of the fact that the barons had been ordered to send it, under seal of the exchequer, to be enrolled in the chancery.[4] The settlement is referred to subsequently in a fine of 1305[5] and in the Close Roll of 1329,[6] and at the time in writs addressed on 4 June 1292 to the justices in eyre at Hereford and Lancaster, which are enrolled both on the eyre and memoranda rolls.[7] From them it appears that Maud de Dagworth, the eldest sister, with the consent of her sisters Lora and Beatrice, and in the presence of the barons of the exchequer, assigned the office of the ushery to John de Dagworth (her son, still under age) and to Philip de Cokefeld (whom the king had already appointed to act as Marshal of the Eyre in the interim) to be performed for her and her co-heiresses. These two deputy-serjeants entered at once into the exercise of the functions of Marshal of the Eyre in the eyres opened at Hereford and Lancaster on the octave of Trinity 1292. It would seem that, the nomination having gone by *droit d'aînesse* to the eldest sister,[8] the profits of the serjeanty were equally shared between the three sisters,[9] for in 1304 Maud and Lora sought the king's licence to alienate their shares of the serjeanty to Maud's daughter Hawise

---

[1] *C.R.C.* p. 220.   [2] *Ibid.* p. 229.

[3] Mem. Rolls, L.T.R. 63, m. 16: *Pro Matillda una sororum Simonis de Scaccario*; m, 16 d: *Pro Willelmo Peyvere.* See also *C.R.C.* p. 230.

[4] Mem. Rolls, L.T.R. 63, m. 16.

[5] Feet of Fines, London and Middlesex, no. 322.   [6] *C.R.C.* p. 507.

[7] Mem. Rolls, L.T.R. 63, m. 37, m. 37 d; Ass. R. 302, m. 1, 408, m. 1.

[8] 'La verge fut livree a Maude pur ceo qel fut leynesce.' B.M. Harl. MS. 1062, fo. 1 d.

[9] It will be noted that neither the account of the editors of the *Dialogus* (p. 24) nor that of Mr Bolland (*Yearbooks of Edward II*, XVI. p. xlvii) is entirely correct.

and her husband Reginald de Herlizoun. The barons were directed to inquire whether the king would suffer by such an alienation, and they replied that it seemed to them that it would not be to the king's loss to grant the licence 'Quia seriantia est nunc dispersa in tres participes et per concessionem huiusmodi erunt due parte (*sic*) unite. De valore eiusdem ignoramus, quia in Itineribus Justiciariorum plus valet quam alio tempore'.[1] Maud and Lora, however, soon changed their minds; on 3 November 1305, by a fine before the king's justices,[2] Maud made over her share of the serjeanty to her son, receiving in return a life interest in it. Consequently in 1307 Reginald de Herlizoun petitioned the King[3] for release from his fine of £20 which he had made before the treasurer and barons of the exchequer to have the serjeanty of the ushery of the exchequer, since, owing to Maud's grant, he could not have any advantage from his fine: and he was in fact released from it.[4] John de Dagworth did homage for his mother's third part and took seisin of it in the exchequer on her death in 1308.[5]

In the eyre of Kent in 1313 Simon's widow Petronilla and her second husband John du Boys sought a share in the profits of the office of Marshal of the Eyre, as her lawful dower. Her plea was disallowed on technical grounds; she had brought an assize of novel disseisin and had not specified the place where the profits of the bailiwick lay. Later Canterbury and Rochester were named, and it was then pointed out that the profits of the office arose in any county of England where an eyre was held.[6] In this suit John's aunt Lora Peyforer and his cousin Hamo Peverel, who had by now inherited the rights of the third sister Beatrice, were defending their purparties of the serjeanty along with him; but that John himself was exercising the office on their behalf appears from his petition to the king that he may exercise it without hindrance,[7] and by the king's letter of 15 October 1313 to the justices, bidding them let him exercise his rights and take his profits.[8] In the next general eyre, that of London

[1] Mem. Rolls, L.T.R. 74, m. 25 d.
[2] Feet of Fines, London and Middlesex, no. 322.
[3] *Rot. Parl.* I. 474 b.
[4] *C.R.C.* pp. 86–7 (1308).
[5] Mem. Rolls, L.T.R. 78, m. 50; *C.R.C.* p. 34.
[6] *Eyre of Kent* (Selden Soc.), III. 141–2, 212; *Yearbooks of Edward II* (Selden Soc.), XVI. 208–9.
[7] Ancient Petitions, File 194, no. 9665. 'A nostre seignour le Roy prie soun lige Bacheler Johan de Dageworth soun mareschal de fee en les heires par mi le reaume' (etc.).   [8] Ass. R. 382, m. 228 (printed *Eyre of Kent*, III. 228).

in 1321, another dispute over the serjeanty arose, and in this the same three litigants figure—John, Lora and Hamo. In the petition addressed to the king and his council on the matter, however, only Lora and John are mentioned:[1] John had bought out his cousin Hamo, by licence of the king;[2] and in 1325, according to a second petition, John had succeeded to Lora's purparty, and 'the bailiwick of the ushery with all its appurtenances has now come into the hand of the said John de Dagworth as his right'.[3] As a result, apparently, of these petitions, John's claim was once more officially endorsed, and the justices of the eyres of 1329 were ordered, in a long letter which rehearses the history of the serjeanty from the death of Simon,[4] to admit John to the Marshalsy of the Eyre. The occasion of this letter would seem to have been the difficulties raised by the justices and the king's counsel when John claimed his serjeanty on the second day of the eyre of Northamptonshire, 7 November 1329. As reported in the yearbooks, the presiding justice Scrope first objected that the claim should not have been made till Wednesday, the proper day for all claims of franchises, when Aldborough said that the claim was to exercise the office from the opening of the eyre.[5] Dagworth's counsel gave proof that homage had been done for the said serjeanty, and it was then objected first that homage had only been done for the inherited third and not for the purchased two-thirds (on which the reporter comments 'that a man or woman may do homage twice'), and then that the homage was for the office of ushery of the exchequer and Dagworth had not shown how the office of the marshalsy was connected with that of the ushery.[6] The shortest answer to these legal subtleties was the king's letter close, which Dagworth procured, as we have seen, on 12 December 1329. The letter of 28 October 1330,[7] giving similar orders to the justices in eyre at Derby, states that Scrope had testified before the king that Dagworth was admitted to the office in the eyre of Northampton, and another

[1] Ancient Petitions, File 8, no. 381. The date of this must fall between 1321 and 23 January 1325, when the writ for Lora's inquisition post-mortem issued. *Inq. Post Mortem*, VI. 402.   [2] So the next petition states.

[3] Ancient Petitions, File 8, no. 383 (printed *Rot. Parl.* I. 426–7).

[4] C.R.C. p. 507. Lora, whom Andrew Horn in the *Liber Custumarum* [R.S.], p. 297, describes as John's wife, is here called his grandmother. For her two husbands, stepbrothers, and the serjeanty inherited by the first, see *Knights of Edward I* (Harleian Soc.) *s.v.* Leveland, Peyforer.

[5] B.M. Add. MS. 5924, fo. 1d.

[6] B.M. Egerton MS. 2811, fo. 246.

[7] C.R.C. p. 71.

letter of 12 May 1331 [1] ordered the sheriff of Nottingham and Derby to deliver to Dagworth his perquisites after the eyres in those counties. It seems, then, that Dagworth exercised the functions of marshal in the last eyres that were carried through to a conclusion in England.

In 1331–32 the Patent Rolls record the granting out of fractions of the whole serjeanty; to Roger de Bedfield, for life, half the serjeanty of the ushery of the exchequer, with all profits and power to appoint a deputy; [2] to the same Roger, for life, two quarters of the serjeanty in the Common Bench, [3] and to John Hovel another quarter. [4] The other half of the ushery had been granted to John Dymmoke for life; but the Marshalsy of the Eyre was retained in the hands of Dagworth and his heirs, as well as the fivepence a day during the session of the exchequer which the ushery brought in, apart from all fees. [5] The 'impartible bailiwick' was thus in a finely mangled condition when, on 27 July 1332, John de Dagworth died and was succeeded by his son Nicholas. [6] On 7 October 1357, by a fine before the king's justices at Westminster, John the son of Nicholas finally granted away the whole serjeanty, including the Marshalsy of the Eyre, by royal consent, to John Gaunt, for £100. [7] The history of the serjeanty need be traced no farther, [8] as we are primarily concerned with the Marshalsy of the Eyre, and the general eyre was defunct even before the Dagworths had surrendered the office.

It remains to consider what precisely were the duties of the Marshal of the Eyre. Mr Bolland shows that he had a share of the fees, and suggests that he had also some billeting duties. [9] Mr Bolland's reviewer in the *Law Quarterly Review* suggests that he had duties in connection with the custody of prisoners. [10] In all the disputes as to the serjeanty, however, the fees and perquisites of the office are clearly regarded as of greater importance than the duties; it may therefore be as well to begin with a statement as to those fees and perquisites which, so far as I know, has not been noted hitherto. It is enrolled on the record of the Cambridgeshire eyre of 1272. [11]

[1] *C.R.C.* p. 233.   [2] *P.R.C.* p. 175 (10 Oct. 1331).
[3] *Ibid.* p. 217 (6 Nov. 1331).   [4] *Ibid.* pp. 328–9 (11 Sept. 1332).
[5] *Inq. Post Mortem*, VII. 310.   [6] *Ibid.*   [7] Feet of Fines, Middlesex, no. 359.
[8] Miss D. M. Broome gives details both of the holders and their deputies in her thesis on *The Exchequer under Edward III*.
[9] *Eyre of Kent* (Selden Soc.), I. xxiii.
[10] *Law Quarterly Review*, April 1923, p. 255.
[11] Ass. R. 85, m. 10. A good many other eyre rolls have been searched in vain for similar entries.

Die Lune proximo post mensem Pasche venit Laurentius de Scaccario coram
Justitiariis hic et petiit feudum suum tanquam marescallus domini Regis itinerantibus scilicet:

Coram justitiariis ad placita—

De quolibet brevi placitato vel pace fracta de recuperante . . .	iiij d.
De quolibet brevi recuperante per mangnam assisam	ij s.
De quolibet retorno per jurata xxiiij militum	ij s.
De quolibet duello vadiato	ij s.
De quolibet fine levato	iiij d.

De quolibet homine faciente homagium coram justitiariis, superiorem
pannum vel v s.

Et similiter coram Justitiariis ad coronam:—

De quolibet hundredo quod respondit per xij coram Justitiariis . .	xij d.
De qualibet „ villa „ „ „ xxiiij „ .	ij s.
De qualibet villa ad primum ingressum	iiij d.
De quolibet incarcerato et acquietato per patriam	iiij d.
De quolibet dampnato	superiorem pannum
De qualibet carta lecta coram justitiariis	ij s.
De qualibet meretrice	iiij d.
De quolibet doleo vini pudridi	doleum vacuum

Et post recessum Justitiariorum barreragia coram Justitiariis ad placita et ad
coronam, etc.

These last perquisites of the barriers are mentioned again in 1331
as if they were regarded as especially valuable, when the sheriff of
Nottingham and Derby is ordered to let John de Dagworth have the
barriers made for the sessions of the justices in eyre in those counties,
and all other things pertaining to the office of the barriers.[1] The
empty casks were presumably the fruit of that tour of inspection of
the alehouses which Mr Bolland describes.[2] In 1285 the second
Statute of Westminster, under the heading *de custodibus hostiorum in
itineribus, virgam portantibus coram Justitiariis de Banco*,[3] gives a list of
fees, revised in the downward direction for the most part, though
some are new. The fees for the grand assize and the duel are reduced
to a shilling; the fees from the men doing homage, from the hundred
jury, and from the acquitted prisoner are unchanged, as well as the
fee for each writ pleaded; the fee for reading a charter is abolished.
A fee of fourpence for each jury guarded is new, as is the fee of one
shilling from each pardoned outlaw whose peace is proclaimed by
the crier, but both by omission, and by express abolition, the fines
are substantially reduced. There is a further reference to the fees in the

[1] *C.R.C.* p. 233.   [2] W. C. Bolland, *The General Eyre*, p. 41.
[3] c. 44. See *Stat. Realm*, I. 93.

case of *Scoland versus Grandison* in the eyre of Kent, when 2 marks are paid to the marshals and clerks where the total damages are £15,[1] and 20 marks to the clerks, 100s. to the marshals, 100s. to the sheriffs' clerks and 20s. to the criers where the total damages are 140 marks.[2] This seems a great increase on the earlier tariff, and gives one a clue to the importance which the Dagworths attached to their claims.

The functions of the marshal are given under four heads in the records of 1329–30; he is crier (*praeco*), marshal and usher, and he has the office of the barriers. Some light is thrown on these duties by the controversy with the mayor and citizens of London in 1321. According to the account of the *Liber Custumarum*[3] and the year-books,[4] which is confirmed by the eyre roll,[5] the mayor and citizens claimed to have their own porter (*janitor*) outside the gates of the Tower, the king's porter being within; and their own usher (*ostiarius*) without the door of the hall where they ought to plead, to introduce the barons and others of the city who ought to plead, the king's usher being within the door; and to have their own serjeants with rods, no serjeant of the king intermeddling with anything pertaining to that office. They asserted that their claim had been allowed and enrolled in the eyres of 1252 and 1276. According to the *Liber Albus* it had been allowed in 1244 also.[6] The eyre roll of 1276 supports the claim of the city,[7] which was allowed by the justices when it had **been made clear that no fees or profits of any sort were being claimed**—'ut de feodo marescalli, ostiarii seu clamatorum vel aliorum ministrorum coram justitiariis itinerantibus'.[8] John de Dagworth and his parceners, however, protested that whether the citizens' officials took profits or no they were being ousted from their profits, since by reason of their serjeanty 'coram justitiariis Domini Regis hic in itinere suo virgas portare, clamatores ponere et feoda quae marescallorum feoda nuncupantur capere debeant',[9] as they did before the justices of the bench, and had recently done in the eyre of Kent. In his petition to the king of 1321–24 John declares that though no fees were taken by the officials of the city the justices'

---

[1] *Eyre of Kent* (Selden Soc.), I. 176.   [2] *Ibid.* I. 184.
[3] *Munimenta Gildhallae* [R.S.], II. 295, 301–2.
[4] B.M. Harl. MSS. 453, fo. 12; 1062, fo. 1; Egerton MS. 2811, ff. 22, 24 d, 25 d.
[5] Ass. R. 547 a, m. 1.   [6] *Munimenta Gildhallae*, I. 77.
[7] B.M. Add. Charters, 5153, m. 1.   [8] *Munimenta Gildhallae*, II. 302.
[9] *Ibid.* 364.

own marshals took them instead, and points out with the wisdom of the serpent that the king stands to lose by this as well as the Dagworths, since during the minority of the heir (as from 1284 to 1291) the profits of the serjeanty were in the king's own hands.[1] It is possible that the justices were really taking these fees on the king's behalf.[2] The yearbooks of the eyre disclose the fact that the serjeants of the city did take fees, in spite of the undertaking of the mayor and citizens, and that on this pretext the 'liberty', as the justices called it, was taken into the king's hands,[3] although the Recorder declared that what was taken was 'not fee, but courtesy'.[4] This confiscation may account for John's difficulty in making good a claim that had been allowed only seven years before, in the eyre of Kent.

From the details of this controversy one gathers that the function of the usher was to keep the door of the hall where the eyre was held and to announce the names of litigants—'to introduce those who ought to plead'. The duty of the marshals proper seems to be identified with that of the serjeants who bear the rods, and to be of a disciplinary nature. We have seen that he takes fees from prisoners, whether found guilty or acquitted, therefore he probably has custody of them, like the Earl Marshal.[5] In one of the yearbooks of the eyre of Northampton John de Dagworth claims 'de porter verge en court,...et de prendre profit solom lestatut[6] com apent a criour, com en porter verge deuant les justices, et de mettre criours, et de garder les dozeins'.[7] Similar to this 'guarding' of the hundred juries, for which it will be remembered the marshal claimed a special fee, is the part played by a marshal in the Northampton eyre. One of the coroners had not his rolls by him, and said they were in the town, and the court allowed him to go and fetch them under the guard of the marshal.[8] The duty of the crier was presumably to make the

[1] Ancient Petitions, File 8, no. 381. As a matter of fact, some nineteen eyres were held in the period of Simon's minority.

[2] See, however, below, note 8.

[3] B.M. Egerton MS. 2811, fo. 24d. *Scrop.* 'Vous avez entendu coment le mair e les aldermans unt clame loffice de marschals cy en cest eyre et clamaint le profit com le fee par qai le fee devait al Roy, e leur servaunts par eux assis unt pris le fee par qai nous prioums qe la franchise sait seisi.'

[4] *Ibid.* fo. 25d.   [5] Madox, *Exchequer*, p. 729.

[6] *sc. Stat. West.* II. c. 44.   [7] B.M. Egerton MS. 2811, fo. 245d.

[8] B.M. Add. MS. 24063, fo. 2d. At this point of the eyre, however, Dagworth's claim had not yet been allowed, and it is possible that the marshal was a dependent of one of the justices. Such a marshal is mentioned at the Gloucestershire eyre at Bristol in 1285, as having been the agent of Richard de Boyland—'Quidam

general proclamations of which many are mentioned in any eyre report, and to summon or announce litigants. Andrew Horn says that on the first day of the London eyre of 1321 Sir John de Dagworth's crier called many times for the sheriffs of London.[1] From *Scoland v. Grandison* it appears that different deputies exercised the offices of marshals and of criers. It will be remembered that the inquisition of 1284 speaks of two serjeant-criers and ushers.[2] It is possible that the external duties which seem to be associated with the office may have arisen from a combination of these disciplinary and proclamatory functions. As crier the marshal had to announce that the rates of lodging in the inns were not to be raised because of the eyre, and that the justices and their clerks, the king's serjeants, the dozens and the men of the vills were to have their lodging gratis.[3] From a charter to the city of York cited by Mr Bolland one gathers that the marshal might assign lodgings to persons during the eyre— presumably to those entitled to free accommodation.[4] The fee payable by the *meretrices*[5] suggests some kind of external supervision of the town where the eyre was held, and so does the perquisite of the empty wine-casks.

The 'office of the barriers' may indicate some regulation of the duel, if trial by battle was used. On the other hand, they may merely have been the temporary wooden erections necessary to keep the crowd at a suitable distance, or to mark off the different courts from each other if different business was being conducted simultaneously.

Johannes de Wycham, valettus predicti Ricardi portans virgam coram eo in predicto itinere.' *State Trials of Edward I* (Camden Soc.), pp. 5, 6. As Madox says (*Exchequer*, p. 729), 'the word Marshall seems to have been sometimes used with latitude'. Such a multiplicity of officials is contemplated, and deprecated, in the *Statutes of Westminster*, I. cap. xxx, which mentions 'Justices' marshals' as well as 'criers of fee', in forbidding the exaction of excessive fees.

[1] *Munimenta Gildhallae*, II. 289.

[2] *Inq. Post Mortem*, II. 317. Cf. *Rot. Parl.* II. 448, where the marshal and crier try in vain to enforce silence before justices of oyer and terminer sitting at Ipswich, 1339.   [3] B.M. Add. MS. 24063, fo. 5.

[4] *Cal. Charter Rolls* (1312), p. 187, cited *Eyre of Kent* (Selden Soc.), I. xxiii. Cf. clause in various borough charters, 1155–99: 'Quod infra civitatem illam nemo capiat hospitium per vim vel liberationem marescaldi.' If this refers to the Marshal of the Eyre, it is by far the earliest mention of him. *Rot. Cart.* p. 5. It is more likely, however, to refer to the king's marshal. See Madox, *Exchequer*, p. 33, Ballard, *Borough Charters*, p. 87, and Bateson, *Leicester Records*, I. 147–8.

[5] Cf. the office of marshal *de meretricibus* in Round, *King's Serjeants and Officers of State*, pp. 96–8.

The holding of an eyre certainly necessitated the erection of temporary structures of some sort,[1] and whether as rod-bearer or as usher, the marshal had some office connected with them, and claimed them later as his perquisite.

There is much, then, that still remains obscure in the history of the Marshalsy of the Eyre, but it is to be hoped that further light may be forthcoming, both from the unpublished yearbooks of the eyres, and the comparatively unexplored field of the assize rolls.

[1] *Munimenta Gildhallae Londiniensis*, I. 59, II. 287; C.R.C., p. 493 (3 Sept. 1329).

X

The General Eyres of 1329–30[1]

On 3 September 1329 commissions for the holding of a general eyre were issued, the one to Geoffrey le Scrope and his fellows for the Monday after All Saints at Northampton, the other to William Herle and his fellows for the Monday after Martinmas at Nottingham.[2] Orders were sent to the sheriffs to make preparations locally, to the king's serjeants to be ready to plead his pleas, to the treasurer to hand over the rolls of the last eyres in those counties, and to the chief justice of the Common Bench to adjourn all pleas concerning those counties to the eyres.[3] The whole vast machinery of a general eyre had been set working, and this after an almost complete intermission for a generation. There is no evidence for the holding of more than two eyres in the whole reign of Edward II: the famous eyre of Kent of 1313, and the almost equally famous eyre of London in 1321. There is positive evidence that no eyre had been held in Northamptonshire since 1285,[4] or in Nottinghamshire since 1280.[5]

In the records no explanation is given of this return on the part of the new government to the practice of Edward I. In the reports, however, are preserved accounts of two speeches by the two presiding justices which not only clear up a point in the history of the general eyre as an institution, but also throw some light on the general administrative history of the opening years of Edward III's reign. So far as I know, these speeches have never been printed, and the incidents they describe are not noticed in any of the chronicles or records of 1327–30.

The first point that calls for comment is that such speeches should have been made or reported at all. It has been suggested that the speech made by the presiding justice at the opening of the eyre was practically a 'common form', that varied very little from the time of Henry III to that of Edward III.[6] One report of Scrope's speech is of this type,[7] and it is possible that variations from the standard

---

[1] Reprinted from the *English Historical Review*, April 1924.
[2] *P.R.C.* p. 439.   [3] *C.R.C.* pp. 492–3.   [4] Ass. R. 632.
[5] Ass. R. 683.   [6] W. C. Bolland, *Eyre of Kent* (Selden Soc.), I. xxvi.
[7] Rylands MS. 180, fo. 1 b. Cf. Staunton's speech in *Eyre of Kent*, I. 2.

did not as a rule seem important to the student of law, but happily some of the reporters at Northampton, and at least one at Nottingham,[1] found it worth while to give fuller versions, perhaps from that growing literary or dramatic sense which is traceable in the fourteenth-century reports,[2] perhaps because Scrope's speech purported to give an outline of the history of the eyre, which in 1329 must have been almost as much of an antiquity to the budding lawyer as presentment of Englishry.[3] For most of those present at Northampton and Nottingham it must have been the first eyre of their lives; an historical discourse might well seem appropriate.

In the next place, Scrope's speech contains the statement that has haunted the text-books for centuries and perplexed so many modern scholars, namely, that in the good old days the eyres went every seven years. Britton had put into the mouth of Edward I the command that justices itinerant should be assigned to hear the articles of the eyre every seven years;[4] Scrope definitely says that they went throughout the realm every seven years. 'En temps des progenitours cesti Roy Eyres soleient estre de sept aunz en sept aunz par tut le Roialme.' And this in spite of the fact that he had in his possession the rolls of the two last Northamptonshire eyres, for 1269 and 1285, when if Edward I had really observed the seven-year rule there should have been rolls in existence for 1292, 1299 and 1306. Only of the reign of Henry III is such a statement approximately true.[5] But **this report is the source of Selden's dictum to this effect in his *Notes upon Hengham*, 'So seies Scrope in *temps* E. III':[6]** and later historians have taken it from Selden.

[1] Of seven reports of the eyre of Nottingham which have been examined, only the Cambridge manuscript given below includes the speech.

[2] I am indebted for this suggestion to Mr H. G. Richardson.

[3] In the eyre of Nottingham 'Russel pria qe les justices les voleit encenser coment il deuent presenter [englescherie], car il dit qe le temps fut taunt passe puys ceo qil auaynt presente qil ne sauaynt coment ceo dust estre. *Herle* Nous ne sumes pas venutz ceo pur vus aprendre coment vous deuez presenter . . . e il ne les voleit pas dire.' (Cambridge University Library MS. Hh. 2. 4, fo. 266.)

[4] Britton, ed. F. M. Nichols, p. 3.

[5] It seems probable that there were eyres in Northamptonshire in or about the following years: 1232, 1239, 1247, 1253, 1261, 1269. See *Oxford Studies in Legal and Social History*, VI. 106–10.

[6] Selden gives the reference 'fo. 143a' for this statement, and MS. Egerton 2811 has the note 'Kel 143a' against Scrope's words. [Mr Hall has located the reference in Keilway's *Reports* (1602), not in Scrope's opening speech, but as an *obiter dictum* of his in a Quo Warranto case. See *E.H.R.*, 1959, pp. 90–2.]

The chief interest of Scrope's speech, however, which it shares with Herle's, lies in the fact that it professes to describe a concerted policy carried out, if not by the ill-famed Mortimer, at least under his auspices, to restore peace and order to England. There are four features of this policy: first the appointment of keepers of the peace, secondly the passing of strict laws against highway robbers, armed gangs, and maintainors, thirdly the appointing of justices of oyer and terminer with a new and comprehensive commission, and lastly the initiation of a general eyre. For all these measures we are to see the parliament of Northampton of April–May 1328 as the focus; the parliament whose work in ratifying the unpopular Scottish peace seems for most contemporary and later historians to have obscured the importance of its police legislation, though in later years the Statute of Northampton was to form the second chapter, so to speak, in the code administered by the justices of the peace.

The first step taken by the new government, the appointment of keepers of the peace throughout the realm, was not the new device which Scrope's speech would seem to suggest. The Patent Rolls of Edward II's reign [1] are widely sprinkled with commissions to *custodes pacis*, and with mandates to them to enforce the Statute of Winchester, and at less frequent intervals recur commissions to justices of oyer and terminer for the punishment of those 'vagabundos, vulneratores, verberatores et manutenores' whom the guardians of the peace had, in theory at least, committed to jail. *Custodes pacis* had been appointed for the whole country in the spring of 1326, [2] and justices of oyer and terminer in the autumn, [3] though the latter commission had been revoked by Edward II 'for certain causes' on the eve of his downfall. [4] But disorder still prevailed. Scrope's picture of the complaints from all quarters is corroborated by the wording of the petition presented in Edward III's first parliament of January–February 1327 at Westminster, 'La commune prie sovereynement qe bones gentz et leaux soient assignez en chescun cunte a la garde de la pees qe ne sount meintenours de mausbaretz en pays et quil eient power de chastier les mesfesurs solom ley et resun'. [5] From the popular point of view the *custodes pacis* were unsatisfactory because

---

[1] *Parl. Writs*, II. ii, part 2, *passim*. Dates 1307–26. See also below, pp. 163–172.
[2] *Ibid.* p. 282.
[3] *Ibid.* pp. 287, 291.
[4] *Ibid.* p. 294 (2 Oct. 1326).
[5] *Rot. Parl.* II. 11.

they had no power to punish, but only to inquire, to detain, and to send up reports to Westminster.[1] The Statute of Westminster provided for the appointment of good men and lawful to keep the peace in each county,[2] and the appointments were made before the parliament was fairly over.[3] But the powers of the new *custodes* were no greater than those of the old, and soon further steps had to be taken.

On 24 April 1328 a parliament was opened at Northampton in the course of which various measures were passed for the better keeping of the peace. Armed and mounted men were not to be present when justice was being done by any of the king's justices or ministers, or in fairs or markets, and the officials of shires, franchises, and boroughs were to enforce this.[4] Justices assigned to inquire into the keeping of the Statute of Winchester were to have power to punish and not merely to report to the king in parliament 'whereof no man hath yet seen any issue'.[5] Lastly, justices were to be assigned 'as in the time of the king's grandfather' to inquire, both at the suit of the king and of the party injured, into all manner of felonies, robberies, homicides, conspiracies and oppressions, done both by ministers of the king and by others, and to inquire into the misdeeds of sheriffs and other officials and to punish them.[6] These terms and the reference to Edward I recall the Statute of Rageman, and the scope of activity of the justices as well as the procedure sketched are those of the eyre, yet on the whole it seems that the promise of this clause of the statute was fulfilled in the commissions of oyer and terminer issued on 15 May,[7] the day that the parliament rose. Four different groups of judges, men 'skilled in the law'[8] as the statute had said, were dispatched to the different counties of England to inquire into and punish breaches of the peace. If the commission be compared in detail with those of the previous reign, it will be found to be the completest yet issued. The commissions of 1320, issued in response to a petition from the knights and burgesses, had anticipated many of its

[1] E.g. 'De toto vero facto in hac parte et de nominibus malefactorum predictorum consilium nostrum apud Westminster distincte et aperte de mense in mensem per vestras literas certioretis' (*Parl. Writs*, II. ii, part 2, p. 75).
[2] 1 Edw. III, st. 2, c. 16.
[3] *P.R.C.* pp. 88–90 (8 March 1327).
[4] 2 Edw. III, c. 3.   [5] 2 Edw. III, c. 6.
[6] 2 Edw. III, c. 7.
[7] *P.R.C.* p. 297.
[8] E.g. Willoughby, Toudeby, Herle, Denham, Mutford, etc.

features, including the authorization of procedure by bill,[1] but though special inquiries into the conduct of officials had been held by justices assigned in the past,[2] it was a new thing for all these powers to be held by the same justices. The extent of the work involved may be gauged from the bulk of the records extant for Lincolnshire,[3] one of the five counties assigned to Stonore, Cambridge, and their fellows. Inquiries were made into the oppression and extortion of sheriffs, coroners, sub-escheators, and their clerks, bailiffs and their servants, constables and keepers of prisons and bailiffs of liberties with their underlings. Scrope and the other justices of the King's Bench had a similar commission for every county in which they might hold the pleas *coram rege*.[4] By these means arrears were to be cleared up, and offences previous to May 1328 punished. Other measures were taken later in the year to enforce the new statute. On 16 September the sheriffs throughout the country were ordered to make proclamation of the clause forbidding assemblies of armed men, and to arrest offenders against it.[5] On 10 November renewed commands were sent to all sheriffs to enforce the statute, and on 11 November they were ordered to hold inquests into the names of offenders and to send the returns duly sealed to the king.[6] In like manner inquests had been held into the keeping of the Statute of Winchester under Edward I.[7]

We may now turn to the account of these matters given in the reported speeches of the justices. Herle's account, though less circumstantial than Scrope's, is clearly more correct. He omits all reference to the keepers of the peace, assigns the appointment of justices of oyer and terminer to the parliament of Northampton, and the decision to hold a general eyre to the council at Windsor to which Scrope also refers. Of this council, summoned for the morrow of St Mary Magdalen (22 July 1329),[8] we have the writs, the terms of

---

[1] 'Dicti iustitiarii recipiant querelas omnium et singulorum coram eis conqueri volencium de transgressionibus eis factis contra pacem Regis et eas audiant et terminent et eis iusticiam faciant per billas sicut per brevia Regis' (*Parl. Writs*, II. ii, part 2, p. 155).

[2] *Ibid.* pp. 135, 154, 161, 287.

[3] Ass. R. 516 (60 ms.).

[4] Patent Roll, 2 Edw. III, part 1, m. 7 d.

[5] *C.R.C.* p. 413. The date is incorrectly printed 16 October.

[6] *Ibid.* pp. 420–1.

[7] *Parl. Writs*, I. 388–9 (20 Jan. 1287).

[8] Close Roll, 3 Edw. III, m. 18 d. Printed *Report on the Dignity of a Peer*, IV. 390.

which go to confirm the account in the reports.[1] The *colloquium* in question was to be held 'touching the tranquillity and quiet of our people'—the conventional phrase for police concerns. It is noteworthy that the proportion of lawyers summoned is high. Thirteen judges or counsel at least are named,[2] and eight of these had been summoned to no previous council or parliament for which the writs are extant. Three of these new-comers, like Scrope himself, had been on the commissions of 15 May 1328; whilst there were seven *custodes pacis* of the years 1327-29 amongst the other magnates summoned to Windsor. At this council, according to one report of Scrope's speech,[3] complaints were made 'more straitly than before' as to the violation of the peace; the king applied to the magnates there assembled for a remedy, and at their suggestion ordained a general eyre, for two circuits, north and south of Trent,[4] to begin at the county of Northampton, 'because it is in the middle of the kingdom'.[5] According to another version of Scrope's speech,[6] however, the decision to hold an eyre was made 'in full parliament, with the consent of the commonalty of the realm', and the provision for the eyre is linked on to a promise of the magnates not to maintain the causes of indicted persons. Just such an undertaking on the part of the king and the magnates is included in chapter vii of the Statute of Northampton, which defines the very extensive functions of the justices sent out in 1328. It seems highly probable that the pros and cons of a general eyre had been discussed at Northampton, whether or no chapter vii of the statute was intended to cover one. Even before this an eyre had actually been proclaimed for January 1328 at Canterbury,[7] and had only been revoked at the last moment[8] because so many of the magnates bound to attend it were also due at the parliament at York in February, and the king had declared that he could by no means dispense with the presence and counsel of the

---

[1] 'Quia super magnis et arduis negotiis nos et statum regni nostri ac tranquillitatem et quietem populi eiusdem regni intime contingentibus vobiscum et cum ceteris...prelatis magnatibus et proceribus dicti regni die dominica in crastino sancte Marie Magdalene proximo futuro apud Wyndesore colloquium habere ordinauimus et tractatum....'

[2] Geoffrey le Scrope, Herle, Malberthorpe, Willoughby, Travers, Henry le Scrope, Wodehouse, William de Denham, Cambridge, Aldeborough, Middelton, Baynard, Oliver de Ingham.

[3] See below, (i).   [4] See below, (iii).
[5] See below, (ii).   [6] See below, (iii).
[7] *C.R.C.* p. 189 (4 Dec. 1327).   [8] *Ibid.* p. 244 (17 Jan. 1328).

justices of the eyre—Geoffrey le Scrope, Stonore, Friskeney, Willoughby and Bereford—in the said parliament.[1] The idea of holding a general eyre cannot therefore have originated at Windsor in July 1329, though there seems no reason to doubt the statement that a final decision was taken there.

In spite of probable errors[2] and manifest inconsistencies, then, these reports have an historical value as evidence of a conscious and continuous policy of which the revival of the moribund institution of the eyre is one feature. Herle and Scrope appear to have followed some agreed outline in making their speeches. The reports are also of interest in affording some supplementary evidence of the close connection between the eyres of 1329-30 and the Statute of Northampton. From the eyre rolls it was already clear that new articles of the eyre were being administered at Northampton, Nottingham and Derby, but only headings, not the full text of these new articles, were quoted on the record. The reports give two versions of these new articles, one in Latin and one in French. The Latin version is written on the back of the last page of a report of the Nottinghamshire eyre and it seems to be in the same hand as the report. The French version is an integral part of the report of the Northamptonshire eyre. Both versions are printed below, and illustrate the close connection with legislation which characterizes the articles of the eyre from 1272 on. The first of the *Novi Articuli* in the Egerton Manuscript, the first of those in French in the Lincoln's Inn and Additional Manuscripts, is based upon the Statute of York of 1318 and had been administered in the London eyre of 1321. The four Latin articles that follow in the Egerton Manuscript refer explicitly to the Statute of Northampton and are based on chapters iii and iv of that statute. The French articles in the other versions follow the wording of the statute closely, though not mentioning it by name; the first and second are based, like the Latin ones, on chapter iii, the third on chapter xv, and the last on chapter xiv, though on that part of it which is not covered by the third and fourth Latin articles. It is possible, though not probable, that different articles were administered at Nottingham and Northampton, or, again, both versions may

---

[1] Scrope is the only one of these justices whose name is recorded as having received a writ of summons to the parliament of York (*Report on the Dignity of a Peer*, IV. 381).

[2] (i), below, assigns the appointment of guardians of the peace to the parliament of Westminster, not Northampton.

be incomplete, as both, of course, are unofficial.[1] Some of the articles had very likely been administered in the local inquests of the autumn of 1328.

The reporter of the Tanner Manuscript (iii) makes Scrope declare at Northampton that the eyre was to be carried from county to county throughout the realm. So far as the evidence goes, only four counties were duly visited, Northamptonshire, Bedfordshire, Nottinghamshire and Derbyshire; in Kent an eyre was begun but not carried through.[2] The policy of the first parliaments and councils of the reign was not abandoned, but modified; the eyre, it would seem, was eliminated from the programme and other and newer means adopted. The statutes made at Westminster in November 1330 indicate this change. Justices of assize and of gaol delivery are to go on circuit three times in the year, and the authority of the guardians of the peace is more clearly defined,[3] and more significant still, justices of the bench and of assize shall have power to inquire concerning maintainors, conspirators, and all such folk 'as well as justices in eyre should do if they were in the same county'.[4] The Statute of Westminster in 1331 augments the powers of justices of gaol delivery to deal with robbers and disorderly persons,[5] and in March 1332 another solution of the problem is attempted. 'Q'en chescuns Counte d'Engleterre soient des plus Grantz de mesme le Counte assignez Gardiens de mesme le Counte par Commission le Roi.... Et eient les ditz Grantz poer d'oier et terminer auxibien felonies faites par ceux qi sont issint a arester et prendre, come par ceux qi serront enditez devant eux.'[6] This appointment of magnates to try those arrested by the keepers was merely a temporary expedient. The transformation of the keeper of the peace into the justice of the peace,[7] with power to

---

[1] The French version seems the more reliable of the two.

[2] Ass. R. 389. An eyre in Durham was also projected, but revoked in consideration of a payment from the men of the liberty (C.R.C. 1333–7, pp. 138, 182).   [3] 4 Edw. III, c. 2.

[4] 4 Edw. III, c. 11.   [5] 5 Edw. III, c. 14.

[6] Rot. Parl. II. 64. As Dr Beard has pointed out (Office of Justice of the Peace, p. 38), we have here a perfectly regular statute, and it is cited as such on the Patent Roll (Calendar, p. 298), though it is not to be found on the Statute Roll. Proceedings on a commission issued under this statute are recorded, Ass. R. 520 (1333).

[7] The commissions of May 1329 and of February 1332 had in fact given the power to hear and determine to the keepers of the peace, but they had been speedily revoked. For the whole story see B. H. Putnam, 'Keepers and Justices of the Peace', in Trans. R. Hist. S. 1929, pp. 19–48.

hear and determine, was, ultimately with the extension of the functions of the justices of assize, to provide the efficient substitute for the inefficient general eyre. No complete general eyre was held after 1332.[1]

The relation of this episode in administrative history to contemporary politics must be largely a matter of conjecture. In the five years which it covers, two *coups d'état* occurred, but they do not seem to have caused any breach of continuity in administrative policy. It is tempting to associate the experiment of the revival of the eyre and the abandonment of that experiment with Sir Geoffrey le Scrope, chief justice under Edward II, under Isabella and Mortimer,[2] and under Edward III, confidential servant of both father and son,[3] presiding justice at Northampton and prolocutor of the four parliaments of 1332.[4] His continuance in office under two revolutions offers a striking parallel to the continuity in administrative policy: he was summoned to every one of the seven councils or parliaments held from 1327 to 1330: the allusions in his speech at the eyre to the time of the king's grandfather[5] are paralleled in the Statutes of Northampton, and it was he who expounded the whole matter in the parliament of 1332 that gave the guardians of the counties judicial powers. It is even conceivable that it was his indispensability as the king's right-hand man that led to the abandonment of the experiment of general eyres, as it had led to the abandonment of the Kentish eyre of 1328. However that may be, his speech at Northampton and Herle's at Nottingham constitute a definite addition to the history of the decline and fall of the general eyre.

---

[1] The eyre of Kent, begun in 1333, was abandoned half-way, as was the eyre of London of 1341.

[2] Scrope appears to exercise his functions as chief justice without a break, as well before as after the pardon of 1 March 1327 (*P.R.C.* p. 28). Foss, in his *Judges of England*, gives an erroneous account at this point.

[3] See J. C. Davies, *Baronial Opposition to Edward II*; *Parl. Writs*, II. iii, Alphabetical Digest; N. Harris Nicolas, *Scrope and Grosvenor Roll*.

[4] *Rot. Parl.* II. 64, 66, 67, 69. [See also E. L. G. Stones in *E.H.R.*, 1954, pp. 1-15.]

[5] [A writ of 11 Oct. 1337 addressed to Scrope, CJ, (Coram Rege Roll no. 310, Rex m. 42), refers to the customary holding of eyres *de septennio in septennium* in the time of the King's progenitors, and to the rarity of such eyres since 1307. Their lack, it says, is to be supplied by the itinerating King's Bench. I owe this information to Professor Stones.] ., 06, 67, 69.

MANUSCRIPTS OF THE EYRES OF NORTHAMPTON
AND NOTTINGHAM

[In the John Rylands Library Bulletin, vol. 34, pp. 388–431, Mr R. V. Rogers gives a list of the seventeen manuscript reports of this Eyre of Northampton, seven of which have been cited here.]

The following manuscripts of this Eyre of Nottingham have been examined, but only the first contains Herle's speech:

Cambridge University Library: MS. Hh. 4. MS. Hh. 3. 9.
British Museum: Egerton MS. 2811. Add. MSS. 5924, 5926, 34789.
Lincoln's Inn: MS. 137 (1).
[Harvard Law School: MS. 3.]

A.   SCROPE'S SPEECH

(i)

Lincoln's Inn MS. 137 (2), fo. 243 d, collated with Lincoln's Inn MS. 137 (1) and Egerton MS. 2811, fo. 243 d, with which it is practically identical. The punctuation has been added.

Et puis sire G. dit: Beaux seignurs, les uns de vos qestes cy venuz savez [sic] Seuent la cause pur quey cest Eyr est ordeyne, et plusurs ne mye; par qi a parlement dreyn tenu a Northamton pleintz vindrent a notre seignur le Roi de totes costes de Roialme, qe le peuple fut si malement demene par diuers oppressions des grauntz, et par extortion de meintenurs et duresses des baillifs, et homicides et larcyns faitz de tut partz en le Roialme, de quoi plusurs de totes partz qi se sentirent grauez prierent de ceo [eide et][1] remedie. Les pleintz oyz, le Roi et les grauntz a ces parlement esteauntz par comune assent ordinerent de tute partz en le Roialme en checun counte gardeyns de la pees, de tiels tortz et trespas homicides et [felonies][2] redrescer. Nyent aresteaunt la dite ordinance, al counseil le Roi tenuz a Wyndesore, ou assemble furent touz les grauntz de la terre, les pleintz[3] de tote partz vindrent au Roi de meffetz auantditz plus estreytement qe auant ne fesoient, priauntz des meffez[4] remedy; par qi le Roi pria a touz qi illeusqes furent assemblez qe eux ordynereient voie coment la pes de sa terre put meu estre salve et garde, et coment tiels meffes en meillour manere purent estre redresse. Entre queux cest choses furent parlez et debatuz, et monstre fust illeusqe qe la pees ne fut mye bien garde et meyn-

---

[1] The words within brackets are taken from Lincoln's Inn MS. 137 (1).
[2] From Lincoln's Inn MS. 137 (1); 137 (2) repeats *homicides*.
[3] Lincoln's Inn MS. 137 (1) reads *pleintifs*.
[4] Lincoln's Inn MS. 137 (1) reads *meffesantz*.

tenu com auant ces temps auoyt este en temps des altres Rois; pur ceo qen
temps des progeniturs cesti Roy Eyres soleient estre de sept aunz en sept
aunz par tut le Roialme, par queux la pees de la terre fut bien meyntenu et
garde et droit fait as riches et as poures. Par qi grauntz illeusqes assemblez
[assentiront qe Eyre seroyt par tote la terre, sur qi la comune illeoques
assemblez pria al Roy]¹ qil voleit a ceo acorder, par qi la pees de sa terre
put estre salue et garde et les ditz meffetz et trespas estre redresces; et le
Roy a lour request a ceo acorda. Par qi entre vos grantz, nos vos char-
goms de par le Roi, et prioms, com a vos seignours et amiz, qe vos ne
sustinez meyntenours des malueise quereles ne gentz rettez de malueise
fame, mes qe vos soiez eydauntz [et consaillant]² qe la pees nostre seignur
le Roi soit garde, et qe les ditz meffesours soient puniz, issint qe cours de
loy se face come auant ces hures fut fait par reson del Eyre auant dit.

(ii)

Add. MS. 5924 (British Museum), fo. 1 d.

Et puis dit sire G. la cause pur qoi le Eyre fut ordine en parlement a
Norhamton et a Wyndesore par comun consail, pur ceo qe la pees de la
tere ne fut pas tenue com deuoit estre et soleit en temps de progenitours
le Roi, qant les Eyres furent tenuez de vij aunz en vij aunz. Pur qoi le Roi
a donqe ordine ceste Eyre, solom les articles adounqe ordenez, et solom
lestatut auaunt fait, et comence en ceo counte pur ceo qe cest en millewe
de son realme etc.

(iii)

Tanner MS. 13 (Bodleian Library), fo. 312.

Scrop rercherca la manere coment le Roi en plein parlement, par commun
assent des prelatz et des touz les grauntz du Realme et de tute la comu-
nalte, aueit grante, por establissement de la pees, Eir par mi tut son realme:
cest assauer, un pair des Justices de cea Trente, et altres de la, a errer de
counte en counte par tut le realme; et coment les grantz granterent al Roi
qe nul hom endite ou en tagle ne sereit par euz meintenuz contre la lei.

B. HERLE'S SPEECH

Cambridge University Library, MS. Hh. 2. 4, fo. 265.

E puys Herle dit qi la cause de cest eyre fut qi la comonalte de la terre,
a parlement le Roy tenuz a Northamton, mist peticion qi la pes de sa terre
ne put pas [estre] tenuz ne meyntenuz come estre dut. Sur qi le Roy e son

¹ The words within brackets are taken from Egerton MS. 2811. Lincoln's Inn
MS. 137 (2) omits the reference to the commons and merely has *prierent au Roi*.
² The words within brackets are taken from Egerton MS. 2811.

counseyl ordina qi certeynz justices fussent assignez en checoun counte
denquer de checoun maner de felonyes &c e transgressions a la suyte de
Roy e des autres, e a oyer e terminer &c. E puys apres, a counseyl le Roy
tenutz a Wyndesore, autre peticion fut mys de par la comune e par defaut
qi lour primer request se mustra pas en ouer', ou cest petition fut moustre
a les graunz de la terre, ou assentuz fut par touz qi, pur la pes de la terre
sauver, qi justices furent assignez de eyrer par tut la terre; issint qi le Roy,
taunt com en luy est, ad oy votre peticion, e nos ad assignez de tenir cest
eyr, e a moustrer qi notre pouer est tiel, e qi nos auons pouer a tenir totez
maners des pleez.

C. THE 'NEW ARTICLES' OF THE EYRES OF 1329-30

(a) The Latin Version.

Egerton MS. 2811.
  fo. 225 d, 'Incipiunt articuli de Itinere' (Vetera capitula).
  fo. 226 (in margin), 'Incipiunt Nova Capitula' (Nova Capitula and Articles
     on the Statutes down to Mortmain article of 1313).[1]
  fo. 227, Novi Articuli.

De ministris Regis qui ratione officii sui custodire debent assisam de
vinis et victualibus qui marchandizaverunt de vinis et victualibus illis in
grosso vel ad retallium dum ad officium illud fuerint intendentes post
statutum inde editum apud Eboracum in tribus septimanis Sancti Michaelis
anno R. E. filii R. E. xij°.[2]

De hiis qui fuerunt armati et cesserunt de nocte vel de die in feriis vel
mercatis in praesentia iusticiarum vel aliorum ministrorum domini Regis
officia sua facientium vel alibi in terrorem populi vel in perturbacionem
pacis post statutum apud Northampton inde editum anno R. E. tercii a
conquestu secundo. Et qui huiusmodi armatos ceperint quos et quando
et quas armaturas et quantum valuerunt.

De vicecomitibus et aliis ministris Regis et dominis libertatum et
eorum ballivis et maioribus et ballivis Civitatum Burgorum Constabu-
lariis et Custodibus pacis infra custodias suas qui huiusmodi armatos non
ceperint iuxta idem statutum.

De pannis qui ponuntur ad terram quae non sunt ulnerati per
ulneratorem Regis in presentia maiorum et ballivorum ubi maior
est et ballivorum ubi maior non est per mensuram contentam in
eodem statuto.

De maioribus et ballivis ubi maior aut ballivis ubi maior non est in villis
aut locis ubi huiusmodi panni venerunt qui non fuerunt parati ad ex-

---

[1] For standard version of articles down to 1321 see Oxford Studies, VI. 92-101.
[2] This seems to be the only place where this article is found in Latin.

CLC

aminacionem facere de huiusmodi pannis temporibus quibus requisiti fuerunt per voluntatem [1] Regis absque aliquo capiente de mercatoribus pro examinatione predicta etc.

Expliciunt articuli de itinere anno Regni Regis etc.

(b) The French Version.

(1) Lincoln's Inn MS. 137 (1) (no pagination).
(2) Lincoln's Inn MS. 137 (2) ff. 241–2 d.
(3) Brit. Mus. Additional MS. 24063, ff. 3–5.
(4) Harl. MS. 239, fo. 41 b.
(1) 'Incipit Iter de Norhampton.'
(2) 'De itinere Norhamton. De articlis Itineris.'
(3) 'Articli Itineris Norhamton.'
(4) fo. 39, 'Hic incipiunt articli Itineris apud N. anno tercio.'

[Articles up to Mortmain article in Latin: then as follows:]

Dez ministres le Rey en Cytez et en Burghz qi par reson de lour office deyuent garder lassise dez vins et dez vitaillez qi les ount en marchaundise des vins et des vitaillez en gros et a retaille tant com eux furent intendauntz au tel office puis lestatut de ceo fait a Euerwyk a iij semaines de seint Michel lan de son reyn xij^{me}.

Item de ceo qui sount venuz deuant les Justices le Roi ou altres ministres le Roi en fesant lour office a force et armes ou ount force mene ou chivauche arme en feyres et en marchez ou aillours en affray de sa pees queux il sount.

Item si Justices le Roi en lour presence vicomtes et autres ministres le Roi en lour baillies seignors des franchises et lour baillifs en yceles et meires et baillifs en citez et en burghz deyns mesmes les citez et Burghz Burghalders conestables et Gardeyns de la pees dedeyns lour gardes eyent fait execution de tiel trespassours solom ceo qest contenu en lestatut queux il sont et qi tiels trespassours ont suffert aler despuniz.

Item des seignors des feyres qen le comencement de lour feyres ne ont pas fayt crier e publier en yceles com longement les feyres se tendront par qi les marchauntz sount illeusqes plus longement qe fere ne deyuent par defaute de tiel crie nyent faite et queux il sont.

Item si meire et baillifs des villes eyent fait endentures entre eux et launeour le Roy des drapz forfetz au Roi qi ne sont pas de assise et livere mesmes les endentures chescun an al Escheker pur charger le dit auneour a respoundre illeusqs des ditz forfeytures qant des draps et le pris de checun.

[In (4) only:] Expliciunt articuli Itineris North.

---

[1] Probably an error for *ulneratorem*.

XI

Some Early Inquests before 'Custodes Pacis'[1]

In the Public Record Office *List of Plea Rolls*, Assize Roll 262 is described as follows: 'Essex. 1 Edward I. Inquisitiones de feloniis etc. in hundredo de Tendring. 1 m.' This description is both inadequate and incorrect. The two membranes which compose the roll record inquests held before 'custodes pacis' of the county of Essex in the years 5 Edward I (1277) and 1 Edward II (1308) respectively. It is because they appear to be the oldest examples of a kind of record rare in itself and hitherto hardly noticed that they are here described. Records of three inquests held by 'custodes pacis' in the reign of Henry III are calendared among the miscellaneous inquests in the exchequer for the years 1263 and 1267.[2] The writs, however, deal with individual cases and special conditions, and bear out Lambarde's description of these officials as 'extraordinary' guardians of the peace.[3] Their existence is explained by the special conditions arising out of the struggle between the king and the baronial party. The inquests given below are concerned with the keeping of the peace in the more normal and general sense, and they fall into line in the series of records illustrating the evolution of the office as justice of the peace.

As membrane 1 is merely headed 'the first year of King Edward', and membrane 2 'the fifth year of King Edward', it is necessary to give the evidence for assigning them to 1308 and 1277 respectively. The second membrane is only a fragment, half obliterated and torn at the foot. It is, however, written clearly and far more carefully than the other, and states definitely that the inquests were held by Sir Richard de Tany, 'custos pacis', in the county of Essex. Details as to the history of the Tany family are given in the *Victoria County History* for Hertfordshire,[4] and the facts relevant to our inquiry are to be found in the Inquisitiones Post Mortem. Sir Richard de Tany the elder, sheriff of Essex and Hertfordshire in 1259–61,[5] died in 1270, when his son Sir Richard de Tany the younger was aged thirty and

---

[1] Reprinted from the *English Historical Review*, July 1925.
[2] *Cal. Misc. Inq.* I. nos. 278, 326, 2114.
[3] *Eirenarcha* (1610), p. 18. See also the mandate to a 'custos pacis' of 4 July 1264, *P.R.C.* p. 331.   [4] III. 317.   [5] P.R.O., *Lists and Indexes*, IX. 43.

more.[1] The younger Richard is mentioned in the Hundred Rolls of 1274 as holding the manors of Estwyk in Hertfordshire (Braughing hundred) and Elmstede in Essex (Tendring hundred) and claiming rights in two other Essex hundreds.[2] He was fined nine marks for trespass of venison by the justices of the forest in Essex in 1277.[3] He died in 1296, leaving his estates to his son Roger,[4] who died in 1301, leaving a son Laurence as his heir.[5] In the fifth year of Edward I, then, there was a Richard de Tany, of weight and substance, in Essex; in the fifth year of Edward II the representative of the family was named Laurence.

This evidence is corroborated by the reference to Ralph de Tony, lord of Wolcomes Stouhe, that is, Walthamstow. For this family the Inquests Post Mortem are less complete, and the genealogies given by Morant and Blomfield are not correct, but the proofs are adequate. Roger de Tony of Walthamstow died in 1264,[6] and his heir (unnamed) was still in the king's wardship in 1274.[7] In 1278, however, Ralph de Tony is mentioned on the Hertfordshire eyre roll as lord of Walthamstow,[8] and in 1276 and 1277 he was being employed by Edward on the Welsh marches.[9] In 1303 Robert de Tony was the lord of Walthamstow,[10] and he died in 1309, leaving no heir but his sister Alice de Leyburn.[11] Thus in the fifth year of Edward II the lord of Walthamstow was not a Tony at all.

Internal evidence thus points to 1277 as the date of membrane 2, and is confirmed by external evidence. On 12 July 1277 Edward I issued letters patent to the sheriffs and bailiffs of liberties in twenty-nine counties, bidding them see that peace was better kept in their parts, the more so as he and many of his nobles were going on an expedition to Wales. They were to use diligence in swearing men to arms, and in arresting and imprisoning malefactors; and for the better accomplishment of this the sheriffs were to cause to be elected in full county one of the more upright and powerful men of the country who was not going to Wales, who should take an oath to assist both sheriffs and bailiffs whenever required in the keeping of the peace and the arresting of evildoers. On his return from Wales the king would requite both the sheriff and the elected person for

---

[1] *Inq. Post Mortem,* I. 248.   [2] *Rot. Hund.* I. 140, 153, 162, 191.
[3] *C.R.C.* p. 534; cf. *P.R.C.* p. 193.   [4] *Inq. Post Mortem,* III. 201.
[5] *Ibid.* IV. 12.   [6] *Ibid.* I. 188.   [7] *Ibid.* II. 54.
[8] *Plac. Quo War.* p. 284.   [9] *P.R.C.* pp. 169, 222.
[10] *Feudal Aids,* II. 151.   [11] *Inq. Post Mortem,* V. 101.

their trouble and expense, according to their zeal in carrying out his commands.[1] The Patent Roll of 2 September 1277 contains a mandate to John de Bretun, whom the sheriff and community of Norfolk have elected to be 'custos pacis nostrae' in that shire.[2] Although no such mandate for Essex has been traced, it seems evident that Richard de Tany was elected to the office of 'custos pacis' in the shire court of Essex in July or August 1277, and held the inquests recorded in Assize Roll 262 between 24 August and 20 November 1277.[3]

The date of the other membrane is fixed partly by the references to the Statute of Winchester, which show that the first of Edward I is an impossible date, and, more exactly, by the words 'on Saturday, the morrow of the Purification'. In 1308, the first year of Edward II, the 3rd of February fell on a Saturday. The commission appointing Sir Hugh de Nevile and Hugh le Blund, with the sheriff, to be 'custodes pacis' for the county of Essex is to be found, dated 24 December 1307, on the Patent Roll, and is printed in full in *Parliamentary Writs*.[4] The directions to inquire into the existence of forestallers and the observance of the Statute of Winchester correspond exactly to the scope of the inquests printed below.

A few points of interest may be indicated. That such inquests were held by 'custodes pacis' early in the reign of Edward I is, I think, an addition to our knowledge. Lambarde was apparently not aware of evidence for their power to receive indictments earlier than 3 Edward III,[5] though he suspected its existence. A passage in the records of the state trials of 1291 reinforces our evidence. The bailiff of the bishop of Lincoln's hundred of Banbury quotes a writ from the sheriff of Oxfordshire commanding him to arrest a criminal who has been indicted before the 'custodes pacis' of the hundred of Bloxham;[6] a writ which further illustrates the co-operation between the sheriffs and bailiffs of liberties urged in the letters patent of 12 July 1277, and reflected in the presentment below as to the hanging of a freeman in Becontree hundred 'against the peace of the lord king and the liberty of the abbess of Barking who holds that hundred'.

---

[1] Patent Roll, 5 Edw. I, m. 9.
[2] *Ibid.* m. 5. Printed in full, Lambarde, *Eirenarcha*, pp. 16–17.
[3] The dated events in the record occurred about St Laurence's (10 Aug.), the Assumption of the Virgin (15 Aug.), and St Bartholomew's (24 Aug.); the sixth year of Edward I began on 20 Nov. 1277.
[4] *Parl. Writs*, II. ii, appendix, p. 8.   [5] p. 20.   [6] Ass. R. 541 A, m. 77.

Another point of interest is the procedure followed in 1277 and 1308 respectively. The 1277 fragment records presentments made in five hundreds: in one case 'per comitatum', in the other cases by the jurors of vills. In the one instance where the jurors are named, they number five, presumably four men and the reeve. There is nothing to show whether the inquests were held at one time and place, or in a perambulation of the 'custos'. In 1308 we have the full presentments for Tendring hundred, and the beginning of the presentments for Dengie hundred. The presentments are made by juries of varying composition: (1) twelve 'forinseci' with eight men of Manningtree; (2) twelve men of Great Oakley; (3) thirteen men of Colchester, with twelve men of the hundred of Lexden, six men of the hundred of Tendring, and two others. The inquests are held on 3 February, 4 February, and 6 February, at three different places in Tendring hundred, and the forestallers of Colchester are to be called up again on 13 February. On the question of procedure it is useful to compare a Northamptonshire record of 1320, the only other unequivocal record of inquests before 'custodes pacis' that I have traced, though it is highly probable that records of a similar sort, as yet unidentified, are to be found among the assize rolls or elsewhere.[1] In 1320 two mandates were issued to 'custodes pacis', on 18 June and 7 August.[2] Assize Roll 640 contains the actual letter close of 7 August, addressed to the two 'custodes' of Northamptonshire, endorsed 'execucio istius brevis patet in rotulo eisdem consuto'.[3] The annexed roll begins with the writ of 18 June, and contains the record of inquests held at Northampton on 18 August 1320, according to the procedure therein described.[4] The sheriff summoned to Northampton all the chief constables and sub-constables of the different hundreds, twenty-four knights or freemen from every hundred, and four men and the reeve from every vill, to do and inquire as the king commanded according to the tenor of the commission and according to the Statute of Winchester. The presentments, made by hundreds, are followed by a command to the sheriff to arrest all the persons above indicted, and keep them safe till further orders, and to this is added the note 'qui adhuc nullum supradictorum indictatorum arestauit, ut

---

[1] E.g. in Ass. R. 473–5 (Leicestershire).

[2] Both are printed in full, *Parl. Writs*, II. ii, appendix, pp. 148, 150–1.

[3] Ass. R. 640, m. 5.

[4] It has now been edited for the Northamptonshire Record Society by Miss M. Gollancz (1940).

dicitur'.[1] The return attached to the writ is, in fact, one of those lists of names of offenders which the central government demanded from the 'custodes' on several occasions in the reign of Edward II.[2]

Whilst interesting on the formal side, the main importance of the records printed below lies in the light they throw on the local efforts to put in force the Statute of Winchester, and on the developing activities of those officials who were under Edward III to be transformed into justices of the peace.

Assize Roll 262, m. 2. [1277.]

Inquisiciones facte per dominum Ricardum de Tany custodem pacis domini Regis in comitatu Essex' Anno Rengni Regis Edwardi quinto.

¶ Dicunt Iuratores de Hatfeud Peuerel sc. Willelmus atte Bregge, Willelmus Eylmer, Elias de Marisco, Willelmus Botere, et Petrus Page, quod Marcele uxor Motti de Okham die dominica proxima ante festum Sancti Laurencii Anno supradicto depredata fuit de omnibus bonis suis et domus eius fracta per homines Ricardi de Coleworth' scilicet per Robertum Carectarium qui manet cum eodem apud Borham et per Willelmum fillium Willelmi Botere et Willelmum Cocum ad valorem xxx sol et amplius. Ista recepta fuerunt ad domum Roberti fillii Huberti. **Hundr' de Wyham.**

¶ Item dicunt Iuratores de Fairstede quod Ricardus Sonce molendinarius qui manebat ad molendinum Nicholai de Giney, Radulphus Wracke et Sturling' de Borham sunt fractores domorum. Et quod Elias filius Sacriste de Fairstede est latro.

¶ Presentatum est per comitatum quod Willelmus Sapi senescallus Radulphi de Tony domini de Wolcomes Stouhe cepit quendam hominem liberum de eadem villa et ipsum suspendidit sine secta et sine visu ballivi hundredi, contra pacem domini regis et contra libertatem abbatisse de Berkinge que tenet hundredum integrum libere de domino rege. **Bekentr'**

¶ Dicunt Iuratores de Haningefeud quod die Iouis proxima post Assumcionem Beate Marie venit Ricardus seruiens Templariorum apud Neuelande in Haningefeud et intrauit domum Roberti Marescalli inde vi et armis contra voluntatem eiusdem Roberti cepit et adduxit et fregit portas suas et uolnerauit eum, unde huthesium leuatum fuit. **Chelm'-ford**

¶ Item dicunt quod idem Ricardus fregit domum Xristiane Beneit de Suhaningefeud et unam supertunicam precii xij s. asportauit, videlicet die Ascencionis anno E. iiij°.

[1] Ass. R. 640, m. 6 d.   [2] See above, p. 153, n. 1.

¶ Dicunt Iuratores de Borham quod Galfridus seruiens abbatis de Waltham, Ricardus le Messor, Iohannes carectarius eiusdem abbatis metebant et asportabant unam acram seminatam in auena ad curiam dicti abbatis...

Dimid'
Herlawe

Dicunt Iuratores de...

m. 2 d.

Frouswell

Dicunt Iuratores quod die Sancti Bartholome Anno supradicto venerunt magister Hugo Biged et manupasti sui, videlicet Michael Eylbern et Willelmus de Beyfeld, Petrus de Koyfe, Radulphus le Noreis, ad domum Galfridi Camerarii in Stevintone. Et domum suam fregerunt, hostium et fenestras et contra voluntatem suam intrauerunt et ea que inuenerunt asportauerunt maliciose et contra pacem. Et ibidem enormia fecerunt quousque patria et tota vicinitas cum hutasio venerat. Et exierunt. Et ad domum dicti magistri Hugonis receptati fuerunt. Et ad...succ'...aliq...quierantes et adhuc Idem Magister Hugo minatur dictum Hugonem de Steue...

Assize Roll, 262, m. 1. [February 1308.]

Essex
Hundr' de
Tendr'
Maningtre

Essex Tendr' Hundr'   Neuill[1]

Inquisitio facta coram Domino Hugone de Neuile et sociis suis[1] apud Manitr' die Sabbati in crastino Purificationis Beate Marie Anno Regni Regis E. primo per xij iuratos[2] videlicet Iohannem de Badele, Sayer' de Brittlenggesheye, Iohannem filium Walteri, Willelmum le But, Iohannem Rosse, Aunus' de Petr', Willelmum Adam, Nicholaum Gernon, Thomam Batin, Robertum de Peyton, Willelmum Pigace, et Willelmum de Helleye, Forinsecos; et Adam de la Riuere, Edmundum filium Golfridi, Willelmum Batin, Warinum Mol, Robertum de Bexston, Iohannem Vine, Thomam Caperon, Nicholaum de Stinnerie de Maningtre Iuratos et...

qui dicunt per sacramentum quod Willelmus Magge de Cattewad', Iohannes le Blok de eadem, Thomas Pycot' de eadem, Stephanus Brente de eadem, Briocus[3] Cissor de Manitr', Bartolomeus Cissor de eadem, Robert Pertrich[3] de eadem, sunt forestallarii et forestallant villatam de Manitr' ab omnibus mercimoniis venientibus per aquam et terram ad predictam villatam [4]ita quod illi qui bona sua vellent in propriis personis suis vendere non possunt propter huiusmodi fore-stallatores.[5]

[1] 'Iusticiario domini Regis' has been written after 'Neuile', crossed out, and 'et sociis suis' written in over the line.
[2] 'homines fideles' has been crossed out before 'iuratos'.
[3] 'p.m.' is written in over these names.
[4] to [5] Written in over the line.

Item dicunt quod ittinera uersus Colecestr' et alibi sunt ita stricta
in villa de Ardley apud Boscum de Crockeleford prioris Sancti
Botul' ¹quod homines vix audent equitare vel pedibus ire propter
latronum insidias² et hoc ad nocumentum totius patrie et contra
statutum ¹Wynton'² Et iter versus Colecr' ad ecclesiam de Ardleye
est tam strictum pro defectu bosci Radulfi Pycot' quod vix homines
audent ire.

Manyngtre

Item presentant quod Thomas Alfild³ uulnerauit quemdam
mulierem ad domum Godini sutoris contra pacem et est communis
imperturbator pacis.

Item presentant quod Rogerus le Barker uulnerauit dictum
Thomam noctanter contra pacem.⁴

Item presentant quod Ricardus Miles, Gerardus Pykerel de Manitre
sunt forestallarii ut supradicti de piscibus et omnibus aliis mercimoniis per terram et aquam. Ita quod venditores non possunt sua
mercimonia per se propter huiusmodi forestallatores vendere ad
dampnum totius patrie.

Inquisitio capta apud Akle Magnam coram domino Hugone de
Neuile Custode pacis Domini Regis Die dominica proxima post
festum Purificationis Beate Marie Anno Regni Regis Edwardi primo
per xij homines iuratos, scilicet per Ricardum Brennote, Saherum
Caperoun, Iohannem le Cok', Walterum de Hewode, Iohannem
Houmfrey, Henricum Tresdeners, Iohannem Braymnel, Iohannem
de la Forde, Hugonem de la Roklaunde, Willelmum Pistorem,
Thomam le Ferour', Radulfum Russel.

Qui dicunt per sacramentum quod Walterus le Cogger', Radulphus Ylot,³ Willelmus³ Brote,³ Robertus le Stur',³ Willelmus
Petifraunk', Radulfus Stace, Adam Chimbel,³ Galfr' le Bout',⁵
Willelmus Godefrei³ senior, Willelmus Godefrey³ junior, Valen-
tinus de Soutwold,³ Willelmus Squyrel, Adam ate Char',³ Henricus
Bene,⁶ Adam Colyn,³ Ricardus de Sutwolde,³ Adam Smye,³ omnes
de Herewyco; et Ricardus de Rysing' de Magna Holaunde, Iordanus
de Barythes Welle de Thorp, Willelmus Thedain³ de Magna Holaunde sunt forestallarii de omnibus mercimoniis venientibus tam per

Herewych

Akle
Tendr'

---

¹ to ² Written in over the line.
³ 'p.m.' is written in over these names.
⁴ The next two presentments, 'Item presentant quod Godin' sutor resectus
dictum Rogerum post insultum factum. Item presentant quod Thomas
Alfild est communis verberator', have been crossed out.
⁵ 'Rogerus Godefrei' is written here and crossed out.
⁶ A cross is marked above this name.

terram quam per aquam uersus Herewycum et alibi in Hundredo de Tendring'. [1]Et recipiunt allecia pisces a nauibus et batellis et ad voluntatem suam ponunt precium, videlicet pro lasta i marcam vel xx s., et postea vendunt pro v marcis et amplius et pro medietate soluunt et aliam medietatem sine precio recipiunt ad dampnum totius patrie.[2]

Item presentant quod boscus de Trendhey non est amputatus ut preceptus fuit, per quod via est tam stricta pro defectu amputationis Thome de Greylee et comitis Oxonie quod homines propter latronum insidias vix audent anbulare.

Colc'
Tendr'

Inquisitio capta apud Colecestr' die Martis proxima post festum Purificationis Beate Marie Anno Regni Regis Edwardi primo per xij homines iuratos, videlicet per Warinum filium Willelmi, Robertum Oliuer, Alexandrum Tabernar', Sayherum de Doniland, Iohannem Tinctorem, Iohannem de Burstall', Matheum le Verrer, Willelmum Pronale, Iohannem Edward, Ricardum Attegate, Ricardum le Barber, et Willelmum Grey, Petrum de Asington' de Colc'; Walterum de Codewell, Willelmum Mot, Adam clericum de Messing', Robertum Vincent, Iohannem Batekyn, Ricardum Fabrum, Robertum Best, Iohannem Bonherbe, Iohannem Chimyn, Robertum Gernon, Willelmum Quethe, Stephanum Hoter de Lexhedenn; Walterum de Hewode, Thomam filium Stephani, Willelmum Sperburn', Iohannem Munte, Walterum Bunde, et Thomam Vere de Tendringg'; Thomam de Fulho, et Petrum Wylde.

isti habent
diem martis
ante festum
sancti
Valentini
apud Colc'

Felonia

Qui dicunt per sacramentum quod Walterus de Gloffar' de Branketre, Iohannes Houel de Branketr', Iohannes de Lond' piscator in Colc', Iohannes Menewy,[3] Walterus Trewe de Branketr', Willelmus Sartrie, Iohannes de Tendringg', Simon filius Bartholomei de Colc' sunt communes forestallatores omnium bonorum venalium venientium tam per terram quam per aquam ad forum de Colc' et Cogeshale; et Petrus Fingerer emit duo pecia correi tannatoris de Rogero Alnote precii iiij s. que Idem Rogerus furabatur de Simone filio Bartholomei et idem Petrus sciuit ea fuisse furata.

Dicunt etiam quod Gilbertus Makerel est communis latro de meremmio et de aliis minutis latrociniis et consuetus est contra noctem deuillare et in aurora diei redire. Ideo plus suspicatur de eo quod est latro ⁋ et quod Simon Radebrych' noctanter et contra

_____

[1] to [2] The sentence is written in over the line and in the margin, with a mark to show the place of insertion.

[3] 'Colc'' is written over this name.

pacem intrauit domum Ricardi de Coln' apud Srebbestrete per
quandam fenestram et asportauit clates et stramen dicti Ricardi ad
valenciam vj den. ¶ et quod Amicia Spillewater receptauit quendam
Iohannem de Holebrok' sepius noctanter et de quo est grauis suspicio latrocinii quia noctanter venit et recedit, et quod Matildis
Motshole est communis receptatrix de aucis et gallinis furatis in
suburbio, et quod Iohannes Finger receptauit Iohannem de Markesh'
de quo est grauis suspicio latrocinii quia noctanter venit et recedit, et
quod est receptator latronum.

Dicunt et quod Gilbertus Makerel furabatur et furtiue asportauit
tunicam de burello de domo Iohannis le Spicer videlicet die Iouis
proxima ante festum Sancti Bartholomei ultimo preteritum ad
valenciam vj d. et quod Rogerus Alnete furabatur duo pecia correi
tannatoris de tannaria Simonis filii Bartholomeu' precii iiij s. ¶ et
quod Iohannes Baron de Hewham fecit insultum Galfrido Lewy die
veneris in festo Purificationis Beate Marie ultimo preterito et dictum
Galfridum cum quodam baculo in capite grauiter percussit et contra
pacem et est communis malefactor ¶ et quod Willelmus Basset
insultum fecit Iohanni Garde die dominica proxima post festum
Purificationis Beate Marie ultimo preterito et dictum Iohannem in
domo sua propria grauiter percussit, apud Hewstrete de nocte ¶ et
quod Ricardus[1] Sayher stetit in hostio matris sue in Hewstrete sero
diei mercurii proxime ante festum conversionis Sancti Pauli ultimo
preterito, et quidam Rogerus Jolifboy per viam transiens canem
matris dicti Rogeri Sayher cum una petra iecit, et dictus Rogerus
Sayher interrogabat eum quis esset, cui noluit respondere, et quia
noluit respondere dictus Rogerus Sayher eidem Rogero Jolifboy
insultum fecit ipsum cum pugno percussit. ¶ Et quod Hugo
Carnifex est communis forestallator, et Katerina la Vaus, Iohannes
profite, Petrus le Wylde, Iohannes filius Ricardi Holdeman sunt
communes forestallatores omnium bonorum venalium ita [2]quod
homines vendentes non possunt per se vendere propter huiusmodi
forestallatores[3] per terram et per aquam. ¶ Et quod Willelmus
Holdegate non venit ad portam de Estgate apud Colc' custodiendam
sicut summonitus fuerat ¶ et quod parcus[4] Abbatis Sancti Iohannis
Colc' apud Grenstede non claudatur iuxta formam statuti Wynton'
[2]ad dampnum totius patrie propter latronum insidias[3] ¶ et quod iter
ducens versus Maldon iuxta boscum de Srebbe [2]quod est domini
Iohannis de Belhus[3] non elargit secundum formam statuti ad dampnum propter latronum insidias totius patrie.

Coln'

trans-
gression'

trans-
gression'
contra
statutum

[1] A cross is marked above this name.
[2] to [3] Written in above line.
[4] A cross is marked above this word.

m. 1 d.

Coram iustic' de transgressionibus et de feloniis.[1]

Deng'
Hundr'
Maldon.

Inquisicio capta apud Maldon die mercurii proxima post festum
Purificationis Beate Marie Anno Regni Regis Edwardi primo per xij
homines iuratos videlicet per Willelmum de Birche, Thomam le
Palmere, Willelmum de Callyngg', Thomam Forester, Iohannem
Spicer, Willelmum Reynber', Rogerum Draper, Thomam Symple,
Radulphum Pilke

(The rest is blank.)

[1] In a fifteenth-century hand.

XII

The Quo Warranto Proceedings under Edward I[1]

On Edward I's return from the East in 1274 he ordered a general inquiry to be held throughout England into the misconduct of local government officials and the usurpation or misuse of franchises by magnates and others. The statistics produced by this inquiry are usually known as the Hundred Rolls. The action taken upon this information was firstly legislative—the passing of a series of statutes, from those at Westminster in the spring of 1275 to those at Gloucester in August 1278; and then administrative and judicial—the sending round the country of justices in eyre empowered to deal with complaints of official misconduct and to examine and adjudicate on all claims to franchises. Claimants were to appear before them, and if it was found that they actually held any franchise, a writ of Quo Warranto would be served on them, requiring them to show by what warrant they claimed to have the liberty of wreck, or gallows, or view of frankpledge, or return of writs, or whatever it might be.[2] The judicial proceedings thus initiated went on all through the reign of Edward I and into those of his son and grandson, so long as the general eyres continued, and the records of such proceedings are to be found in the eight hundred and odd pages of the *Placita de Quo Warranto* published by the Record Commission in 1818.

The narrative given above is generally accepted and needs no revision. There are, however, as it appears to me, some misconceptions current as to the general significance of Edward I's 'attack upon the franchises', and as to the development of his policy; and it is the purpose of this article to attempt to set them in a clearer light.

In the average text-book, Edward's policy is represented as an entirely new departure. In the reign of Henry III, we gather, a weak and slipshod administration was suffering all kinds of feudal privileges and encroachments on the royal power to multiply unchallenged. The new, strong, business-like king tackles the question in a

---

[1] Reprinted from *History*, July 1926.
[2] See F. Pollock and F. W. Maitland, *History of English Law*, I. 574 ff., for a description of these liberties.

thoroughgoing manner, using the new and effective weapon of the writ of Quo Warranto. To make good his claim to any franchise, the holder must produce a royal charter—'no plea of long-continued usage is admitted as a defence'.[1] Edward's methods, however, prove too drastic. The indignation of the baronage at this attack on their privileges finds a spokesman in Earl Warenne, who, producing an old and rusty sword, declares to the justices, 'This is my warrant! My ancestors who came over with the Conqueror won their lands by the sword, and by the sword I will defend them against all usurpers.'[2] So Edward finds it prudent not to press his claim; recedes from his first position, 'No franchise without a charter', and strikes a compromise. In 1290, by the statute of Quo Warranto, he grants that continuous possession of a liberty from before the coronation of Richard I shall be a sufficient answer to the writ of Quo Warranto, and the proceedings before the justices after this date show 'a complete change in the law, or in the king's theory of the law'.[3]

This account needs revision in three respects. In the first place, neither the policy nor the use of the writ was new; in the second place, the story about Earl Warenne cannot be accepted as it stands; and in the third place, there are certain facts, which seem to have been unknown even to Maitland, which make it doubtful whether the statute of 1290 does represent any departure from Edward's original intentions.

I. We have first to consider the government's attitude towards franchises under Henry III, and the previous history of the writ of Quo Warranto. Legal historians have long known that this writ was in use at least as early as the reign of Richard I.[4] Several cases, for instance, are to be found in the rolls of the king's court in 1194 and 1198 of clergy answering the query by what warrant they hold their churches.[5] An Essex eyre roll of 1229 shows us the tenant of a mill on the royal demesne answering to such a writ,[6] and Bracton's Notebook contains many such cases. In all these instances, however, inquiry is made as to the holding of lands, not of liberties, and such a use of the writ was quite distinct and, as Maitland points out,[7]

---

[1] E. Jenks, *Edward Plantagenet*, p. 166.
[2] T. F. Tout, *Political History of England*, III. 149.
[3] Maitland, *Select Pleas in Manorial Courts* (Selden Soc.), pp. xxi, lxxvii.
[4] *Abbreviatio Placitorum* (Rec. Comm. 1811), p. xi.
[5] *Pipe Roll Society*, XIV. 33, 66; *Rotuli Curiae Regis* (Rec. Comm. 1835), I. 142.
[6] Ass. R. 229, m. 18.   [7] Pollock and Maitland, *op. cit.* II. 661.

liable to abuse.[1] But alongside these practices we also find
Henry III's government using the writ in precisely the same way as
Edward I for the inquiry into the tenure of franchises. Bracton's
theory that all 'regalities' or royal liberties cannot be held by a
private person 'unless it be given him from above' is more than
the legist's ideal that Maitland would seem to suggest;[2] it was a
theory that was being applied in practice by the king's courts. In
1238 the justices in eyre in Devon are summoning lord after lord of
the private hundreds of the county to show by what warrant they
hold their hundredal liberties, and in hundred after hundred the lords
are pleading ancient tenure, in some cases, 'from the Conquest'.[3]
In a few instances they produce charters. The record of most of these
cases is not complete; they are generally referred to some other
authority, probably the council. From the eyre rolls that survive for
the period 1234-38 it seems probable that the inquiry was confined
to the south-western circuit.[4] But from 1254 onwards the justices in
eyre, as part of their ordinary routine work, were charged to inquire
into the assumption of liberties without warrant,[5] and cases to correspond are found on the eyre rolls.[6] Moreover, the clergy protest, in a
series of articles presented to the king in 1257, against the attack on
the liberties of the Church by the Quo Warranto inquiries, which,
as they declare, infringe Magna Carta, whereby all those liberties
which they had hitherto used had been confirmed to them.[7]

Edward I then is in no way making a new departure. He is using
a recognized weapon, and reviving, on a more comprehensive scale,
a procedure used by his father's government, on principles already
familiar to the justices and pleaders of the law courts.

[1] Miss M. H. Mills pointed out to me an order to the Barons of the Exchequer
in 1230-31 not to summon men to show by what warrant they hold their lands
except by the king's special command: P.R.O., Mem. Roll, K.R. 10, m. 5.
[2] Pollock and Maitland, op. cit. I. 528-9, 572; cf. L. Ehrlich, in Oxford Studies in
Social and Legal History, VI. 68.
[3] Ass. R. 174, mm. 34-38, etc. See also M. H. Mills, in Trans. R. Hist. S. 1927,
pp. 117 ff.
[4] [I owe this information to Mr C. A. F. Meekings of the P.R.O. For inquiries
into liberties under Henry III, see now Powicke, Henry III and the Lord Edward
(1947), pp. 110-15.]
[5] Oxford Studies, ut supra, VI. 23.
[6] E.g. Ass. R. 233, m. 50.
[7] M. Paris, Chronica Majora [R.S.], VI. 363-4. The bishops complain especially
of the theory that a grant in general terms does not cover special rights—an
argument put forward constantly by Edward's lawyers, 1278-1307.

II. The story of Earl Warenne must now be examined. The authority for it is the chronicler Walter of 'Hemingburgh', and students of Stubbs' *Charters* may have noticed that the passage in question, printed on pages 431–2 of the eighth edition, has been omitted in the ninth. Professor Rothwell, who has restored to 'Hemingburgh' his proper appellation of Guisborough, says that the story is clearly a later interpolation.[1] He also notes that it is told twice, once of Warenne and again of Clare.[2] However that may be the narrative misrepresents the character of the Quo Warranto proceedings. It states that the king, soon after the passing of the Statute of Gloucester in 1278, sent justices to inquire by what warrant men held their *lands*, whereas the tenants were only required to answer concerning liberties—rights like those of toll, warren, or jurisdiction. And there are other divergences between the Chronicle and the records. The eyre rolls show the earl in a very different attitude.[3] In Surrey, Sussex, Yorkshire, Lincolnshire and Norfolk he or his attorney appears before the justices, armed not with a rusty sword but with legal arguments, and pleads in due form as to his title to his liberties. In Surrey and Sussex (1279) he says, and the juries uphold him, that he has held his liberties from time immemorial, and the justices allow him to keep them.[4] In Yorkshire (1280–81) he makes the same plea, and the matter is referred to a jury; the final result is not stated.[5] In Lincolnshire (1281) he claims return of writs and other liberties in Stamford, under a charter given him by Edward himself in 1263. The king's counsel points out that the liberties in question had been unlawfully usurped by Edward himself when he was lord of Stamford, and that he, being, as he was then, a private person, had no power to grant usurped liberties; as he has no other warrant, the earl loses these franchises.[6] In Norfolk (1286) the king claims two private hundreds held by the earl, alleging that Richard I had held them.[7]

---

1 [*Chronicle of Walter of Guisborough*, ed. H. Rothwell, Camden Series, vol. lxxxix (1957), p. 216.]   2 [*Ibid.* p. 259.]

3 Professor Tout's references (*Pol. Hist.* III. 149, n. 1; cf. his article on John de Warenne in *Dict. Nat. Biog.*) are not to the Quo Warranto proceedings, but to Kirkby's inquest of 1285, and to a later inquest into knights' fees in 1303. The sort of resistance described was not infrequently made by lords who had the return of writs and thus had a right to exclude the sheriff and his staff. Refusal to plead before a royal justice would be more serious.

4 *Plac. Quo War.* pp. 745, 750–51.   5 *Ibid.* p. 191.   6 *Ibid.* pp. 429–50.

7 According to the Hundred Rolls, they had been given to the earl's ancestors by Henry I. *Rot. Hund.* I. 454.

The end of this case is not recorded on the eyre rolls, but as to another liberty, that of free warren, the king's counsel admits that the earl has had it from time immemorial, and the court allows him to keep it.[1] There is nothing in these legal records to suggest that Earl Warenne headed a movement of successful opposition to the royal policy, and the nearest approach to an appeal to the sword is the argument put forward in the Sussex eyre, that the earl's ancestors had faithfully adhered to King John at the time of the loss of Normandy and had been granted their rights of warren in compensation for the loss of their Norman lands.[2] If the incident inserted in the Chronicle ever really occurred it is more likely to have been at the time of the inquests of 1274–75, or at some other inquest when lands as well as liberties were inquired into, without any judicial proceedings, rather than in the Quo Warranto Pleas of 1278–90.

III. We come lastly to the question whether Edward I did, for one reason or another, moderate his claims and accept a compromise. It may be pointed out that the cases just cited are not consistent with the theory worked out by Maitland in 1888 and adopted by all who have since written on the subject, namely, that the statute of 1290 does constitute such a compromise, and form a landmark in the legal proceedings. In the two earliest eyres, as we have seen, the earl's plea of immemorial tenure is allowed, and no demand is made for a written charter. In 1286, four years before the statute of 1290, the king is claiming a franchise because his ancestor Richard I held it. To prove or disprove the truth of Maitland's contention that the change in the law is plain if we compare the pleadings before 1290 with those after 1290[3] would need a detailed examination of a vast bulk of plea rolls, unprinted as well as printed.[4] But even a cursory inspection will produce other cases, besides Earl Warenne's, in which immemorial possession without written grant is allowed to be good warrant well before 1290.[5] It is true that the lawyers pleading for the king sometimes deny this. But it is judgments, rather than arguments, that we must go by; the bench, not the bar. Some of the extreme assertions of royal prerogative which Maitland quotes are later than

[1] *Plac. Quo War.* p. 485.   [2] *Ibid.* p. 750.
[3] *Select Pleas in Manorial Courts*, p. lxxvii.
[4] [Such an investigation is being made by Professor Sutherland of Iowa University.]
[5] *Rot. Hund.* II 302 (W. de Faucunberg, A. de Everingham); *Plac. Quo War.* pp. 783 (Bishop of Worcester), 799 (Abbess of Wilton).

1290, when, according to him, such claims had been abandoned.[1] As he himself says, in these rolls we hear no statements of the law that can claim to be impartial,[2] and if, as has recently been suggested,[3] any man might plead in the courts on behalf of the king, ambitious lawyers may well have had a motive for making extravagant claims for the crown. Such arguments would not, however, bind the king in any way, or be evidence of the official royal policy. 'It is open to anyone to sue in the king's name and so make the king apparently say what is not true', said Herle in 1315.[4]

The evidence of the plea rolls, then, does not seem to bear out Maitland's view, but we are not dependent only upon them. A record which escaped his notice comes very near an official statement of policy at the beginning of the campaign. This consists of some official memoranda, of which apparently the only extant copy is to be found at the end of two manuscripts of Bracton now in the British Museum and Lambeth Libraries.[5] Internal evidence enables us to attribute these notes to the early spring of 1279. Three of the five items have no bearing on our subject; the other two are pronounce-ments as to Quo Warranto procedure, coming, one from the king's council, the other from the justices of the two benches.

The origin of these statements was apparently a query from the justices then sitting in eyre at Canterbury. Gilbert of Clare, an even mightier baron than Earl Warenne, had already in the parliament of Gloucester prayed to be left in the peaceful possession of his liberties, and not be disturbed 'contrary to the law of the land'.[6] Now, summoned to show by what warrant he held the hundreds of Washlingstone and Littlefield in Kent, he had objected that he was not bound to answer the king, since the king was not mentioned as a party in the writ of Quo Warranto.[7] The form of the writ had, in fact, been called in question, and the justices refer the matter to head-

[1] *Plac. Quo War.* pp. 122, 676-7, cited Pollock and Maitland, *op. cit.* I. 573. Both belong to 1292.
[2] Pollock and Maitland, I. 573.
[3] *Yearbooks of 8 Edward II* (Selden Soc.), pp. x-xii.
[4] *Ibid.* p. 76.
[5] Royal MS. 9 E. XV. fo. 216: printed by Palgrave, *Parl. Writs,* I, 383-4. See below. A similar entry is to be found at the end of Lambeth MS. 92.
[6] *Rot. Parl.* I. 8. The Chronicle of Lanercost, like Guisborough's interpolator, attributes to him, not to Earl Warenne, the production of a sword as his warrant. *Chron. de Lanercost,* p. 168.

quarters. The king's council, with his justices, resolve that the form of the writ is perfectly sound.

Such writs [as to the holding of hundreds] have been used to be made and pleaded in these same words in the time of the king's predecessors, as is clear from the old plea rolls now in the Exchequer. Therefore the earl must plead to the writ, and show by what warrant he holds the hundreds in question.

The second, and more important, ruling is that of the two benches, and is headed by the names of the ten judges responsible for it. It begins by giving the correct form of the writ, and then proceeds to answer the objection raised by Gilbert of Clare's attorney.

It has been objected that this writ is insufficient, since in every writ that can be pleaded the name of the person to whom the defendant must answer ought to be mentioned. This does not hold good with this writ, because... when it is used in this way, it is perfectly clear that answer must be made to the lord king, even though his name is not expressly mentioned in the writ. It has also been objected that the writ ought also to state that the liberty in question belongs to our crown. To this objection we reply that although it is necessary to add the words 'which belongs or ought to belong to our crown' in writs of Quo Warranto concerning the tenure of manors—for there are many manors which do not belong to the crown—...it is not so with regard to liberties, because every liberty is royal and belongs to the crown, *or to him who has sufficient warrant, either by charter or from time immemorial.* If therefore the wording were 'which liberty belongs to our crown' we might seem to admit that a liberty might exist which could not belong to the king.

This judicial pronouncement not only puts in a nutshell the official, Bractonian, theory that all seignorial authority is delegated and every franchise is royal in origin, but it incidentally declares what constitutes a good title. Charter *or* immemorial tenure is sufficient warrant of a liberty; and so the king's counsel says at Canterbury in answer to Gilbert of Clare, echoing the judges' ruling: 'There is no other warrant than ancient immemorial custom or the king's special charter, neither of which the earl can show.'[1]

This rule, laid down when the Quo Warranto proceedings had only just begun,[2] was adhered to throughout Edward's reign: it

---

[1] *Plac. Quo War.* p. 338.
[2] The first eyres under the Statute of Gloucester began on 3 Nov. 1278. The eyre at Canterbury began on 21 Jan. 1279.

would seem, indeed, that any change that took place was rather in the direction of greater stringency than of more leniency in asserting the royal claims.[1] But disputes might still arise as to the exact meaning of 'time immemorial'. How far back was the memory of man supposed to stretch? Even before 1290, as we have seen, there are signs that the beginning of Richard I's reign was regarded as a landmark, and the reason is pretty clear. It had been laid down in 1275, in the Statutes of Westminster, I, cap. 39, that in proving seisin in a writ of right none were to go back further than the time of Richard I. But until a term was officially fixed in pleas of Quo Warranto, claimants might go on alleging long seisin[2] and justices continue referring the matter to the king and council for decision, as Britton describes,[3] thus causing delay and annoyance.[4] The passing of the statutes of 1290, following on the directions to the exchequer officials cited by the Dunstable annalist,[5] probably did give real relief; not so much as representing a change of royal policy as in setting a limit to the law's delays.[6]

As to the general effect of the Quo Warranto proceedings, there is little to add to Maitland's summary.[7] Few, if any, franchises were abolished.[8] In almost every case where a liberty was found to be unwarranted, the king was willing, for a substantial fine, to restore it to its late holder and give him a charter. It would be a mistake, however, to think that this is evidence of the futility of the proceedings.

---

[1] Note, for example, the eyre of Devon, *Plac. Quo War.* pp. 164 ff., and the account given by the Dunstable annalist of the severity of the justices assigned to finish off the Quo Warranto proceedings (*Annales Monastici* [R.S.], III. 360). These justices are probably to be identified with Gilbert de Thornton and his fellows, appointed to hear and determine the king's pleas (*C.R.C.* 1288–96, p. 94), but no records of their proceedings are extant. Of the two gentlemen described by the annalist as having lost their liberties for want of written warrant, one, Robert fitz Walter, had had his liberty allowed in the eyre of Northampton of 1285, under a charter from King John (Ass. R. 619, m. 69d), and his heir had it allowed under the same charter in 1330 (*Plac. Quo War.* p. 573). It is possible that these two liberties were taken into the king's hands temporarily for failure to appear or some other technical legal blunder.

[2] *Diutina seisina.*   [3] Edited by F. M. Nichols, I. 76–7.

[4] 'Judgments upon pleas of Quo Warranto were greatly delayed, because the justices...were not certified of the king's pleasure therein.' *Stat.* 18 *Edw. I: Statutes of the Realm*, I. 107.

[5] *Annales Monastici* [R.S.], III. 360. See also Mem. Roll, L.T.R. 63, m. 36.

[6] See, for a slightly different view, G. T. Lapsley, 'John de Warenne and the *quo waranto* proceedings in 1279', in the *Cambridge Historical Journal* for 1927.

[7] Pollock and Maitland, *op. cit.* I. 574.   [8] But Gilbert lost the two hundreds.

From the point of view of Edward I, the whole campaign must have been very well worth while. He was far from wishing to do away with private jurisdictions and have all the work of local government done by royal officials alone. What he wanted was to get it down in black and white what rights his subjects might lawfully claim, and to assert in an unmistakable manner the principle that they held these rights from him, and only so long as they exercised them to the good of the realm. If the exchequer also profited largely by fines and fees, so much the better. But that his policy was a striking innovation, or that he modified it in face of sturdy baronial opposition, are views which seem to me no longer tenable.

A

Close Roll, 7 E. I, m. 10d.

Rex vicecomiti Kanc' salutem. Summone per bonos summonitores Gilbertum de Clare comitem Gloucestr' et Hertford' quod sit coram iusticiariis nostris ad primam assisam cum in partes illas uenerint ostensurus quo waranto tenet hundreda de Wathelestan et Littelfeld in comitatu predicto. Et habeas ibi summonitores et hoc breue. T. R. apud Westm. xxj die Ianuarii.

B

MS. Reg. 9 E. XV, fo. 216.

Concordatum est per consilium Domini Regis et justiciarios suos London' quod breve quo waranto de hundredis versus talem non est viciosum immo bene conceptum. Et consimilia brevia per eadem verba fieri et placitari consueverunt tempore predecessorum Regis, ut patet in antiquis rotulis placitorum ad scaccarium existentibus. Et ideo talis respondeat. Et quo ad hoc quod talis petit iudicium si ad huiusmodi breve debeat respondere desicut auus et pater eius quibus ipse comes successit obierunt inde seisiti; concordatum est quod quia Rex vel antecessores eius per alia brevia in consimilibus casibus de libertatibus placitare non consueverunt, predictus comes respondeat ulterius, et doceat quo waranto predicta hundreda tenet vel quomodo seisina eorundem pervenit ad antecessores eius.

C

Bene concordatum est per Magistrum Thomam Beck, J. de Kyrkeby, R. de Hengham,[1] N. de Stapeltone,[1] W. de Wymburne,[1] T. de Weylaunde,[2] W. de Heliun,[2] J. de Lovetoft,[2] W. de Brumpton[2] et R. de Leycestr'[2] quod breue quod dicitur Quo Waranto formatum super illos

---

[1] Justices of the Bench 'ad placita regis', 6 E. I. *C.R.C.* 1272-9, p. 503.
[2] Justices of the Bench at Westminster, 6 E. I. *C.R.C.* 1272-9, p. 503.

qui tenent libertates que ad coronam pertinent sine waranto sufficiens est in tali forma :—

Summone per bonos summonitores talem quod sit coram nobis vel talibus iusticiariis nostris tali die ostensurus quo waranto tenet visum franci plegii in tali manerio. Et habeas ibi summonitores etc.

Et ad hoc quod obiciunt quidam quod breve predictum minus est sufficiens in principio, in hoc quod in qualibet breui placitabili debet fieri mencio cui actori pars defendens debet respondere, non est verum in isto breui quod est speciale in actione Domini Regis, quia in multis locis invenitur istud breue placitatum, nec tunc fit mencio quod pars defendens ad aliud sit summonita quam ad ostendendum quo waranto etc; quia cum breue illud tantum modo deseruiat Domino Regi et non alii evidenter potest et debet intelligi quod Domino Regi est responsabilis, licet in breui non exprimatur. Ad hoc etiam quod obiciunt quod breue illud in fine est insufficiens in hoc quia dicitur 'quo waranto tenet vel habet talem libertatem' etc., non adiiciendo 'que est de corona nostra vel spectat ad coronam nostram', eorum objectioni bene potest respondere quod licet in breuibus quo waranto tenet talem manerium necesse est mencionem facere quod est de corona nostra vel quod debet esse in manum nostram tanquam escaeta nostra de terris Normannorum, multa enim sunt maneria que nec sunt de corona nec de terris Normannorum, propter quod in peticione tenementi conveniens est quod exprimat causam peticionis sue; sed non est sic de libertatibus, quia quelibet libertas regia est et ad coronam pertinet nisi ille qui eam habet sufficiens habeat warrantum vel per cartam vel a tempore cuius non extat memoria. Propter quod non est necessarie quod breve dicat 'que libertas est de corona nostra', quia si clausula illa poneretur, uideretur innui quod aliqua sit libertas que ad Regem pertinere non posset.

XIII

The King's Government, as administered by the Greater Abbots of East Anglia[1]

We are all familiar with the idea of the England of the Middle Ages as a land of private jurisdictions, of specially privileged tracts of land, of franchises and palatinates. Professor Pollard has clinched the contrast of medieval and modern ways of thought in his epigram, echoed by Maurice Hewlett: 'Magna Carta was a charter not of liberty but of liberties.' The champions of law were not claiming a liberty in which all had an equal share, but each man's own liberty, warranted by a charter, upheld in the courts:

> Liberty for a man to hang
> His villein on his own park trees,
> Freedom to make freedom a thing
> Not to be hop'd for![2]

liberty of gallows, of wreck, of pillory and tumbril, of view of frankpledge, of the assize of bread and ale.

It is with certain local examples of such liberties or franchises that we are now concerned; but whilst the privilege and the power attaching to them should not be minimized, there is another aspect of the liberty which has, I think, been rather disregarded by modern writers. We are so accustomed to look on feudalism as antagonistic to the royal power, as a force making for decentralization and lawlessness, as the irreconcilable enemy of good government, that we have failed to grasp the fact that the magnates, secular and lay, in whose hands these great powers lay, were charged also with a heavy responsibility. This responsibility was not merely moral but legal. The liberty was held, as the judges hold their offices, so long as it was well administered; for defect of good order and justice the king could, and not seldom did, take it into his own hands. A particularly

[1] Read to the Cambridge Antiquarian Society 8 March 1926. Reprinted from their *Communications*, Vol. XXIX (1928).

[2] The liberty of gallows or 'infangthef' gave to the lord the right (also possessed by the hundred courts) of hanging the red-handed or manifest thief, whether he were freeman or villein. Tenurial relationships were not involved.

explicit statement of this conception occurs in 1302, in connection with the great palatinate franchise of the bishop of Durham. Certain royal messengers carrying writs into the palatinate had been attacked and imprisoned, and the bishop had taken no steps to punish the offenders; his liberty was, therefore, taken into the king's hands:

Because the bishop, since he holds the said liberty, is so far the king's minister for upholding and carrying out in the king's name and in due manner what belongs to the royal authority within the same liberty; so that he ought to do justice to all and singular there, and duly submit to the lord king's mandates, although by the king's grant he receives the profits and issues thence arising. For the royal authority extends throughout the whole realm, both within the liberties and without.[1]

This judgment clearly and briefly defines the two aspects of the liberty or franchise. The king has granted to its holder certain valuable rights and powers, defined by charter or custom, and further defined by successive judgments given in his courts. By virtue of this grant the lord of the liberty does certain things which elsewhere are done by the king or his officials, and keeps for himself profits of various kinds which elsewhere go to the king's exchequer. But in so far as these rights and duties are governmental, not proprietary, public, not private, the franchise-holder is the viceroy or agent of the king—responsible to the king, and liable to forfeiture, like any other government official, for maladministration as, for instance, the abbot of Crowland permanently forfeited his right to have a gaol because of his repeated unjust detention of prisoners;[2] and as the private and public functions are closely intertwined, he will, in case of such forfeiture, in all likelihood lose, for the time being, certain other profits which have no logical connection with his franchise, but are his fair dues as a landlord. In examining some features of the greater ecclesiastical liberties of East Anglia, I shall ignore the whole field of their holders' activities as landlords, in so far as it is possible to keep these distinct, and regard them solely as viceroys—administrators of the king's government.

The ecclesiastical franchises in this fertile corner of England were extensive. There was first the great Peterborough liberty—the eight hundreds of Oundle, in northern Northamptonshire: then Thorney Abbey's one hundred of Normancross in Huntingdonshire; Ramsey Abbey's two hundreds of Hurstingstone, Huntingdonshire, and

---

[1] *Placitorum Abbreviatio*, p. 257.   [2] *Yearbooks*, 20 Edw. IV, Trin. Term.

Clackclose, Norfolk; Ely's two hundreds in the marshes of North Cambridgeshire, five and a half hundreds of Wicklaw in South-East Suffolk, and the hundred of Mitford in Norfolk; and, lastly, the eight and a half hundreds of Bury St Edmunds in West Suffolk. The liberties of Bury and Ely will be the main subjects of discussion, with some reference to Peterborough and only a few to Ramsey, about which there is a good deal already in print.

Of all these liberties, Thorney is the only one that originates this side of the Norman Conquest. It is highly probable that as administrative districts some of them have a very ancient origin. Bede, in his *Ecclesiastical History*, speaks of a district belonging to Oundle, and though the Peterborough charters attributed to Edgar are forgeries, there seems no reason to doubt that the district known as the eight hundreds of Oundle in the twelfth century, of which to-day the soke of Peterborough is the sole remaining fragment, was bestowed on the abbey in the tenth century, when it was refounded by Bishop Aethelwold. The Isle of Ely, again, is probably very ancient, though not as ancient as was once thought. Mr Miller has shown that it cannot be identified with Etheldreda's dower or with the *regio* over which her first husband was ealdorman.[1] But when the house at Ely was refounded for monks by Aethelwold and Edgar, it was natural that both lands within the Isle and royal rights over the Isle should be bestowed on it. Edgar, however, granted to St Etheldreda the soke not only of the two hundreds in the marshes but also the five and a half hundreds of Wicklaw in Suffolk,[2] a compact block of territory of which Woodbridge is nowadays the natural administrative centre. Wicklaw has been identified by Mr Redstone of Woodbridge as a hill in the parish of Hacheston, but this identification is not certain. The *Liber Eliensis* in a later passage[3] speaks of this as the six hundreds belonging to Southborne—presumably Sudborn near Oxford: but in the Middle Ages it was most frequently known simply as the liberty of St Etheldred. By 1066 St Etheldred also had the soke of the hundred and a half of Mitford in Norfolk; very probably this is the gift mentioned in the *Liber Eliensis*,[4] when Aethelwold obtained from Edgar Dyrham with all that pertained to it, since Domesday describes the soke of Mitford hundred as being annexed to the manor of East Dereham.[5]

[1] [Miller, *op. cit.* pp. 10-15.]   [2] *Liber Eliensis*, II. 5.
[3] *Ibid.* II. 41.   [4] *Ibid.* II. 40.   [5] *D.B.* II 214.

The liberty of Bury St Edmunds has, as such, a later origin: it was bestowed upon the saint by Edward the Confessor. But here also we seem to trace an older unit. The eight and a half hundreds annexed to the royal vill of Bedricsworth, where the saint's body lay, had been the dowry of Cnut's wife Emma, as the Isle of Ely had been that of St Etheldreda: and it came into the hands of the crown on her forfeiture, and was granted out again by her son.[1] Of this donation the following story was told by the monks in the fifteenth century, according to a manuscript in the University Library. Edward the Confessor came to Bury township on the feast of St Edmund, and Abbot Baldwin took him round the monastery. When they came to the refectory, it chanced that the king found the young monks at their midday meal eating barley bread. 'My lord abbot', said the king, 'wherefore are these young kinsmen of mine feeding on barley bread?' 'The possessions of the monastery', replied the abbot, 'do not suffice for them to have wheaten bread.' Then said the king, 'Ask what you will of me, and I will give it, that so they may be better fed, and may take their part in the divine service with greater alacrity and vigour'. So the abbot, having taken advice, asked of the king the manor of Mildenhall and the eight and a half hundreds with all their liberties, as the king himself held them, and the king, having heard him, replied, 'Unwisely have you demanded for yourself and your successors a great and continual labour—*grandem et continuum laborem*. I would more willingly have given you three or four manors. Nevertheless, for the reverence I bear my kinsman the saint, I will freely grant your request', and thus by divers charters sealed with his seal he bestowed upon Saint Edmund, as fully and freely as he held it himself, the aforesaid manor and the eight and a half hundreds which are now called the liberty of St Edmund.[2]

The liberty of Ramsey Abbey also owes its origin to Edward the Confessor, who granted the monks the soke over Clackclose hundred, which Domesday shows them enjoying. To this Hurstingstone hundred in Huntingdonshire was added by Henry I. The hundred of Normancross was granted to Thorney Abbey by William II.[3]

Not only are these districts older, as local government units, than the monasteries which administered them, they survived the monasteries' own dissolution. According to Kelly's *Directory* for Cam-

[1] *Eng. Hist. Rev.* 1909, p. 418.
[2] Camb. Univ. Lib. MS. Ff. 2. 29, fo. 65.
[3] Camb. Univ. Lib. Add. MS. 3021 (Red Book of Thorney), fo. 19.

bridgeshire, 'Cambridgeshire includes two shires or jurisdictions—
the shire proper, and Ely'. The Isle of Ely is not only a parliamentary
constituency, it has its own county council and its own coroner. A
hundred years ago it was even more notable. Down to 1836 the
bishop of Ely still nominated a chief justice for the Isle, who could
hear and determine all criminal and civil pleas in the island. Under
King Charles II, as under King John four hundred and fifty years
earlier, the bishop could claim his franchise and get cases transferred
from the king's court at Westminster to his own court at Ely. The
bishop's chaplain, writing in 1812, says that this is no longer usual,
and that residents in the Isle do frequently sue in the king's court at
Westminster, and that cases are taken out of the bishop's court into
the king's without the bishop's protesting. Yet he does not seem to
consider the survival an abuse.

'This jurisdiction, being considered as a matter of gain, is not worth
having,' he says, 'yet as it gives the see of Ely some peculiar powers and
privileges, no bishop would be willing to part with it. But with respect
to the inhabitants of the Isle this Franchise is a matter of great convenience;
since they have justice administered as it were at their very doors, in all
pleas of the Crown; and in most civil cases they need not, unless they
think fit, have recourse to any other place for justice but the Bishop's
court of Pleas belonging to this jurisdiction.'[1]

The liberties of St Edmund and St Etheldreda have also left a
permanent stamp upon Suffolk local government. To this day the
county is divided into 'the geldable' and 'the franchises'; there is a
session for St Edmund's at Bury, and for St Etheldreda's at Woodbridge, and there is a separate grand jury for St Edmund's.[2]

Most remarkable of all is the survival of the soke of Peterborough,
though it has lost six of the original eight hundreds. Like Ely, it is a
separate administrative county, with its own county council, coroner,
chief constable and police. What is more, it has its own separate
Commission of Gaol Delivery. Though there is no longer a liberty
gaol, as there was up to 1877, the justices of the liberty, selected as
required from time to time from the bench of J.P.s, have power to
try all felonies and inflict capital punishment. It is the only county
franchise which still retains the power to punish by death, and once
at least in this century the right has been waived.[3]

[1] James Bentham, *Cathedral Church of Ely* (1812), Appendix, p. 25.
[2] Kelly, *Directory of Suffolk* (1925), p. 2.
[3] In 1903; see Gaches, *Liberty of Peterborough*, p. 70.

These modern survivals are not of purely antiquarian interest. They throw a light backwards on to the history of the whole system of franchise government; for unless they had served their purpose efficiently and met the needs of the countryside at least as adequately as other methods of local government, these liberties would not have survived the dissolution of the monasteries, and been continued in existence by 'that majestic lord who broke the bonds of Rome', and who showed by his whole policy, and in especial by his 'Act for recontinuing Liberties in the Crown',[1] that he had no intention of tolerating lesser *imperia in imperio*.

A document of the latter part of the fifteenth century reflects a similar view of the relationship of monarch and liberty. There is in the Bodleian Library a most interesting statement drawn up by the abbot of Bury St Edmunds as to the duties of his chief steward or seneschal, to which I shall have to refer later. Having laid down various rules, as to the enforcement of the king's law and the execution of the king's writs by the steward, he says: 'What time this rule was kept, it was noted and holden the most notable franchise of good rule in the land.' Here you have the proper pride of the viceroy, not the jealousy of the landlord.

Let us turn now to consider the actual machinery of government, through which this 'great and continuous labour' of doing the king's work was carried on. The key to the situation, we shall find, is, in each liberty, this same high steward or seneschal. The fullest details as to his office and functions are to be found in the records of St Edmunds. If in the days when Jocelin of Brakelond wrote about Abbot Samson, the abbot was still himself actively exercising his public functions, by the thirteenth century the steward had taken all this work off the abbot's shoulders. To quote the Bodleian document again:

The abbot of Bury gave out of his revenues certain manors to a steward, to support the rights of his church and his franchise, so that he and his brethren might quietly praise and serve God....If any misdoers should rebel, the steward should deal with them as right and law would, so that the abbot should in no wise be troubled nor vexed with such foreign matters.[2]

[1] 27 Hen. VIII, c. 24.
[2] Bodl. Suffolk Charters, 134. A copy in the Egerton MSS. (B.M.) has been printed by Lord Francis Hervey, *The Pinchbeck Register*, II. 357 ff.

The stewardship was hereditary in the family of Hastings, who traced their descent from a certain Ralph to whom it was said to have been granted by William the Conqueror. From the time of Henry I down to the present day the descent of the office is clearly traceable: in the latter part of the fourteenth century it passed by the female line to the Grays of Ruthin, later to the Howards, and it is now in the hands of the Herveys, the present marquis of Bristol holding the title. The office was a serjeanty, by which certain manors were held; but, as a matter of fact, pretty early in the Middle Ages the hereditary steward delegated the actual work to a sub-steward and only retained the responsibility himself. These under-stewards are very generally called stewards in government documents, such as the Hundred Rolls of 1275. They had to take an oath to the abbot, and once at least, as we shall see, the abbot removed an under-steward for incompetence without waiting for the hereditary steward to act. It must have been strenuous work, to which a nobleman would be unable to devote his time, for it was roughly equivalent to the work of a sheriff, and sheriffs were very busy people. The steward was the connecting link between the crown and the liberty in matters of administration, jurisdiction and finance. The scope of his functions is very clearly defined in a document which occurs in three at least of the Bury registers, and probably belongs to the reign of Edward I. 'Note that the office of steward extends to the keeping of the liberty which belongs to the crown, and to executing the king's writs: but he is not to intermeddle with the manors except by the special command of the abbot.' [1] That is to say, he has no concern with the estates, only with the governmental work of the abbey. His pivotal position is well illustrated by a story of the reign of Edward I. Somewhere about 1290 the abbot of St Edmunds appointed Robert de Verdun as under-steward at the nomination of Sir John Hastings. In 1293 two sudden deaths occurred in the liberty; a boy of 12 years was found drowned in Livermere, and a man at Melford lighting a church lamp was crushed by the fall of the heavy weight that kept it up. The relatives of the dead persons sought for the coroner to hold the inquests, but he was not to be found, nor was the steward. Robert of Verdun was in fact taking a holiday; he had gone off to distant parts without asking the abbot's leave, and left his bailiwick unkept. Thus there was no one to compel the coroner to do his duty: the job would have fallen to the sheriff elsewhere, but the sheriff

[1] *Pinchbeck Register,* I. 337.

could not intervene in the liberty without special orders. The desperate relatives came to the abbot and begged a remedy, as they dared not bury the bodies without the coroner's inquest, though the whole neighbourhood was suffering from the stench. The abbot at once deprived Robert of his office and appointed a new under-steward, to the great indignation of Sir John Hastings.[1]

The steward, then, had to see that all the officials of the liberty did their duty—coroner, hundred bailiffs, clerks, constables, bedels and the whole crowd of officials who were supposed to enforce the king's law in western Suffolk.

He had also judicial duties; he held the 'great court' at Bury, which corresponded to the shire court in the rest of the country; the central court for all the eight and a half hundreds, held at the beginning of Edward I's reign at Catteshall, to the east of the town, and later at Henhow, just outside the town, probably on the tract now known as Shirehouse heath. Besides this, again like the sheriff, he went round the different hundreds holding tourns twice a year, at which the view of frankpledge was held and the articles of the tourn inquired into by the hundred juries, and greater and lesser criminal offences presented. On such occasions he handed over to the bailiffs of the hundreds estreats or lists of the fines and amercements imposed at these courts, for the bailiffs to collect and pay over to him.

His fiscal duties had two aspects—those looking to the king and those looking to the abbot. He was responsible for levying all fines, amercements and dues owed to the king, whether payments for writs, fines imposed by the justices in eyre, or customary payments. Some of these dues had, by the terms of the abbot's charters, been transferred by the king to him; the steward would have to collect them and pay them to the abbot. Others, not so granted by charter, he would have to pay in at the king's exchequer. To quote the fifteenth-century statement again:

The steward should yearly make clear accounts in the king's exchequer for all manner things appertaining to the said franchise, and collect all debts of the green wax and in the said exchequer make livery thereof, and acquit the abbot of all things whereof account ought of custom to be made in the exchequer; and he should answer to the abbot of all green wax that by point of charter should grow to him within the said franchise.

[1] *Pinchbeck Register*, I. 461 ff.

The steward might also have to represent the abbot in other places as well as the exchequer; at the shire court held at Ipswich for the rest of the county, and in the king's courts at Westminster, or before the travelling justices. This will naturally arise out of his duty of upholding the rights and privileges of the abbot and the liberty: and the perquisites allowed him are calculated with a view to such activities. Ordinarily he is allowed four horses, of the abbot's providing and feeding, and board and lodging for himself, a clerk, a serjeant and three grooms, extended by a later agreement to nine men and eight horses. If he has to go to London or Ipswich on the abbot's business, the abbot pays his expenses. He is also allowed four gallons of ale a day, half of the kind the abbot drinks, and half of smaller ale. He may turn out his horse to graze in St Edmund's meadows. In winter he is allowed six candles, in summer four, of the same quality that the prior is allowed; if he is lucky enough to get better ones, it is by grace and not of right. He has grants at Christmas, Easter, and St Edmund's day; $4\frac{1}{2}d.$ each time in the earlier record, $2s.$, $1s.$, and $1s.$ in the later.[1]

But more important than any of these perquisites were those arising from his duty of executing the king's writs in the liberty. The abbot of Bury St Edmunds had the return of writs, as had the abbots of Ramsey, Ely and Peterborough; and this franchise was exercised by the steward, to the exclusion, as he asserted in 1293, of the abbot himself. It is worth being fairly precise on this point, as one often hears it asserted of these great and ancient liberties that 'The king's writ did not run in them'. What exactly took place if a resident of West Suffolk wished to go to law with his neighbour over a piece of land, and sued out the king's writ, say, of Novel Disseisin? In the Bodleian Library[2] there is a roll of memoranda by a sheriff of Suffolk in the reign of Edward III, in some such form as the following: 'Received such and such a writ—passed it on to the steward of St Edmunds—who either has reported that he has done what was commanded him, or has done nothing about it.' Examples of writs, so transmitted, are extant for various liberties; for instance, those of the abbot of St Albans and the bishop of Lincoln; they are addressed by the sheriff to the steward or bailiff of the liberty and run something like this: 'We have received the command of the king in these words: [and the writ is quoted verbatim] wherefore we command

---

[1] *Pinchbeck Register*, I. 337; Camb. Univ. Lib. MS. Ff. 2. 33, fo. 142.
[2] Suffolk Rolls, 4.

you to execute this writ and report to us what you have done in the matter.' If the steward failed to take action, and the sheriff reported **as much, the litigant would get another writ of** *non omittas propter libertatem,* **by virtue of which the sheriff** could enter the liberty and execute the writ himself. The liberty of return of writs, that is, the right to prevent the sheriff and his staff from executing them in the franchise, was conditional on the franchise holder's seeing that the king's work was properly done by his own officials.

In the Chronicle of Peterborough we have a rebuke addressed to the sheriff for unjustifiable interference. It is worth noting as illustrating the relation of two different lords of liberties, as well as the working of franchisal government. In 1279 the sheriff of Northamptonshire had quite regularly passed on to the bailiffs of the soke of Peterborough a writ for replevying the beasts of the abbot of Ramsey, which the abbot of Peterborough had distrained for arrears of rent, etc., but the sheriff having formally handed on the matter to the officials of the liberty, then proceeded to come into the soke to replevy the beasts himself, alleging that the abbot's hundred courts could not hear a plea in which the abbot himself was a party. The abbot promptly obtained a letter from the king, ordering the sheriff to respect the liberties of Peterborough and to cease from interference.[1] Another case, of the year 1284, illustrates the normal working of the franchise. The abbot and one of his hundred bailiffs were summoned for forcibly taking three beasts of John de Vere's. The abbot replied that he had the return of writs in his liberty, and that his bailiff of the hundred of Huxlow had taken the beasts on a mandate from the sheriff that he should distrain him for 20s. which John owed the king's chancery for three writs obtained from the chancery. The case turned on whether the place where the distress was taken was in the abbot's liberty or no; as it was, he won the case.[2]

This case illustrates very well the importance of the writ system in extending the king's control over the liberties. It was the universal spread of royal justice that opened a breach in the walls of a liberty, and transformed its lord from a semi-independent magnate into a 'minister of the king'. As we shall see, it was a valuable privilege; but it also involved heavy responsibilities, and above all, it fitted the lord's liberties into a national scheme of administration. In a large

[1] *Chron. Petroburgense* (Camden Soc.), p. 33.
[2] *Ibid.* pp. 69–70.

part of their activities they were simply acting as royal agents. If the king's writ could not run without their endorsement and co-operation, it was very much to their interest that it should be passed on and executed as speedily as possible; for if not they risked first the invasion of their liberty by the sheriff, and finally, if they were obstinately neglectful, the forfeiture of the liberty itself, for not up-holding the king's law and enforcing his mandates.

It was to their pecuniary advantage, also, that the writs should be executed. There were perquisites and pickings to be had out of this business, especially if it led, as it did in the majority of cases, to a distraint—a taking of beasts. To compel attendance in court, pay-ment of a debt, or rendering of a service, the normal initial pro-ceeding was to distrain the cattle of the recalcitrant party, or, if they were poor, their coats, their pots or their pans. For each beast so impounded, the litigant paid a fixed rate—primarily for its food—for each day that the beast was in the lord's close or the sheriff's pound. The steward of St Edmunds 'has all the oxen which have to be distrained under the king's writs or pleas arising within the liberty';[1] and this was probably the most valuable of all his perquisites.

The records of Peterborough, Ely and Ramsey are not so numerous as those of St Edmunds, of which the Cambridge University Library has a fine selection. There seems here no trace of a hereditary steward-ship, though Ely has a hereditary constable. But though we do not know so much about their stewards, they appear to be doing much the same work. We see the steward of Peterborough in 1275 at the county court of Northamptonshire (as St Edmunds' steward went to Ipswich county) claiming the jurisdiction of the abbot in a case of assault and murder. Twenty-nine men of the liberty were appealed by the widow in the county court, and in spite of the resistance of the sheriff, the steward, Robert of Sheffield, succeeded in getting them transferred to the gaol of the liberty. The case went up to the king's council, which upheld the charter of the abbot, and ordered the trial to be held at Peterborough.[2]

Again, a succession of Ely stewards come before us. When, in 1299, the justices in eyre move on from Cambridge Castle to Ely, just as at Cambridge they demanded a list of all the sheriffs who have exercised office since their last visit, so at Ely they demand and get a list of all the stewards who have held office at Ely, and so done

[1] Camb. Univ. Lib. MS. Ff. 2. 33. fo. 142.
[2] *Chron. Petroburgense*, p. 22.

sheriff's work, since 1286. Of the six persons named, two had also been sheriffs of Cambridgeshire, one before, the other after their stewardship—Robert Hereward and William of Sutton.

From the creation of the bishopric in the reign of Henry I the administration of the Suffolk and Cambridgeshire liberties of Ely was separated: the bishop was lord of the Isle, the prior and monks of the five and a half hundreds of Wicklaw. There were therefore two stewards: the steward of the Isle, and the steward or chief bailiff of the five and a half hundreds, who resided at Melton, where the ancient gaol of the liberty still stands. The liberty gaol at Ely now serves, like Cambridge gaol in its later days, as a record office.

The steward of Ramsey[1] again, like those of Ely, Peterborough and St Edmunds, represents his abbot when necessary in the king's courts, and holds the tourns (or leets as they are called in Norfolk and Cambridgeshire) like the sheriff, in the hundreds and manors, thus travelling round the liberty and supervising the work of the lesser officials. Here again we have evidence that these stewards were of the same class as that from which the sheriffs were drawn; in one case (Walter of Stukely) the same man serves in turn as steward of Ramsey and sheriff of Cambridgeshire and Huntingdonshire, and in several cases the same family names occur in both lists.

Of the other officials whose competence extended over the whole of the liberty, the most important was the coroner. We have already heard of a coroner of St Edmunds neglecting his duty in the reign of Edward I, and lest it should be thought that liberties were more liable to suffer in this way than districts under direct royal control, I may mention, by the way, that precisely parallel charges had been made in Devon a little earlier, against the county coroner for refusing to hold inquests, and against the sheriff for failing to make him do so, the Devonshire county gentry complaining bitterly of the public nuisance. Each of these great liberties had its own coroner who kept the pleas of the crown, so that no profits arising from crimes or sudden deaths should be lost to the government. It was a responsible position, and the coroner of St Edmunds might well be expected to be a man of some standing. By a lucky chance, we have the will of a man who served both as coroner and clerk to the steward of the liberty, and is mentioned frequently—and generally to his discredit—in the Hundred Rolls of 1274–75. This man, Henry of Helhoughton,

---

[1] A list of Ramsey stewards is given in Ault, *Private Jurisdiction*, pp. 145–6. See also his *Court Rolls of Ramsey Abbey* (1928).

took bribes to let people off serving on inquests; he instigated the accusation of innocent men, he arrested men who had not been regularly indicted and kept them in prison till they paid to be released, and took fees for holding his inquests, which he should have held gratis. His will, dated 19 June 1274,[1] reveals the fact that if a clerk, he was married, for he leaves legacies to his widow, to three sons and two daughters and to their nurse, Agnes de Lansele; that although supposed to be an upholder of the law, he encroached upon the king's highway both at Risby, where he held land, and at Helhoughton; that if a layman, he could read, for he left 'one of my books called a codex' to a nephew; that he held land in Bury St Edmunds and in two other villages besides Helhoughton, where his court or manor house was and where he had a chaplain of his own. His little gifts to friends and servants are numerous, and suggest a kindly man. His legacies to the poor, to chaplains of churches, to Dominicans, Franciscans, and the monks of St Edmund, and his provision for his funeral masses would suggest the devout son of the Church—but that the first two items of the will rather lead one to suspect a guilty conscience, or, perhaps, a very businesslike other-wordliness. 'I leave half a mark to repair the parish church of St James, because of the tithes I have forgotten or failed to pay. I leave my charger and armour to the shrine of St Edmund, for all my trespasses done against the blessed Edmund and his church.' The villagers of West Suffolk might complain that Henry had unjustly extorted money from them; what lay heavy on his conscience when he came to die was not so much what he had taken, but what he had kept—those perquisites of royal government which had long ago been bestowed by one king and saint upon another king and saint.

We have considered the administration of the liberty as a whole, mainly in the light of the St Edmunds evidence; we have now to turn to the parts. If the unit of estate management (with which we are not concerned) was the manor, the unit of royal administration was the hundred, whose bailiff, with his assistants, carried out the steward's commands on the spot. There is a wealth of material for illustrating hundredal administration; I shall draw mainly on the Ely material, since both thirteenth-century court rolls and fourteenth-century bailiffs' accounts are extant for the hundreds of this liberty.

The hundred bailiff was, as a rule, appointed by the steward: a hereditary bailiff is mentioned for one of the St Edmunds hundreds

[1] Bodl. Suffolk Charters, 75.

by Jocelin of Brakelond, but the post is no longer hereditary in the thirteenth century. He entered into a bond for good conduct with the abbey. In one of the Bury Registers at the British Museum there are copies of the indentures for the seventh year of Henry VI for the hundreds of St Edmunds, which are let out for terms varying from one to five years.[1] The bailiff is to hold hundreds, leets and tourns; to certify inquests to St Edmund; to levy the fines and amercements owing both to St Edmund's court and to the exchequer, and to render account for them to the abbot, the steward and the coroner; to keep the rolls on parchment and hand them over at the end of his term; and to hear pleas of contracts, etc., up to 39s. 11¾d. The annual sum payable ranges from £6. 13s. 4d. for Risbridge hundred to £35 for the double hundred of Blackburn. The formula addressed to the good folk of the hundred adds that the bailiff has full power to distrain and do all things necessary for carrying out these duties.[2]

These indentures give the outline of the hundred bailiff's function. He is the executive, judicial and fiscal subordinate of the steward of the liberty. He carries out the orders contained in the writs; in many if not all cases, he holds the three-weekly hundred courts; and he collects both 'the king's debts', under the mandates sealed with the green wax of the exchequer; the fines and amercements arising out of the pleas of the great court of St Edmunds, the intrinsec shire; those arising out of the tourns held in his hundred twice a year by the steward; and those arising out of the courts that he himself holds. He also collects the ancient customary dues, payable generally twice a year, that go by the name of sheriff's aid, hundred scot, assised rents, hundredor's aid, cert-money, head penny, or whatever the local name for them may be.[3] We have a good survey of the fiscal side of his activities, to take these first, in some of the accounts for the Ely hundred of Mitford in the fourteenth century.[4]

In 1379 Richard of Welby, bailiff of Mitford hundred, Roland Lucas his sub-bailiff for half the year, and Nicholas Payn his sub-bailiff for the other half-year, render account to Thomas Arundel, bishop of Ely.

[1] Add. MS. 14848 (Registrum Curteys), fo. 53.
[2] Add. MS. 14848, fo. 321 b (18 Henry VI).
[3] See N. Neilson, 'Customary Rents', in Vinogradoff, *Oxford Studies*, II. 2, pp. 119 ff.
[4] Bodl. Norfolk Rolls, 99.

Receipts: Arrears from previous year   £19. 3. 10.
     Sheriff's aid   22/8
     Cert-money payable at view of frank-
       pledge from 18 villages   22/5½
     Perquisites of the leet in 14 villages   £7. 9. 0.
     Perquisites of 17 hundred courts   49/6
     Perquisites of fairs and markets   60/1

Total receipts, including arrears from last year   £39. 14. 0½
Fines and amercements arising in the king's courts   31/5.

Outgoings: Richard Welby's fee   100/-
     Parchment for keeping court rolls of hundreds and leets,
       and for return of writs   2/-

Balance due £34. 12. 0½.
     of which £4 is allowed to Nicholas Payn and
     £6. 2. 5. to R. Lucas.
∴   Total due is £24. 9. 7½.

In the diocesan registry at Ely there are some accounts for the hundred of Wisbech in the years 1489–90, but they are almost certainly incomplete, as they make no reference to hundred courts, leets or customary payments. They are simply accounts of the fines and amercements arising from the sessions of the justices of the peace at Ely at Easter and in August. 54s. 10d. is due, and 8s. 4d. is remitted because it cannot be collected.

Thomas Ketyll, bailiff of Wisbech, accounts firstly for
     100/- of arrears from the previous year.
     17/6 for fines and amercements arising from the sessions of the
       Justices of the Peace of the Isle of Ely, held at Ely on Wednesday
       before Palm Sunday.
     37/4 for similar fines from the sessions of St Peter's ad Vincula.

Total due 154/10.   Paid down 46/- (? 46/6).
     Fines remitted 8/4.
     Still owing 100/-.

The appearance of the justice of the peace is significant of the supersession in the fourteenth and fifteenth centuries of the sheriff and shire court and, to some extent, of the hundred bailiff and hundred court for the purposes of local government by the new 'maid of all work', the J.P., who was to do for the Tudor kings what the sheriff had done for the Angevin kings.

This leads us to consider the judicial work of the hundred bailiff. The Ely records are good evidence of the dwindling importance of the courts held by the hundred bailiff. At Ely there is an incomplete series of court rolls for the hundred of Wisbech belonging to the years 1302-7. There is also a series for the hundred of Wichford for the year 1366-67 which, though complete, is very bald and uninteresting. The vast majority of cases are cases of debt, and the number at each court is very much smaller than at the earlier date. In the intervening sixty years the J.P. has come into existence, and his sessions are stealing the petty criminal jurisdiction of the hundred.

Certain facts, however, emerge. At both dates the hundred courts are held on a fixed day of the week—Tuesday at Wichford, Thursday at Wisbech, at regular three-week intervals, except in the New Year, where there is a four-weeks' interval. I think some sort of Christmas holiday for court-holders was general. Thus you get your full tale of seventeen courts in the year. At the Martinmas court of Wichford a long string of persons who owe suit pay a lump sum down to be released from attendance for the next twelve months. Among those owing suit to the hundred of Wisbech may be noted two women—one the prioress of Eton and one a lay-woman.

If the Wichford rolls of Edward III's reign are uninteresting, the Wisbech rolls give a very fair notion of the kind of business conducted every three weeks by a hundred bailiff in the reign of Edward I. For further light we can also refer to the court rolls of the Ramsey hundred of Clackclose. I do this the more willingly, as the latest historian of Ramsey, Dr Ault of Boston, doubts whether the hundred court of Clackclose ever met.[1] There is in the Record Office solid reason—fourteen membranes of court rolls—for believing that it met and did business in the years 1282-84.[2] It is to this roll we owe a charming vignette of medieval piety, for it was at the court held at Downham Market on 12 February 1284 that Avelina Perlet sued Robert Hall of Boughton for attacking her by force and arms upon the king's highway between Wereham and Boughton upon Easter Sunday, 1282, and robbing her of a missal worth 20s., a manual worth 2 marks, and two rolls of songs worth 6d. We should like to know if the songs were carols or the more secular songs of some

[1] In his *Private Jurisdiction in England* (1923), p. 100; but in *Court Rolls of Ramsey Abbey* (1928) he prints extracts from the Rolls of Clackclose Hundred, pp. 145-69.
[2] P.R.O., Court Rolls, 192/67.

village choral to which Avelina was proceeding, her spiritual duties performed—but all we learn is that she won her case and recovered the value of the stolen goods, plus damages.[1]

This is a plea of detention of chattels, another example of which may be cited from a Wisbech roll of 1302. Two men of Leverington agreed at Michaelmas to lay out £8 jointly, repayable at Christmas, for trading purposes, and one having put down £4 and only received 40s. back, sued the other for the remaining 39s. 11d. It will be remembered that the Statute of Gloucester of 1278 was interpreted to prohibit any plea involving 40s. or upwards being heard in a shire or hundred court. The plaintiff lost his case.

Cases of trespass occur frequently in the Wisbech rolls. Joan Pelham complains that Stephen Malebraunche fell upon her one Sunday at Leverington, with various other men unknown, beat her, ill-treated her, drew blood from her and finally flung her on to a fire. Richard Baxter complains that Peter of Domerham assaulted him at Wisbech, violently entering his house, and frightening his wife so that he lost her services for a week. Damages were assessed at 18d. He also accuses him of public defamation, by calling him 'false man', whereby he lost a bargain involving five quarters of wheat. Seemingly he lost this plea. More unusual is the complaint of John, the son of Geoffrey Gerard. Thomas of Rotherwick, a man of Tydd, to whom John had entrusted a hound, had, contrary to the custom of the country, neither tied her up nor shut her up at the breeding season, and by mismating with all manner of strange dogs the breed of her offspring had been spoiled, for which he claims 6s. 8d. damages. Thomas asserts that such tying-up is the custom of boroughs and towns, not of country villages like Tydd, and demands a jury. Unfortunately the verdict of the jury is not enrolled.

Pleas of debt and of contract are very common, as, for instance, when Richard Dunham buys two quarters of wheat for 10s. at the end of February, undertaking to pay on the Good Friday following, but pays nothing until July. His creditor claims 6s. 8d. for the intervening four months. Or again, John Aleyn leases 26 acres of William of St Ives for a rent of 22s. for the whole year, to be paid at Michaelmas and Easter, and William pays nothing; or a woman claims 2s. 3d. due to her for minding a cow—two years' pay in

[1] P.R.O., Court Rolls, 192/68, m. 2.

arrears. She secures 1s. 10d. On 10 June 1305 Richard Baker is accused of enticing William Pepper away from the service of Thomas Fisher, to whom William was bound from Michaelmas to Easter. The jury finds for Fisher, who gets 40d. damages.

Two or three times we are reminded of the great world outside the Isle. There is an interesting case that appears to arise out of *Quia Emptores*. John Aleyn takes the beasts of Richard Baker by way of claiming the service owed from his tenement—6d. a year and two suits to his court. John Aleyn's tenant had formerly been Roger Batere, who enfeoffed Baker to hold of the chief lord of the fee according to the statute, and as Baker refused to render the services to John Aleyn he was distrained. Baker says that Aleyn has already admitted that Batere held the land by those services, and Batere is still alive, so that he is asserting that he has two tenants of the same tenement. It would seem that Baker refused to accept the working of the new statute.

Another point of contact with the governmental policy of Edward I is to be noted in a case at the court held on 16 February 1306. Walter Tolmer complains that John Nunne had accused him un-justly, bringing a 'malicious bill' before the justices of Trailbaston sitting at Ely in June 1305, asserting that he had burgled John's house. The jury had found him innocent, but as a consequence of his journey to and from Ely to answer this frivolous charge he had lost a horse worth 20s. Apparently Walter got his damages. The refer-ence is interesting both as showing the universal use of a nickname first invented in the previous year, and also as alluding to the pro-cedure by bill—the individual petition as contrasted with the pre-sentment of an accusing jury, a procedure discussed at length by Dr Bolland, and shown recently by Dr Jacob to be at least as old as 1259. It will be noted also that the justices of Trailbaston, like the justices in eyre, sat in the Isle itself.

Edward I's name itself is heard in the court on 10 June 1305, when Hamo de Walton brings a writ of right addressed by the king to the bishop. 'Do right to Hamo concerning this piece of land, for unless you do, the sheriff of Cambridge shall.' So the command goes out that all free tenants are to attend the next court. The average agree-ment about suit to a private hundred court included the condition that the suitor should attend the court twice a year and on such other occasions as a thief is to be judged, or the king's writ to be pleaded, due summons having been given. This is a case in point.

Another aspect of hundredal jurisdiction is illustrated by the appearance from time to time on the record of the prior of Ely, who 'claims his court' in cases where one of the parties is his man or lives on his manor. It would appear from the entries of the affeerors at the end of each court day that he claimed rather the money profits arising out of the case than the actual jurisdiction: for sums are sometimes noted as being due to the prior, whilst most are described as being due to the bishop.

Besides evidence as to the kind of cases that came up before the hundred bailiff every three weeks, we have some light on the actual conduct of the business. There are no cases, such as Miss Levett found at St Albans, of litigants or suitors losing their temper and using violent and unruly language. We do hear, however, of 'a great altercation' between the prior of Ely and Thomas Doreward as to which of the two should have jurisdiction over Stephen Hamund. We find the suitors of the court holding a discussion as to whether William Cavendish is to be allowed to claim 38s. 6d. from William Okey, who sold him a piece of land 16 perches short of the supposed extent. They decide that Okey need not pay, though he has agreed to do so. In another case they refuse to allow a woman to wage her law to prove that she did not come by night and steal the seal of another woman. In another case the plea is postponed for lack of sufficient number of suitors. Clearly the suitors were still the judges, even if the hundred bailiff presided and kept the rolls. They have other duties. One suitor is amerced a shilling for refusing to collect the fines and amercements of the court in Leverington when he had been elected for the purpose. It would seem that the affeerors chosen at each court, according to Magna Carta, to assess the amount of the amercements imposed, were also bound to collect them in the different villages of the hundred—Elm, Tydd, Newton, Leverington, Well and Wisbech. The total due for each village is given separately at the foot of each roll, along with the names of the affeerors.

A note at the foot of one roll commands the execution of all the orders enrolled on the record of the last court but one, unless they have been ticked off. The execution of the precepts and mandates arising from the holding of the courts will form a large part of the responsibilities of the hundred bailiff, and it is to this side of his activities that we must now turn, having considered his fiscal and judicial duties.

We have already acquired a pretty good idea of what these executive functions are—levying debts and amercements, impanelling juries, attaching people to be present at the court, distraining them by their chattels if they fail to come. To do this work the bailiff has assistants; summoners to summon people to the courts whenever special attendance is required (a tenant of Ramsey Abbey held his land at Wimbotsham by the service of summoning men to the hundred court of Clackclose); collectors chosen in court to collect the fines and amercements of each court day; sub-bailiffs to help with the records and accounts; bedels to attach and distrain men. The Wisbech hundred court rolls indicate that there was a bedel in each village of the Isle of Ely; he is constantly acting as pledge for the appearance of people in court. The number of the staff varied with the hundred.

The hundred bailiff, as we have seen, is appointed by the lord of the liberty or his steward, and enters into a bond with him for good conduct. But he is also the *ballivus juratus* solemnly sworn, probably in the hundred court, to serve the king's interests; when the justices in eyre come round he has to give an account to them of his bailiwick;[1] and to the men of the hundred, when he is doing the king's work, he is 'the king's bailiff'. A case on the Wisbech roll emphasizes the higher loyalty. Reginald fitzWalter, the king's bailiff, was commanded by the constable of Wisbech, on behalf of the king, to attach John Lowyn, chaplain, and six other men who had beaten and wounded John Digby, so that his life was despaired of. John Digby, now fit to appear in court, accused Reginald of entertaining and countenancing these malefactors, and allowing them to escape unharmed from his bailiwick, contrary to his oath and in contempt of the king. Reginald admits that he did take supper with these malefactors, and was in their company for half a day, but only against his will. They took him by force and compelled him to stay with them so that he could not fulfil his office on behalf of the king without being instantly slain. He begs for a jury, as does John Digby; and the jury find that Reginald acted under compulsion and was innocent of supporting these common malefactors.

Again and again it is made evident that the bailiffs in these liberties are doing the king's work. In the Suffolk liberty of Ely, the men of the Earl Marshal are charged with resisting the bailiffs of the prior when they try to take distresses by command of the king in Carlford

[1] Ass. R. 70, m. 7d.

hundred, in order to levy the king's debts there.[1] The bailiff of Thredling hundred appeals to the king in 1302 for punishment of six men who assaulted him at Debenham when he was trying to attach three others for trespass.[2] In 1276 the king appoints justices of oyer and terminer to ascertain what malefactors and disturbers of the peace attacked and ill-treated three bailiffs of the bishop of Ely while holding his view of frankpledge at Walpole and Walsoken.[3] At both ends, then, from the point of view of the villagers and from the point of view of the king himself, the officials of the liberty are doing the king's work as well as the abbot's work.

The co-operation, no less than the profit-sharing of the crown and the franchise-holder, is well illustrated at the visitation of the justices in eyre. They sit in the liberty, whether of Ramsey, Peterborough, Ely or St Edmunds; they call to account the steward and the bailiffs of the separate hundreds; they inspect the rolls of the coroners of the liberty, they inquire into all manner of crimes and trespasses committed within the liberty by the king's ministers and by others since the last eyre. But they are not infringing the liberty, safeguarded by charter. They may condemn the thief to be hanged, but they do not wish to deprive the abbot of his liberty of the gallows. Richard Canting, found guilty of theft in the eyre of Northampton in 1280, 'was delivered by the justices to the bailiffs of the abbot of Peterborough to be hanged, and as it was evening, and they could not take him to the gallows at Collingham, they borrowed the king's gallows and he was hanged there, but his chattels went to the lord abbot'.[4] So when the justices left the county, they delivered to the abbot a list of all the fines and amercements imposed, and the chattels of thieves, fugitives and outlaws, presented in the eyre, forfeit by right to the king, but granted by charter to the abbot.[5]

The very terms in which the lords of liberties claimed their privileges were the measure of their responsibilities. Richard I had granted to the abbot of Peterborough in the eight hundreds 'whatever the sheriff has in the king's hundreds'[6] and the abbot in 1230 claimed by colour of this charter 'whatever pertains to the sheriffdom'.[7] Even in the twelfth century, much more in the thirteenth and following centuries, the sheriff was liable to find himself in difficulties, and ultimately in the Fleet prison, if he failed to obey

[1] *Rot. Hund.* II. 189.   [2] *P.R.C.* p. 85.   [3] Ass. R. 1228, m. 49d.

[4] *Chron. Petroburgense*, p. 41.   [5] *Ibid.* pp. 119–24.

[6] *Ibid.* p. 125.   [7] *Ibid.* pp. 11–12.

orders from headquarters. So with the stewards and bailiffs of these great liberties; if they had the powers they took the risks of the sheriff. In the exchequer, before the justices in eyre—nay, even at the hands of their rival, the sheriff of the shire, they were liable to be called to account for the non-collection of·royal debts, for the non-enforcement of royal justice, for the non-execution of royal writs. The very wording of the writ of right itself, as Maitland pointed out long ago, made the lord of a private court a royal agent. The matter cannot be more briefly put than it is by the lord of a liberty, himself claiming his privileges in the eyre of Northampton in 1330. 'Robert of Ferrers, my predecessor,' he says, 'had the aforesaid hundred, pleas of *vee de naam*, execution of the lord king's writs and thus consequently was the lord king's servant—*minister domini regis*.'[1] If it has not been possible to sketch more than a rough outline of the administration of these ancient ecclesiastical liberties,[2] reason has at least, I hope, been given for recognizing their lords as the king's ministers—cogs in that magnificent machine built up by the practical genius of our Norman and Angevin kings.

[1] *Plac. Quo War.* p. 581.
[2] [For a full-length picture of the liberty of St Etheldreda, see Miller, *op. cit.* chapter vii.]

XIV

The Decline and Fall of English Feudalism[1]

The student of English history is for ever haunted by the difficulty of determining the sense in which he shall use the word *feudal*. The social, the economic, the legal and the constitutional historian approach it with different mental assumptions. To the social historian, the feudal age is, by contrast with the present day, above all the *Stufenkosmos* of Mitteis. The essence of feudalism, for him, is the consecration of inequality, the insistence on subordination, that *reverentia* which, according to Glanvill, differentiates the vassal's side of the relationship from the lord's. To the economic historian the heart of feudalism is in the disposal of material resources, the organization of the cultivation of land by the exercise of rights over persons. To the legal historian, though he also is concerned with both persons and land, the all-important matter is the contractual relationship— the terms of the bargains by which these relationships are regulated, in which land becomes, as M. Halphen has put it, the guarantee, the tool and the reward of service.[2] The lawyer, in fact, refuses to recognize feudalism until the conditional tenure of land is established, and status is determined by tenure. To the military historian, the essentials in feudalism are the feudal castle and the feudal horseman. The constitutional historian, concerned with the problems of government, sees in feudalism the organization of political life on a contractual basis: the feudal state is one in which landholding is the source of political power, in which the functions of government are bound up with the tenure of land; in which the theories of government are associated with those doctrines of obligation, of deference, of loyalty, which derive from the relationships of lord and vassal. Thus in studying different periods, the social, the economic, the legal and the constitutional historian will each apply his own test to the state of things he finds and declare that this is, or is not 'genuine feudalism', whilst his conclusions will be hotly questioned by those who use a different criterion.

[1] Read at the International Congress of Historical Sciences, Zürich, 1938. Reprinted from *History*, December 1940.
[2] *Revue Historique*, CLXXII. 249.

The student of the English constitution who adopts the generally accepted view that political feudalism was tamed and subjugated to the monarchy by the legal and administrative work of Henry II and Edward I, is confronted by the fact that feudalism was an unconscionable while in dying in England. Not only, as the legal historian will tell him, was English land law more feudal than that of any other country in Europe; not only did the feudal incidents of wardship, marriage and primer seisin survive until 1661; not only, as the economic historian points out, did the manorial courts for copyhold tenants survive into the nineteenth century; but he cannot overlook the franchisal courts, from the private hundred courts, of which fifty-five were still in existence in 1839, to the chancery court of the palatinate of Durham, which is still in existence to-day. And if he turns from the forms to the facts of feudalism, the constitutional historian finds that the magnates of the fifteenth century could command the support of bands of followers, in the law court or on the battle-field, to such an extent as to be able to undermine or defy the authority of the crown. How is this to be explained? Are we to write off the achievements of the two great Plantagenets as a failure and declare that feudalism was in effect the chief force in the state until the time of the Tudor kings?

If Edward I's attitude to feudal institutions be examined, it is clear that his legislation gives no evidence of a desire to eliminate feudalism from English land law; the statutes of *Mortmain*, *Quia Emptores* and *De donis* show that Edward was prepared to enforce his own rights as a landlord whilst safeguarding those of other landlords; the struggle to exact both scutage and fine from his military tenants shows him determined to exploit his feudal rights to the uttermost.[1] His policy with regard to the franchise rests on a different principle. Bracton had distinguished the regalian rights of the crown in matters of peace and justice from those which arose naturally out of the relationship of a lord to his tenants, and Edward I in the Statute of Gloucester and the Quo Warranto proceedings that followed it insisted that such rights could not arise naturally from the tenure of land, but could only be held by royal licence, whether explicit in a charter or implicit in long-tolerated exercise. The cases recently printed by Mr Sayles from the *Coram Rege* Rolls of Edward's reign[2]

[1] See H. M. Chew in *Eng. Hist. Rev.* 1922, pp. 321 ff.; 1923, pp. 19 ff.; *Ecclesiastical Tenants in Chief*, pp. 71 f., 156 f.

[2] *Select Cases in the Court of King's Bench* (Selden Soc.), II. liv.

make it clearer than ever that Edward's aim was not to revoke such franchises, but merely to insist on their definition and the recognition that they were held not absolutely, but conditionally. If the abbot of St Albans had the right to appoint his own coroner for the liberty of St Albans, he took on himself the responsibility for seeing that the coroner's rolls were duly kept, and that the coroner was available when required; when these conditions were not fulfilled the king took back the privilege and appointed a coroner himself.[1] If the bishop of Durham, the first franchise-holder of the kingdom, defied the royal authority and assaulted the king's messengers, he was told that the king's power extended within liberties as well as without, and that he, as the king's minister, was bound to uphold the king's law; and his liberty was taken into Edward's hands.[2] If the earls of Hereford and Gloucester took advantage of the Custom of the March to wage private war on each other, they were told that the Custom of the March existed for the safety of the realm and not for their private convenience: and the liberties were taken into the king's hands.[3] All through the reign the juries of the countryside were being invited to tell the king's justices in eyre what they knew of persons who had had liberties granted to them and had used them otherwise than the grant prescribed.

The term 'feudal' does not properly apply to these regalian jurisdictions. They do not arise out of the tenure of land, and they are exercised over persons who do not hold of the lord who enjoys them. They are franchisal, not feudal. But though Edward I's justices insisted over and over again that such rights could not arise from, or even be annexed to the lordship of the soil, they were in fact exercised by landholders, and the principle of the bargain or contract that these judgments enforce is of the very essence of feudalism. 'No privilege without a corresponding obligation' might have been Edward's motto, and if he took every advantage of the unique position of the crown, which, as M. Halphen has pointed out, can never be a vassal, and which retained from pre-feudal days an ultimate responsibility for justice and peace that could not be surrendered, he found in the maxims and ethics of feudalism an entirely adequate support for his policy. To call that policy anti-feudal is to cut him off from the air he breathed, from the

[1] A. E. Levett, *Studies in Manorial History*, p. 107.
[2] L. Ehrlich, in *Oxford Studies in Social and Legal History*, VI. 68, n. 2.
[3] *Rot. Parl.* I. 73–4.

medium in which he worked, from the political and legal assumptions of his whole life.

The franchises, then, were not perceptibly curtailed by Edward's policy. It was not in his interest to extinguish them; as Mitteis says of Philip Augustus, 'We can clearly recognize the tendency to convert the one-time fiefs into administrative districts governed by officials only, and thus to transform what threatened to be disintegration into decentralization under political control'.[1] The palatinate of Durham could serve his purpose as well as the palatinate of Chester. Even the Welsh Custom of the March might be useful.

But as the fourteenth century advances the doubt arises whether Edward I's work had in fact been done for good. His legal theory as to the franchises is upheld in the early eyres of Edward III,[2] but complaints in parliament suggest that the number and the actual powers of the franchises are on the increase. A petition of 1347 asserts that almost all the land is enfranchised, to the extinction of the common law and the oppression of the people. A petition of 1377 prays that general terms in charters of franchise may be more liberally interpreted, so as to give lords the right to hold possessory assizes without a specific grant. From 1378 to 1394 there are reiterated complaints of grants of franchises which throw an unfair financial burden on the unprivileged or geldable parts of the shire.[3] To what extent were new franchises being granted? and to what extent did their creation withdraw men from the operation of the common law?

Two distinct developments can in fact be traced. The financial grievance was genuine; the debts and difficulties bequeathed by Edward I to his heirs probably account for the practice, followed by all three Edwards, of rewarding or retaining royal adherents by the grant of profitable offices, notably the tenure of hundreds, and this caused hardship both to sheriffs and to the people of the shires who had to make up the missing revenue. But such districts were not cut off from the operation of the common law, even though their issues were diverted from the exchequer into private pockets, any more than they were exempt from statute law by their lords' refusal to contribute to the wages of county members of parliament.

---

[1] H. Mitteis, *Lehnrecht und Staatsgewalt*, p. 690.
[2] R. Keilwey, *Reports* (1688), pp. 137d–152.
[3] *Rot. Parl.* II. 166; III. 24, 45, 94, 222, 280, 290, 305, 321–4.

On the other hand, the greater franchises were undoubtedly con-
solidating their position both in theory and in practice. As the
definition of privilege was widening the gulf between the peerage
and the lesser baronage, so the palatinate was becoming distinct from
the lesser franchise. In the greatest liberties the lords had obtained
leave to imitate the procedure of the crown step by step, as it evolved.
Mr Lapsley has traced in detail this process in the bishopric of
Durham; how the bishop, beginning in 1209, secured the right first
to hold the possessory assizes, then to have his own justices for pleas
of the crown, for gaol delivery, for oyer and terminer; then his own
justice of the peace, his own exchequer and his own chancery. For
these 'regalities' a new term was becoming current, used first by
Bracton, it would seem with reference to the county of Chester:[1] a
palatinate. The writs in a palatinate ran not in the name of the king,
but in the name of the lord of the liberty: men were indicted as
breaking the peace not of the king but of the lord. By the fourteenth
century this status was sufficiently established to be deliberately conferred. In 1339 Edward III granted to Lawrence of Hastings the
same prerogative and honour of a *comes palatinus* in Pembroke that
Aymer of Valence had enjoyed; in 1351 he created for his cousin
Henry of Lancaster the county palatine of Lancaster which was
revived in 1377 for John of Gaunt. This appears to be the first
deliberate erection of a private chancery, which was granted to the
duke of Lancaster 'with whatsoever other liberties and regalian rights
belong to a county palatine'.[2] The term is now fully established;[3] the
bishop of Durham will claim the privilege of a *comes palatinus* in
1372, the archbishop of York will assert in 1414 that the liberty of
Hexhamshire is a palatinate, and the bishop of Ely will call the court
he holds for the *ban leuca* of Ely his *curia palacii*.[4] The mere existence
of the generic term helped to strengthen the self-assertion of the
great franchise-holders and diminish the sense of responsibility which
Edward I's *quo warranto* policy had inculcated. Murder, treason and
robbery went unpunished in Tynedale, Redesdale and Hexhamshire,
the commons of Northumberland asserted in 1414, because they were
so enfranchised and the king's writ did not run there.[5]

A similar flavour of vested interest and irresponsibility attaches to

---

[1] Bracton, fo. 122 d. 'qui regalem habeat potestatem…sicut sunt comites paleys'.
[2] W. Hardy, *Charters of Duchy of Lancaster*, pp. 9–11.
[3] Coke, *Fourth Inst.* cc. 38, 40, 41.
[4] [Miller, *op. cit.* pp. 221–5.]   [5] *Rot. Parl.* IV. 21.

a privilege which is found in most of the palatinates, but is not peculiar to them: the right of special sanctuary.[1] The privilege of offering a permanent asylum to the fugitive criminal enjoyed by many ancient shrines like Beverley, Westminster and Glastonbury, and also by some secular centres, like the sanctuaries of Cheshire, was being both abused and unwarrantably extended in the fourteenth century. Edward Balliol recruited his army from the lawless *grithmen* who were sheltering at Beverley, Ripon, Hexham, Tynemouth and Wetherhal sanctuaries; and the sanctuary men of Chester were a terror to the surrounding counties. In the more sophisticated setting of the capital, the sanctuaries of Westminster and St Martin's le Grand were beginning to offer a home not merely to the felon fleeing for his life, but to the fraudulent debtor evading his legal liabilities,[2] thus provoking from the lords of parliament in 1378 the protest that 'not God, saving his perfection, nor the Pope, saving his holiness, nor any king nor prince could grant such a privilege'. By 1394 the abbots of Colchester and Abingdon were claiming similar extensions of privilege.[3]

The clue to the extension of franchisal pretensions in the fourteenth century is in part at least supplied by the map. Apart from a few ancient ecclesiastical liberties, in which the power to exclude royal officials is limited to a small area surrounding the mother church— the *ban leuca* of Bury, Ramsey, Glastonbury and a few more[4]—the greatest franchises are located in the north and west. For this fact there are both historical and military reasons. The franchises of the northern counties may well have derived originally from pre-Conquest Northumbrian custom;[5] their survival into the sixteenth century is mainly due to the foreign policy of the Edwards and the Henries. The Scottish wars initiated by Edward I in 1295 continued on and off for two centuries, and kept the northern counties in a state that explains alike the creation of that wardenship of the Marches on which the power of the Nevilles and Percies was founded, the retention of the liberties of Tynedale, Redesdale, Hexham, Norham and Bedlington as recruiting grounds for the fighting forces,[6] and

---

[1] See R. H. Forster, 'Durham and North Country Sanctuaries', in *Journal of the British Archaeological Association*, 1905, pp. 118 ff.; J. C. Cox, *Sanctuaries and Sanctuary Seekers*.

[2] I. D. Thornley, 'Sanctuary in Medieval London', in *Journ. Brit. Arch. Assoc.* 1933, pp. 299–315.   [3] *Rot. Parl.* III. 37, 321.

[4] M. D. Lobel, 'The Ecclesiastical Ban leuca', in *Essays offered to H. E. Salter*, pp. 122–40.   [5] See W. Page, in *Archaeologia*, LI. 143–55.

[6] R. Reid, in *Eng. Hist. Rev.* 1917, pp. 487–90. See also the map in her *Council of the North*.

the preservation and hardening of the viceregal powers of the bishop of Durham. On the Welsh Marches, over a hundred lords had each his own chancery, claiming to hold his regalities by right of conquest and not by grant of the crown.[1] The historical fact underlying this claim is that the Anglo-Norman marcher lords had succeeded to the territories and rights of their Celtic predecessors, each a prince in his own lands.[2] Like the franchises of the great Benedictine abbeys, the privileges of these lordships were pre-feudal, but, unlike them, they were post-Conquest. They derived from no royal grant; the first marcher lords were 'conquerors in their own right of lands which had never been within the allegiance of the king',[3] and the Custom of the March had a sanction independent, in their eyes at least, of English law. The military justification for the retention of such special privileges, if it had ever been valid, had ceased to hold good after 1284, as the judgment of 1292 indicated, but Edward I's attempt to bring the Marches under royal law had been abandoned by his successors;[4] the marcher lords continued to settle their private disputes by private war and to maintain the Custom of the March intact within their own lordships. The gap between the northern and the western Marches was filled by the palatinates of Chester and Lancaster. In the greater part of this area 'the king's writ did not run': the authority officially recognized was that of the franchise-holder, great or small.

Yet even these areas were not completely withdrawn from the operation of the common law. The procedure of the king's courts was imitated in the palatinate courts, the stewards and justices who worked there frequently served the king at another stage of their official careers—and in the last resort appeal lay from these courts to the king's council, if not to his bench.

In the lesser franchises of the south and east—whether ecclesiastical franchises like those of Glastonbury, St Albans, Ramsey, Bury or Battle, or lay franchises like those of Clare, Bigod or de Fortibus, whose organization has been described by Mr Denholm-Young—there is the same assimilation of personnel and administration and a

[1] C. A. J. Skeel, *Council of the Marches of Wales*, pp. 1-10; G. T. Clark, *Cartae de ⁻lamorgan*, III. 818-21.

[2] W. Rees, *South Wales and the March*, 1284-1415, pp. 23-6. [See also A. J. Otway Ruthven in *Trans. R. Hist. Soc.*, 1958, pp. 1-20.]

[3] *Ibid.* p. 43.

[4] Mr Rees, however, suggests that Edward himself was to blame for his failure to convert the Welsh lands into true 'shires'. *Op. cit.* p. 33.

closer relation to royal government. The officials of the liberty are aware that they are the king's ministers as well as their lords. An abbot of Bury St Edmunds will take pride in the fact that his liberty has been holden 'the most notable franchise of good rule in the land'. As Mr Denholm-Young says: 'There was no difference in kind but one only of degree between the administrative problems that beset the barons and those of the King', and one notable development of the later Middle Ages brings this out well—the development of the baronial council.

Dr Rachel Reid first called attention to the councils of the great lords in 1921. Since Elizabeth Levett's article on Baronial Councils appeared in 1925 more evidence has been accumulating as to their activities. The records of the Duchy of Lancaster, of the Clare estates and of the Liberty of St Albans, to go no further,[1] indicate how these bodies of paid experts were, like the king's council, combining executive functions with something very much like an equitable jurisdiction, originating possibly, as Holdsworth suggests,[2] in the right of the lord to override custom in the case of unfree tenants, but clearly affecting freeholders also. The Durham records show that such justice might be eagerly sought by litigants,[3] and the petition against it which produced the statute of 1391[4] probably represents the view rather of the defendant than of the plaintiff. The St Albans evidence, stretching over a long period, suggests that as the free tenants more and more sought justice elsewhere and commuted their suits to the abbot's court for money payments, the feudal procedure of the court became transformed to the official and equitable procedure of conciliar jurisdiction.

Both the greater and the lesser franchises, then, showed in the later Middle Ages a power of adaptation to changing conditions, and of serving the needs of the times. The law administered in them differed in little from the common law of the realm; its administration was ultimately in the case of the palatinates, and more directly in the case of the other lordships, subordinated to the king's government. The system approximates pretty closely to the *politisch gebotene Dezentralisation* of Mitteis.

It was not the administrative rights of the franchises which en-

---

[1] N. Denholm-Young, *Seignorial Administration*, pp. 25–30; *Register of John of Gaunt* (Camden Series), I. nos. 1004, 1102, 1111, 1157, etc.; E. Levett, *Studies in Manorial History*, pp. 153–9.

[2] *Hist. of Eng. Law*, II. 378–9.   [3] Lapsley, *op. cit.* pp. 182 ff.

[4] 15 Ric. II, c. 12 (*Stat. Realm*, II. 82–3).

dangered royal authority in the fourteenth and fifteenth centuries. The state of affairs described by Plummer as 'bastard feudalism', by Holdsworth as 'the new feudalism' and characterized by M. Bloch as displaying all the essential features of feudalism, rests not on delegated authority, but on personal relationships, and has its root in economic, social and military developments.

The operation of the laws of inheritance and descent had brought about a vast accumulation of estates, the administration of which necessitated the organization of a great household system consisting of a host of paid dependents. The more efficiently a magnate administered his franchise, or exploited the material resources of his domains, the greater were the potentialities of his personal influence. To this must be added the effects of the wars in Scotland and France, which led to the growth of the system whereby lords contracted to supply the government with troops which they themselves secured by indenture, a practice, as has been recently shown, at least as old as 1297.[1] John of Gaunt's Register for 1370 to 1373 contains numerous examples of these contracts by which knights and squires bound themselves for life to a great lord, at a retaining fee in time of peace, augmented in time of war, with wages by the day for the duration of the campaign supplemented by a fixed share of the profits arising from prisoners' ransoms or loot.[2] But the retainers of a fourteenth-century magnate were not all soldiers; they ranged from legal experts 'feed of the lords council' to any humble neighbour who might be useful. The 600 liveried retainers of Thomas of Lancaster in 1314 included knights, squires, clerks and grooms.[3] The practice of clothing your adherents in a livery has been traced by Mrs Stenton as far back as 1218, when a certain north-country robber was reported as buying 100 marks' worth of cloth to clothe his following of fifteen men 'as if he had been a baron or an earl'.[4] The Cambridge parliament of 1388 was the first to legislate on the subject; and by 1393 it had become necessary to forbid yeomen below the rank of squire to wear livery of company unless they were resident in their lord's household.[5] It is not necessary to-day to insist upon the psychological importance of uniform-wearing. The abuses that became associated with the practice are forcibly expressed in the oath taken by all the members of parliament in 1433 from the king

[1] Denholm-Young, *op. cit.* pp. 23, 167–8. See also J. Conway Davies, *Baronial opposition to Edward II*, p. 50, n. 2. [2] *Op. cit.* nos. 775–870.
[3] *Eng. Hist. Rev.* 1927, p. 192. [4] *Eyre of York* (Selden Soc.), p. 424.
[5] *Stat. Realm*, II. 84.

downwards—'that no lord, by colour nor occasion of feoffment or of gift of movable goods shall take any other men's cause or quarrel in favour supportation or maintenance, as by word, by writing or by message to officer, judge, jury or party, by the gift of his clothing or livery or taking into his service the party, nor conceive against any judge or officer indignation or displeasure for doing of his office in form of law'.[1] Oaths and statutes were equally vain: the citizen who petitioned against the practice found himself forced to rely on it for self-protection and to 'get lordship'. Society was honeycombed by these new feudal contracts whereby a man in effect commended himself to a lord, and bound himself to love what he loved and loathe what he loathed.

The contrast between this new feudalism and the old lay firstly in the fact that from the legal point of view the contract between lord and man was no longer secured by land, and the stability of the tenurial relationship was thus lacking; and secondly that from the constitutional point of view the relationships operated not as a substitute for a national governmental system but within the framework of that system. The lord protected his dependent not by excluding government officials from his franchise, but by intimidating juries; by controlling sheriffs; by nominating justices of the peace or of oyer and terminer, or by getting himself put on the commissions. The dependent rendered his service in the shire court, on a jury, or in the witness-box, no less than as a member of an armed gang. The writs might run in the king's name, and the justices, sheriffs and juries might swear to uphold his government, but in fact the machinery of royal government was manipulated by the magnates, without liberties as well as within. If this is to be called feudalism, it is a parasitic institution, deriving its strength from a system hostile to itself, cut off from its natural roots in the soil, and far removed indeed from the atmosphere of responsibility, loyalty and faith which had characterized the relationship of lord and vassal in the earlier Middle Ages.

Sir John Fortescue put his finger on the economic basis of this power. His proposal for the resumption of franchises by the crown was in no way original; for sixty years a succession of acts with that purpose were being passed, but all loaded with exemptions that made them as futile as the measures against livery and maintenance. No effective remedy could come from a parliament dominated by the lords who were the first beneficiaries of the system which the

[1] *Rot. Parl.* IV. 421–2.

commons bewailed. The Yorkists made a beginning,[1] but it was left
to the Tudors to destroy the ascendancy of the landed aristocracy, to
restore the effective, as against the nominal ascendancy of the law,
within liberties as well as without, and to make royal administration
so efficient that the king's revenue was, as Fortescue had demanded,
greater than that of his wealthiest subject.

Of the means employed for this end the suppression of livery and
maintenance by Star Chamber methods and the confiscation of lands
of attainted rebels are familiar. Harrington in his *Oceana* indicated
the legislation by which economic and thus ultimately political power
was transferred from the old aristocracy to the new squirearchy.[2]
The aspects of Tudor policy which are examined below are the
insistence on the rights of the crown as feudal suzerain, the invocation
of a stricter interpretation of the legal theory of *quo warranto*, and
the abolition or absorption of those franchises which sheltered
lawlessness or opposed a barrier to the effective sovereignty of the
crown.

Fortescue had recommended a stricter enforcement of the royal
rights of wardship and marriage, and Richard III had anticipated
Henry VII in the sending out of commissioners to inquire into all
'lordships, manors, lands, advowsons, wards, marriages, reliefs, es-
cheats, and escapes of felons concealed from the king, and all
alienations of land without licence'.[3] From 1485 to 1508 these
inquests, in effect a revival of the oldest articles of the general eyre,
were being held from county to county,[4] including, as Mr Stewart
Brown pointed out, the county palatine of Chester.[5] Their efficiency
and unpopularity are attested by the protests of parliament and by the
surprised comments of the Venetian ambassadors on the amount of
revenue derived from this source,[6] as well as by the enthusiasm with
which the fall of Edmund Dudley was greeted when Henry VIII
disgraced him, as the indictment put it, 'for procuring of false
inquests of alienation to be found, making out that manors were
held in chief of the crown that were not, refusing livery of seisin
to heirs holding of the crown when they came of age unless they

[1] E.g., by the resumption of some of the northern franchises and the creation
of the palatinate of the Western March under Richard of Gloucester in 1482.
See *Rot. Parl.* VI. 204.
[2] 4 Hen. VII, cc. 12, 19; 7 Hen. VII, c. 2; J. Harrington, *Oceana* (1737), p. 69.
[3] *P.R.C.* 1476–85, p. 543.
[4] See D. Brodie in *Trans. R. Hist. S.* 1932, pp. 156–8; and *P.R.C.* 1485–94, pp. 133–4,
415; 1494–1509, pp. 33, 66, 420–4.   [5] *Eng. Hist. Rev.* 1934, pp. 676 ff.
[6] A. F. Pollard, *Reign of Henry VII*, II. 23–7.

paid extortionate fines'.[1] But Henry VIII had his own methods for achieving similar results; as Holdsworth and Plucknett have shown, the Statute of Uses in 1536 was the outcome of a long struggle with the aristocracy to prevent the evasion of feudal dues by the device of enfeoffment to uses,[2] a device employed as early as 1405 and unsuccessfully attacked by Henry VII in the statutes of 1489 and 1504. The statute of 1536 fixed the responsibility for the payment of feudal dues on the beneficiary of the use, and Miss Brodie has shown that the court of Wards and Liveries, set up in 1540 to take over from chancery the administrative, fiscal and judicial work of enforcing the feudal incidents, had been anticipated by Henry VII's short-lived *supervisor of the Prerogative* who fell with Empson and Dudley.[3]

The second line of attack on feudal irresponsibility can also be associated with Edmund Dudley, though it did not originate with him. His law-reading on the Statute of Quo Warranto, discovered by Miss Putnam and now being edited by Miss Brodie,[4] might well be a programme for the attack upon the franchises by the Tudor judges. But the campaign had begun before he gave his lecture; Keilwey's *Reports* and Brooke's and Fitzherbert's *Abridgements* contain the cases on which his doctrine is based. Miss Thornley has told of the struggle with the sanctuaries,[5] beginning under the Yorkists by administrative methods such as registration, but carried on by Henry VII with the collaboration of pope and of lawyers. A philosopher like More might defend sanctuary as a refuge for the political offender;[6] practical statesmen could only applaud the judgment in Stafford's case in 1487, which abolished the protection which had been legally accorded to the traitor by the special sanctuary since 1388.[7] To pardon treason, the judges declared, belongs to the king alone, and no sanctuary can give more than temporary protection in

---

[1] Coke, *Fourth Inst.* c. 35.

[2] Holdsworth, *Hist. of Eng. Law*, IV. 443–67, 579–80; *Trans. R. Hist. S.* 1936, pp. 121 ff.

[3] *Trans. R. Hist. S.* 1932, pp. 158–9; Holdsworth, *Hist. of Eng. Law*, I. 409; *Rot. Cal.* 1494–1509, p. 591. See also W. C. Richardson in *Eng. Hist. Rev.* 1941, pp. 52–75.

[4] I am deeply in Miss Brodie's debt both for many valuable references and for her great kindness in allowing me to consult her transcript of Dudley's Reading, from Camb. Univ. Lib. M.S. Hh. 3. 10.

[5] *Tudor Studies*, ed. F. Seton Watson, pp. 199 f.

[6] More, *History of Richard III*, ed. Lumby, p. 28.

[7] *Journ. Brit. Arch. Assoc.* 1933, p. 306.

treason.[1] This was only one of the series of judgments by which the legal basis of title to franchise was being restricted under Henry VII. Dudley's doctrines[2] as to the forfeiture of liberties for non-use, for abuse, for non-claim, for false claim, for failure to prove prescription for one type of liberty, to produce a charter in another or to establish allowance in the eyre for yet another can all be illustrated in the Yearbooks. The case of the abbot of Battle in 1494,[3] for instance, when it was ruled that a charter of William the Conqueror gave no title because it was before the time of legal memory, and that a recent allowance of the liberty in the Common Bench gave no title because it was not in the general eyre, forms a significant contrast to the case of St Martin's le Grand in 1440, when the two chief justices had said that allowance of the liberty in eyre was unnecessary since the king could not resume a franchise granted by William the Conqueror.[4] Thus interpretations of the law of Quo Warranto far stricter than those of Edward I's or Edward II's justices were threatening the existence of the franchises well before Henry VIII and Cromwell launched their direct attack in the Reformation Parliament.

The note of battle is first sounded in the undated report on the northern franchises sent in to Cromwell in 1534, which stated that 'the king's rights are attacked by all manner of liberties, his felons and outlaws are clothed and maintained by stewards and bailiffs of liberties, so that his process has no place, and his laws are not dreaded'.[5]

The Welsh marcher franchises were, however, the first to be tackled. Four acts of 1534 struck at their practice of sheltering escaped felons, giving the neighbouring county officials and justices of the peace power to demand the surrender of such fugitives.[6] In 1536 the act 'for making the laws of Wales the same as those of England' extinguished the Custom of the March, absorbed some 136 lordships into five new shires and brought both old and new shires under the English administrative and judicial system.[7]

---

[1] *Yearbook of 1 Hen. VII*, Pasch. pl. 15; Trin. pl. 1.

[2] Camb. Univ. Lib. MS. Hh. 3. 10, ff. 11 d–17.

[3] *Yearbooks of 9 Hen. VII*, Mich. pl. 6; cf. *2 Hen. VII*, Mich. pl. 1, *16 Hen. VII*, Trin. pl. 17.

[4] B.M. MS. Lansdowne 170, ff. 95–95 v. Cited by Miss Thornley, *Journ. Brit. Arch. Assoc.* 1933, p. 310.

[5] *Letters and Papers of Henry VIII*, VII. no. 1669.

[6] 26 Hen. VIII, cc. 4, 5, 6, 11.

[7] 27 Hen. VIII, c. 26.

In February 1536 Cromwell had noted as matters to be discussed with the king for parliament 'specially to speak of the utter destruction of sanctuary. Item for the dissolution of all franchises and liberties throughout the realm, especially the franchise of spirituality.'[1] By April, besides the Welsh act, there had been passed an act drastically restricting, though not utterly destroying, sanctuary rights,[2] and the act 'for recontinuing certain liberties heretofore taken from the crown', by which the power to pardon crimes, the power to appoint justices in eyre, justices of assize, justices of gaol delivery and justices of the peace and power to issue writs, original or judicial, was taken away from every subject.[3] Henceforth no man could be said to break the peace of any one but the king. 'The most ancient prerogatives and authorities of justice appertaining to the imperial crown of this realm that had been taken from it by sundry gifts of the king's progenitors to the detriment of the royal estate and the hindrance and delay of justice' were restored to it. The palatinates had lost their viceregal character; henceforth all stewards and bailiffs of franchises were to come under the same regulations as the ordinary officials of the shire. The surrender of the greater monasteries in the years 1536–39 wiped out the greater number of the ecclesiastical liberties, for the lay successors to the abbots' lands received them with greatly lessened privileges.

Revolutionary as was the work of the Reformation Parliament, feudal and franchisal administration had still a long period of life and, one must suppose, usefulness before it. The courts of the duchy of Lancaster, of Chester, of Durham and of Ely were expressly retained by the act of 1536, though the writs of the local chanceries ran in the king's name and the justices were appointed by him. Chester and Lancaster, as we have seen, were in the hands of the crown; Durham would probably have been converted into an ordinary shire on the death of its bishop if he had not happened to outlive Henry VIII. But in fact it was not until the nineteenth century that these 'peculiars' in local government ceased to function. The clue to their survival is to be found in the protest of the inhabitants of Durham in 1688 against the abolition of the palatinate: they said, 'We were and are born to the sure use and enjoyment of the laws of the county (which are and always have been conformable to the laws of the land) distributed at our doors'.[4] In fact, 5084 writs

---

[1] *Letters and Papers of Henry VIII*, x. no. 254.   [2] 27 Hen. VIII, c. 19.
[3] 27 Hen. VIII, c. 24.   [4] W. Hutchinson, *Durham*, I. 561.

issued out of the Durham chancery between 1825 and 1836 and 150 pleas were heard in the Palatinate Court.[1] So, in 1771, Bentham could write of the bishop of Ely's court of pleas that 'for the bishop it was a matter of prestige rather than profit, but for the inhabitants it was a matter of great convenience since they had justice administered, as it were, at their very doors in all pleas of the crown; and in most civil cases they need not, unless they thought fit, have recourse to any other place for justice than the bishop's court'.[2] The same argument applies to the Courts of Great Sessions which functioned for Wales after the abolition of the marcher lordships, and to the Court of Duchy Chamber of Lancaster which continued to function down to 1835. Until the county courts were set up in the nineteenth century, the courts of the franchises were undoubtedly serving a useful purpose, and the enduring quality of medieval administrative arrangements is attested by the fact that the boundaries of the old monastic franchises are still retained in some cases for the county administrative districts of to-day.[3]

One feature of the palatinates of special interest is their relation to parliament. We have seen that the commons had complained in the fourteenth century that residents in the franchises did not bear their fair share of members' expenses. In Cambridgeshire the contribution of the Isle of Ely was already held to be a third in 1338, and this was compounded for by a payment of £200 in 1431.[4] In the county of Lancaster the practice of representation was established before the creation of the palatinate, and the charter of 1351 empowered the duke to send two members to parliament for the county and two for the borough. Mr Richardson has recently shown how John of Gaunt applied this privilege.[5] Wales and the Welsh Marches were given representation by the act of 1536, and seven years later, the inhabitants of the county palatine of Chester petitioned for representation and obtained it.[6] Durham remained unrepresented until the Commonwealth. Down to 1603 the residents in the palatinate had been exempt from taxation also, in consideration of their hazards and services in Scottish wars, but the Union had removed that pretext. Petitions for representation in 1614, 1623 and 1627, in which

---

[1] *Parl. Papers*, 1836, XLIII. 161–2.

[2] Jas. Bentham, *History and Antiquities of Church of Ely*, 1812, Appendix, p. 25*.

[3] E.g., the isle of Ely, the Soke of Peterborough, and Western Suffolk (Bury St Edmunds).   [4] See below, p. 243.

[5] *Bulletin of John Rylands Library*, 1938, pp. 175–222.

[6] 34 Hen. VIII, c. 13 (*Stat. Realm*, III. 911).

the plea of 'no taxation without representation' was urged by the inhabitants of the palatinate 150 years before the American colonists, were rejected.[1] A petition of 1653 was successful, but in 1660 the inhabitants again lost their members and a fresh agitation began in 1666.[2] Bishop Cosin resisted their demand vigorously, informing them that they were very lucky to be exempt from representation: a bill introduced into parliament was defeated in 1668 by sixty-five to fifty, and it was only during the vacancy of the see that occurred after his death that the borough and county of Durham finally obtained representation in 1672.[3]

The history of Scottish feudalism[4] is illuminating in its similarities and contrasts with English feudalism. The legal theory is more clear cut, the beginning and ending of the system more definite, and the political importance is greater, because the crown failed to secure its own position either by evolving a strong central bureaucracy or by retaining or recovering an adequate royal demesne. Something like the *Leihe-zwang* of the Empire seems to be operative. The lords to whom rights of public justice were granted by the Scottish kings in the twelfth century not only retained their regalities intact, but kept the right to delegate those powers which the English barons lost before the end of the twelfth century; they retained the power to hear appeals from their vassals' courts which the English barons lost in the thirteenth century; they retained down to the seventeenth century the power to hear pleas of the sword and to inflict capital punishment by gallows and pit.[5] Dalrymple, writing in 1758, said, 'In the declension of almost every part of the feudal system the English have gone before us'. An act of 1455 to prohibit further grants of jurisdiction was not observed; at the time of the Reformation the forfeited ecclesiastical franchises were re-granted undiminished to the new secular landlords; Cromwell's attempt to discipline the feudal courts was only partially successful,[6] and it took

---

[1] *Vict. Co. Hist., Durham*, II. 167 f.

[2] W. Hutchinson, *Durham*, I. 539–47; *Vict. Co. Hist., Durham*, II. 172.

[3] 25 Car. II, c. 9 (*Stat. Realm*, V. 795).

[4] For Scottish feudalism, see especially John Dalrymple, *An essay towards a general history of feudal property in Great Britain*, 1758 (2nd ed.); and W. C. Dickinson's introductions to *The Court Book of the Barony of Carnwath* and *The Sheriff Court Book of Fife*, Scottish Hist. Soc. 1937, 1938.

[5] Dalrymple, *op. cit.* p. 235; *Court Book of Barony of Carnwath*, pp. xxvi, liii.

[6] See *Minutes of Barony Court of Stitchell* (1655–1807), ed. G. Green and *Forbes Barony Court Book* (1659–78), ed. J. M. Thomson, Scottish Hist. Soc. 1905, 1919.

two Jacobite risings to bring about the abolition of hereditary jurisdictions in 1747.

Undoubtedly the greater activity both of the regalities (the Scottish equivalents of the palatinates), and of the baronies with less
exalted jurisdiction is partly due to the absence of a royal judicial
system comparable to the English. The chief justiciarship of Scotland
was hereditary down to the eighteenth century; the justice of the
peace was only introduced into Scotland in 1609.[1] If the rolls of the
Scottish barony courts of the sixteenth and seventeenth centuries be
compared with those of contemporary English manorial courts their
greater competence and activity are at once evident; the technique
of the feudal court is functioning effectively in dealing with the
problems of local justice and local administration where in England,
in spite of the additional duties imposed on the leet jury by Tudor
legislation,[2] the business tends to become more and more formal.
Neither the presentment of nuisances by a jury nor the transfer of
copyholds before a steward involved judicial activity; in the seventeenth century feudal jurisdiction in England was really a thing of
the past, whilst the feudal incidents whose existence had been
artificially prolonged by Tudor policy, having contributed to the
unpopularity of James I's and Charles I's government, were finally
abolished in 1660 as part of the financial settlement of Charles II.

To what extent, then, are we to consider feudalism as an operative
reality in England from the fourteenth to the seventeenth centuries?

To the administrative historian it is clear that during the later
Middle Ages the monarchy preserved feudal forms of government
to serve its own ends. As in the earliest days of feudalism, conditions
in the north and west still demanded decentralization and devolution
of government, both military and civil. But the fact that a national
system of royal government existed made it possible to enforce the
feudal contract by non-feudal machinery when necessary. Only on
the Welsh Marches is there any real retrogression; Edward I's claim
that the powers of the marcher lords derived from royal grant and
not from conquest, and that the law of England was superior to the
Custom of the March was not upheld. In the south and east the
feudal and franchisal jurisdictions were part and parcel of the national
system of administration, their functions being recognized and utilized
by the royal government.

[1] Dalrymple, *op. cit.* pp. 240 ff.
[2] Holdsworth, *Hist. of Eng. Law*, I. 137.

But if we turn from the framework of government to the forces moving within it, it is clear that the French wars had produced a revival of the political and social power of the landed aristocracy which in its turn exploited the forms of national government and abused and distorted royal justice. Royal officials became the tools of baronial power. Not till the crown had recovered control of its own machinery could the 'new feudalism' be exorcised. Then the Tudors could with one hand enforce half-obsolete feudal obligations on their tenants in chief, and with the other resume those regalities which, like the privileges and alien loyalties of the church, endangered the unique sovereignty of the crown. Their modifications of the land law and their redistribution of landed property released new social and economic forces which operated in the same direction.

The legislation of Henry VII and Henry VIII, followed by the suppression of the two great northern rebellions, killed political feudalism and dealt a mortal blow to economic and social feudalism. The forms of feudalism survived in administration till the nineteenth century and in the land law till the twentieth century. But the real forces of national life were moving in other channels, and if a traditional deference to the great landholders dominated English society well into the nineteenth century, the balance of economic and political power had long before that been transferred to other hands.

XV

The relation of English Members of Parliament to their constituencies in the Fourteenth Century: a neglected text[1]

In spite of all that has been written about the early history of representative institutions in England, we still know very little about the actual relations between the representatives and the communities whom they represented, or, to use modern language, between the members of parliament and their constituencies. We know more about the theory of representation than about its practice, and our approach to the theory is more often from the side of the central government than from that of the locality, more often from the historical than from the contemporary standpoint.

There are four aspects of this relationship on which some work has been done of recent years, though there is still a wide field for inquiry. The first is of pivotal constitutional importance, and has long been the subject of study; it is the power of the members to bind the communities that elected them. On the association of representation with consent to taxation depends the sovereignty of the British parliament. The latest contribution to this question as it bears on the relation of the member to his constituency is Mr J. G. Edwards' essay which appeared in 1932[2] on the formula *cum plena potestate* in the parliamentary writs of summons. He pointed out that Pasquet was not justified in saying that contemporary chronicles made no reference to the practice of representation; the chronicler Bartholomew Cotton in 1294 had observed 'vocati sunt milites de quolibet comitatu qui haberent potestatem obligandi comitatum'; and by a comparison of the formulae used he showed how the principle was defined and established that the knights had power to bind their shires to the payment of the taxes to which they had assented.

---

[1] Reprinted from *L'Organisation corporative du Moyen Age à la fin de l'Ancien Régime: études présentées à la Commission internationale pour l'histoire des Assemblées d'états*, III, Louvain, 1939.

[2] *Oxford Essays in Mediaeval History presented to H. E. Salter* (Oxford, 1932), pp. 141 ff.

It is possible that this relationship between electors and elected was expressed in commissions, sealed with the borough seal, which the burgesses brought with them to parliament, giving them full powers to act, though even so we find the burgesses of King's Lynn referring to their constituents during a session and asking for further instructions.[1]

In the second place it has been suggested that the electing body entrusted to their representatives petitions to be delivered to the king in parliament. Dr Ludwig Riess considered this the main purpose for which representation was introduced by the English kings, and Dr Pasquet accepts his view that the most important function of the members was to report to the central government the grievances of the localities, especially against the officials of the crown. This function, however, has been assumed rather than proved. It is quite certain that petitions could be and were presented to the king at 'parliaments' to which no representatives had been summoned. On the other hand, when representatives did attend, we cannot prove that, to begin with, they regarded the presentation of petitions as part of their duty. Mr George Haskins has recently investigated, for the last seventeen years of the reign of Edward I, the question of how far the representatives who attended parliaments actually presented petitions.[2] In this period 11 parliaments were attended by representatives, and 63 petitions from constituencies are still in existence. Of the 37 shires represented, 15 sent in petitions; of the 165 boroughs, 40 sent in petitions. But there is absolutely no evidence that these petitions were presented by the elected representatives of the shires and boroughs. Twelve petitions were indeed presented by members of parliament, but these concerned their own private interests and not the affairs of the community they represented. It seems quite possible that they did deliver petitions from their communities, and also from individuals living in those communities, but it has not been proved. The only references yet noticed of the choice of representatives to state the grievances of a community suggest that these were *ad hoc* delegates, not the members already elected by royal command. In 1290 the poor men of Norfolk petitioned *per procuratos juratores*;[3] in 1299 four men were chosen by the mayor and aldermen of London 'ad prosequendum negotia civitatis coram rege

---

[1] M. McKisack, *Representation of English boroughs* (Oxford, 1932), pp. 130–1.
[2] *Eng. Hist. Rev.* 1938, pp. 1–20.
[3] *Ibid.* p. 15.

et consilio in parliamento'.[1] For the reign of Edward I, at least, investigation has failed to produce evidence that the members presented petitions in parliament from their communities. Constitutionally speaking, the common petition presented in parliament is so much more important than the petitions from the separate communities that it is not surprising that comparatively little attention has been paid to the question of the private petition brought up ready made from the constituency. In the fourteenth century however there is more evidence. Miss McKisack has found accounts in the town records of Norwich, King's Lynn, Cambridge and London of the elected representatives being requested to promote petitions in parliament (assisted, it is true, by other burgesses),[2] as well as carrying out various kinds of business on behalf of their boroughs.[3] At the end of the fourteenth century it was certainly considered the duty of members to present the grievances of their constituencies in parliament.

This is made clear, amongst other sources, by a political poem of the date 1403–6 which has been recently discovered,[4] the main theme of which is the superiority of honest truth-telling to diplomatic silence as to defects in Church and State. The *Sothsegger* (truth-teller) is told that:

Of all the mischief and misrule that grows in the kingdom *Mum* (silence) has been the maker these many years, and I will prove this above all from parliament. When knights have come for the commons to a parliament, and are assembled to show forth the sores of the kingdom, they should not spare their speech, but should lance the boils and swellings of the heart, and let out the evil matter, lest the abscess fester inwards. Only by letting out gall and anger will healing come. It were better to burst out thus rather than to rise against the royal power and trouble the kingdom.... The great men and the men of the shires have refrained from speaking in the place that is provided for the discussion of the affairs of the realm and the amending of faults; they will not speak of difficult matters for fear of the peril that might fall, they hide their grievances and let silence rule their assembly, and they bring home again a bagful of unhealed sores that must needs continue to afflict them.[5]

[1] *Interim Report of the Committee on House of Commons personnel and politics* (London, 1932), p. 66, note h.
[2] McKisack, *Representation of English boroughs*, pp. 134–6.
[3] *Ibid.* pp. 136–9. See also *Rot. Parl.* I. 444 (1309).
[4] *Mum and the Sothsegger* (E.E.T.S.), London, 1936. The editors consider this to be the work of the same poet who wrote the fragment discussed below, which appears to have been written 1399–1400, and print the two together as two fragments of one long poem.
[5] *Mum and the Sothsegger*, lines 1115–40. See below, p. 233.

A third possible function of the members in relation to their constituencies that still awaits investigation is that of serving as publicity agents. There were, no doubt, other agencies for spreading the news. Two early reports of parliaments are known; one the famous letter written from Oxford in 1258 describing the proceedings of the baronial reformers there, ending: 'Ferociter procedunt barones in agendis suis; utinam bonum finem sortiantur!' [1] This was copied with other documents into the chronicle of Burton Abbey, but whether it was private or for general consumption one cannot say. The second report was found recently by Mr Richardson and Mr Sayles among the *Parliamentary and Council Proceedings* at the Public Record Office, and printed by them in the *English Historical Review* of last July. [2] It describes the doings of the parliament held at Carlisle in March 1307. It is headed *Noueles de parlement*, and does not appear to derive from an official source. Its editors believe that it was a commercial production; a news letter, directed probably to an ecclesiastical public. Unlike the Oxford letter it does not appear to be supporting any faction or pushing any view: it is not a piece of propaganda. On the other hand, it would seem that the possibility of using the elected representatives as agents of propaganda was realized at an early date, both by the crown and by its opponents the magnates. In 1327, in the first parliament held after the deposition of Edward II, the commons, after taking an oath to uphold the new regime, asked for written records of what had been done in the parliament, and granted by the king and council, to carry back to their shires for proclamation by the sheriffs. [3] In like manner, the deposition of Richard II was supported by the widespread circulation of the tendencious narrative enrolled on the roll of Henry IV's first parliament—a well known example of particularly successful propaganda. [4] But the use of representatives as publicity agents originated, it would seem, with the crown. In 1261 Henry III commanded the presence of representatives of the shires 'that they might see and understand for themselves that he was only aiming at the welfare of the whole community'. [5] In 1275 Edward I summoned knights to his first parliament, not to take an active

---

[1] *Annales Monastici* [R.S.], I. 443–5.   [2] *Eng. Hist. Rev.* 1938, pp. 436–7.
[3] *Rot. Parl.* II. 10b. For the circulation of the documents see *Rotuli parliamentorum Anglie hactenus inediti* (Camden Series), p. 100; *Bulletin of the Institute of Historical Research*, XIV. 146. I owe these references to the kindness of Mr H. G. Richardson.   [4] *Eng. Hist. Rev.* 1937, pp. 40 f.
[5] Stubbs, *Select Charters* (9th ed.), p. 395.

part in drawing up the great Statute of Westminster I, but rather
to hear and understand the reforms in local government which it
contained, and to carry back to the community of the shire the explanation of the new provisions for restraining the corruptions and
oppressions of their sheriffs.[1] In 1283 and again in 1295 and 1307
Edward I was undoubtedly, like his contemporary Philippe le Bel,
making use of the representative system for propaganda purposes;
demonstrating to the communities of shire and borough, on whose
material assistance he was bound to rely, the justice of his own cause
against the villainy of his enemy, whether that enemy were David of
Wales,[2] Philip of France,[3] or the Pope himself.[4] The knights and
burgesses were to carry back to their constituencies what they had
learnt at the fountain head of these high matters of national policy.

As regards the thirteenth century we have no proof that the suggestion I have just made is valid: it is merely a plausible hypothesis.
For the fourteenth century there is a little more evidence. Tout, in
his essay on *The English parliament and public opinion* in the *Mélanges
offerts à Henri Pirenne*,[5] referred to two valuable descriptions of
parliamentary sessions, the one of 1376, the other of 1388. The first
reads like the narrative of an eyewitness, probably a Yorkshireman,
who sat in the Westminster chapterhouse with the elected representatives,[6] and his narrative, at once vivid and ingenuous, gives a
very good notion of the report that a member might have carried
back to his constituents of the speeches and proceedings of the commons in the Good Parliament of 1376. We see the knights pro-
ceeding in turn to the lectern in the midst of the chapterhouse,
murmuring a prayer before they begin, and ending with another.[7]
We also note how the writer conveys the impression that the choice
of Peter de la Mare as speaker for the commons is entirely due to the
excellence of his speech: 'par cause qe le dite sire Peire de la Mare
fuist si bien parlaunt et si sagement rehersaunt les maters et purpose
de ses compaignouns et les enfourmant pluis avaunt qils mesmes ne

[1] It should be noted that the wording *discretioribus in lege* given in *E.H.R.* xxv.
236 (1910) is incorrect; the originals at the P.R.O. read *discretioribus et legalioribus*.
C.219/File 1, No. 1.   [2] *Ibid.* pp. 460–61.
[3] *Ibid.* pp. 480–81.   [4] *Rot. Parl.* i. 219.
[5] *Mélanges offerts à Henri Pirenne*, pp. 545 ff. (Brussels, 1926), reprinted in Tout,
Collected Papers, ii. 173–90 (Manchester, 1934).
[6] He was perhaps a clerk of the chancery. See *Eng. Hist. Rev.* 1938, p. 581.
[7] *The Anonimalle Chronicle*, ed. V. H. Galbraith, pp. 79–92 (Manchester, 1927).
See also A. F. Pollard, in *Eng. Hist. Rev.* 1938, pp. 577 ff.

savoient', whereas the more detached chronicler John Malvern explains that the commons were secretly instigated by the prince of Wales,[1] whose effective agent in the parliament, the earl of March, was the master of Peter de la Mare.

The other reporter who conveys to his readers exactly that view of the proceedings which was desired by the baronial opposition is Thomas Favent, who described the doings of the Marvellous Parliament of 1388.[2] He, however, was describing the events in *pleno parlamento*, not the debates in 'the old meeting place of the commons', and he was almost certainly not a representative.

References to reports made by members to the boroughs who elected them have been noted by Miss McKisack in the archives of London, King's Lynn, Colchester, Grimsby, Norwich and Shrewsbury.[3] The earliest mention of such a report is for London in 1328; the fullest accounts come from King's Lynn, where the descriptions suggest that the return of the representatives from parliament brought 'numbers of burgesses to the Gildhall to hear the news and to learn what they were to be asked to pay'.[4] The reports went into such details as the text of the sermon preached at the opening of parliament.[5]

The last aspect of the relationship which I would mention is the payment of wages by the electing communities to their representatives. The standard rate that they were authorized to claim by royal writ was, as is well known, four shillings a day for the knights and two shillings a day for the burgesses, but Miss McKisack has shown that some boroughs paid as little as one shilling and others as much as twenty shillings a day at times.[6] Other writers have investigated the way in which the money was raised in the shires to provide the salaries of the knights.[7]

So far I have been summarizing the work of other scholars and indicating the gaps in our knowledge; my main object, however, in discussing this subject was to call attention to a source which has been, in my opinion, most strangely neglected by historians, though

[1] Higden, *Polychronicon*, VIII. 386.
[2] *Historia...Mirabilis Parliamenti...per Thomam Fauent*, ed. M. McKisack, in *Camden Miscellany*, vol. XIV (London, 1926).
[3] McKisack, *Representation of English boroughs*, pp. 139–44.
[4] *Ibid.* p. 140.   [5] *Ibid.* p. 141.
[6] *Ibid.* pp. 82–99.
[7] L. C. Latham, *Eng. Hist. Rev.* 1933, p. 455; E. C. Lowry, *ibid.* p. 443; S. B. Chrimes, *ibid.* 1934, p. 306. See below, pp. 236–250, for a fuller discussion.

it has been available in print for nearly eighty years.[1] It is the description by a poet of a parliament of Richard II's reign, and though it is rather, I believe, a satirist's description of a typical parliament than a historical account of the parliament that met in 1397 or 1398, it is obviously as much the work of an eyewitness as the narrative of the Yorkshireman who described the house of commons in 1376. The date when the poem was written can be fixed by internal evidence between August 1399 and February 1400; Richard has been deposed but is still alive. The poem has been printed thrice: by Wright in 1859 in the *Rolls Series*,[2] by Skeat in 1886[3] and by Day and Steele in 1936, for the Early English Text Society.[4] The poet is echoing the manner of the author of *Piers Plowman*, but his attitude is recognizably different; he is a political satirist, with a keen eye for individual characteristics rather than a theologian and moralist, concerned with types.

The poem consists of a prologue, three *passus* and the fragment of a fourth. After referring to the execution of Richard's favourites and the welcome with which Henry was received when he landed in Yorkshire, the poet exhorts Richard to repent—'Now Richard the *Redeles*,[5] reweth on yourself'—and tells him how he has lost the love of his people by lawlessness, extortion and choice of evil counsellors; by the gangs of liveried servants and of overdressed courtiers and violent lawbreakers. The fourth *passus* shows how extravagant expenditure compelled Richard to summon a parliament. Neither fines, forfeitures, feefarms, wardships, profits of the law courts, revenues of the crown lands, nor the wool customs were sufficient, says the poet,[6] for the upkeep of Richard's household, without his applying to a parliament for a grant of tonnage and poundage and for a tenth and fifteenth. The money bags were empty and had to be refilled. So, to translate the middle English of the poem into the language of to-day:[7]

[1] But see A. R. Myers in *University of Toronto Law Journal*, 1939, p. 67.

[2] T. Wright, *Political songs*, 1. 368 ff.. under the title 'On the deposition of Richard II'.

[3] As *Richard the Redeles*, in Skeat's edition of Langland's *Works*, vol. 1.

[4] By Mabel Day and Robert Steele under the title *Mum and the Sothsegger*, pp. 1–26.

[5] *Redeles* = without counsel, ill-advised.

[6] Day and Steele, *Mum and the Sothsegger*, p. 23.

[7] Passus IV, lines 24–93. See below, pp. 233–5. Miss D. Everett, of Lady Margaret Hall, Oxford, has very kindly assisted me with this rendering.

Richard made schemes with his council by night to have a privy parliament to get money for himself. He had writs close sent to the peers and prelates summoning them to appear, and letters patent to the sheriffs to elect such knights as would undertake the duty of representing the shires in company with the great men.

When the day for action arrived, the lords were assembled and also the knights of the shire. According to the usual form, the cause of meeting was first declared and then the king's will. A clerk began with a dignified speech setting forth the main points before them all, and asking above all for money, with flattery to the great men to avert complaints. When the speech was ended, the knights of the commons were commanded to meet on the morrow, before dinner, with the citizens of the shires [1] to go through the articles which they had just heard and grant all that had been asked them. But to save appearances, and in accordance with custom, some of them falsely argued at some length, and said: 'We are servants and we draw a salary, we are sent from the shires to make known their grievances, to discuss matters on their behalf and to stick to that, and only make grants of their money to the great men in a regular way, unless there is war. If we are false to the people who pay our wages, we are not earning them.'

Some members sat there like a nought in arithmetic, that marks a place but has no value in itself. Some had taken bribes, so that the shire they represented had no advantage from their presence [in parliament]. Some were tattlers, who went to the king and warned him against men who were really good friends of his and deserved no blame either from king, council or commons, if one listened carefully to the very end of their speeches. Some members slumbered and slept and said little. Some stammered and mumbled and did not know what they meant to say. Some were paid dependents, and were afraid to take any step without their masters' orders. Some were so pompous and dull-witted that they got hopelessly involved before they reached the end of their speeches, and no one, whether he sat on the bench [2] or whether he was a burgess, could have made out what they wanted to say, there was so little sense in it.

And some of them dashed ahead so recklessly that, like a ship driven by the wind, they would have gone on the rocks, had not the lords warned

[1] The only justification for this strange description is that the poet professes to be a native of Bristol, which had been made a county in 1373.

[2] This phrase might mean: 'Whether he were as learned as a justice of the bench'. On the other hand Mr H. G. Richardson, to whose comments I am much indebted, suggests that the knights of the shire may have sat on benches, while the burgesses were expected to stand. There is so far no evidence for this most interesting suggestion, but compare S. C. Russell, in *American Historical Review*, Oct. 1937.

the master[1] that they had better keep to subjects which were their own business and which they understood; then they lowered their sails and took a wiser course.

Some had been got at beforehand by the council, and knew well enough how things would have to end, or the assembly would be sorry for it. Some went with the majority, whichever way they went, while some would not commit themselves. Some were quite openly more concerned about the money the king owed them than about the interests of the commons who paid their salaries, and these were promised their reward; if they would vote the taxes, their debts would be paid them. And some were so afraid of great men[2] that they forsook righteousness.

At this point the narrative breaks off abruptly. No one, I think, who reads this description, can have any doubt that the poet had himself sat with the representatives and listened to the speeches of his fellow-members. It also seems unlikely that he would see so far below the surface unless he had sat in more parliaments than one—like Chaucer's Franklin, who had been 'full oft time knight of the shire'. He recognized not merely the personal but the political elements in the situation; the motives which led the king to call a parliament, the preliminary arrangements that had been made by the council. Those who were old hands knew quite well that they were going to grant all that the king asked, but they were prepared to stage a debate just for the look of things: whilst others, in direct contact with the council, were ready to warn the less experienced that they would be unwise to make difficulties.

The picture drawn of the parts played by king, council, and lords confirms the interpretation which scholars have of late come more and more to put upon the working of parliamentary institutions in the fourteenth century; the leadership and direction of policy came from the lords, who, by getting their dependents elected members and by the device of sending members of their own order to discuss plans with the representatives, were able effectively to exploit the

[1] Mr H. G. Richardson thinks that this expression may indicate some one in a position of authority such as the Speaker; there were both official and unofficial channels of communication between lords and commons, and we know there were conferences in 1373, 1376 and 1379. But 'the master' may be merely metaphorical.

[2] *Duke* has an unspecialized meaning still in 1399, though it is possible that the newly created dukes of 1397 are intended.

economic and political resources of the commons.[1] But the manipulation of the commons needed skill; all were not as discerning as the poet, and the lords had to warn them off when they failed to recognize their limitations and meddled in high matters of state off their beat.

Though the confirmation of other evidence is valuable, all this might have been gathered from the older political narratives, reinforced by the *Anonimalle Chronicler's* description of the parliament of 1376. What is most striking in this account is the evidence of political conscience in the commoners; of a sense of conflicting loyalties. The dilemma between duty to constituents and duty to patrons, which anticipates the problems of the eighteenth-century parliament, has a peculiarly medieval and a characteristically English twist given to it by the reference to the member's wages. Not once but three times does the poet insist on this. Even if the argument was 'against right'—insincere—it was the orthodox and respectable line to take that the members were servants of their constituencies, that they were paid a salary to look after their interests, and to ventilate their grievances. That was their job; they need go no further. 'If we are false to those who provide for us, unworthy are we to earn our wages.' So those who took bribes from any one, or accepted the directions of the council, or waited for the orders and warnings of their masters, the lords, or told tales to the king in the hope of getting his favour, or voted for a subsidy because the government was in their debt, knew that they were failing in their duty. The shire had no advantage from their presences: 'the commons who paid their costs had no comfort of them'.[2]

This vivid recognition of the obligations a member owed the electors seems to me to be unique at this date, and it is for this reason that I venture to call attention to this source, which is as remarkable for its literary qualities and the political *flair* of the writer, as for the certainty with which it can be dated within a few months of the deposition of Richard II.

[1] For a recent discussion of this subject, see H. G. Richardson, 'John of Gaunt and the parliamentary representation of Lancashire', in the *Bulletin of the John Rylands Library*, vol. XXII, April 1938. For evidence on the other side, of the independence and even initiative of the Commons, see B. H. Putnam in *Trans. Royal Hist. Soc.* for 1929, p. 48 and K. Macfarlane, *ibid.* 1943.

[2] Cf. the parliamentary petition of 1391, quoted below on p. 242.

Mum and the Sothsegger

(1) Fragment M, ll. 1115-40

For of al þe mischief and mysse-reule þat in the royaulme groweth
Mum hath be maker alle þees many yeres,
And eek more and moulde, I may wel aduowe;
And principally by parlement to proue hit I þenke,
When knightz for þe comune been come for þat deede,
And semblid forto shewe þe sores of þe royaulme
And spare no speche þough þay spille shuld.
But berste oute alle þe boicches and blaynes of þe hert
And lete þe rancune renne oute a-russhe al at oones
Leste þe fals felon festre with-ynne;
For as I herde haue, þay helen wel þe rather
Whenne þanger and þattre is al oute y-renne,
For better were to breste oute þere bote might falle
Thenne rise agayne regalie and þe royaulme trouble.
The voiding of þis vertue doeth venym forto growe
And sores to be saluelees in many sundry places
Sith souurayns and þe shire-men þe sothe haue eschewed
Yn place þat is proprid to parle for þe royaulme
And fable of þoo fautes and founde þaym to amende...
Thay wollen not parle of þoo poyntz for peril þat might falle,
But hiden alle þe heuynes and halten echone
And maken Mum þaire messaigier þaire mote to determyne,
And bringen home a bagge ful of boicches vn-y-curid,
That nedis most by nature ennoye þaym þere-after.

(2) Passus IV, ll. 24-93

[Richard] cast it be colis with her conceill at euene,
To have preuy parlement for proffitt of hem-self,
And lete write writtis all in wex closid,
For peeris and prelatis, þat þei apere shuld,
And sente side sondis to schreuys abouȝte,
To chese swiche cheualleris as þe charge wold,
To schewe for þe shire in company with þe grete.
And whanne it drowe to þe day of þe dede-doynge,
Þat souereynes were semblid and þe schire-knyȝtis,
Þan, as her forme is frist, þey begynne to declare
Þe cause of her comynge and þan þe kyngis will.
Comliche a clerk þan comsid þe wordis,
And prononcid þe poyntis aperte to hem alle,

And meved for mony, more þan for out ellis,
In glosinge of grette, lest greyues arise.
And whanne þe tale was tolde anon to þe ende,
Amorwe þei must, affore mete, mete to-gedir,
Þe knyȝtis of þe comunete, and carpe of þe maters,
With citiseyns of shiris ysent for þe same,
To reherse þe articlis and graunte all her askynge.
But yit for þe manere to make men blynde,
Some argued aȝein rith þen a good while,
And said: 'We beth seruantis and sallere fongen,
And ysent fro þe shiris to shewe what hem greueth,
And to parle for her prophete, and passe no ferthere,
And to graunte of her gold to þe grett wattis
By no manere wronge way, but if werre were;
And if we ben fals to þo us here fyndyth,
Euyll be we worthy to welden oure hire'.
Þan satte summe, as siphre doth in awgrym,
Þat noteth a place and no þing availith;
And some had ysoupid with Symond ouere euen,
And schewed for þe shire and here schew lost;
And somme were tituleris and to the kyng wente,
And formed him of foos þat good frendis weren,
Þat bablid for þe best, and no blame serued
Of kynge ne conceyll ne of þe comunes nother,
Ho-so toke good kepe to the culorum.
And somme slembrid and slepte and said but a lite;
And somme mafflid with þe mouth and nyst what þey ment;
And somme had hire and helde þer-with euere,
And wolde no forther affoot for fer of her maistris;
And some were so soleyne and sad of her wittis,
Þat er þey come to þe clos acombrid þey were,
Þat þei þe conclucion þan constrewe ne couþe,
No burne of þe benche, of borowe noþer ellis,
So blynde and so ballid and bare was þe reson.
And some were so fers at þe frist come,
Þat þey bente on a bonet and bare a topte saile
Affor þe wynde fresshely to make a good fare.
Þan lay þe lordis alee with laste and with charge,
And bare abouȝte the barge and blamed the maister,
Þat knewe not þe kynde cours þat to þe crafte longid,
And warned him wisely of þe wedir-side.
Thanne þe maste in þe myddis at þe monþe-ende,
Bowid for brestynge and broughte hem to lond;
For ne had þei striked a strake and sterid hem þe better,

And abated a bonet, or þe blast come,
Þey had be þrowe ouere the borde backeward ichonne.
And some were acombrid with þe conceill be-fore,
And wiste well y-now how it sholde ende,
Or some of þe semble shulde repente.
Some helde with þe mo how it euere wente,
And somme dede rith so and wolld go no forþer.
Some parled as perte as prouyd well after,
And clappid more for þe coyne þat þe kyng owed hem
Thanne for comfforte of þe comyne þat her cost paied,
And were be-hote hansell if þey helpe wolde
To be seruyd sekirly of þe same siluere.
And some dradde dukis, and Do-well for-soke;
....

(Reprinted, by kind permission of the Early English Text Society, from *Mum and the Sothsegger*, edited by Mabel Day and Robert Steele, pp. 59–60, 24–26, London, 1936.)

XVI

The Community of the Shire and the payment of its Representatives in Parliament[1]

Speaking at the Congress of International Historical Sciences at Zürich in 1938 M. Coville advocated the study of 'la philosophie du régime corporatif ancien', and M. de Lagarde has shown how fruitful such an approach to the theory of representation may be.[2] To explain the English representative system, however, we must go further than the writings of William of Ockham. The English have never been remarkable for their devotion to a logical theory, and we are as a rule forced to deduce their theory, or rather their assumptions, from their practice.

I propose to consider the question '*What* is represented in parliaments?' in relation to a practice that is well established and well documented—the payment of the expenses of the knights of the shire—their wages, as they came to be called. These knights, as the documents constantly inform us, are in parliament *pro communitate comitatus*—'pour tout la commune del countee'. Are we to regard this community of the shire as a social order—that of the knights or country gentlemen, as distinct from the burgesses on the one hand and the magnates on the other? Or are we to regard it as a localized community, made up of varying classes and grades of society, held together by a common local tradition and by common responsibilities?

The significance of the word *responsibility* should be noted. Ockham insists that a community must have a real existence if it possesses rights. To this corresponds the conception that a community must have a real existence if it has duties, obligations, liabilities. Professor d'Entrèves[3] has recently insisted on the importance of the conception of political obligation as a clue to medieval political thinking, and suggested that this approach commends itself especially

---

[1] Read (in French) at the *Journées de droit*, Dijon, June 1939.
[2] G. de Lagarde, *L'idée de représentation dans les œuvres de Guillaume d'Ockham*, Bulletin of the International Committee of Historical Sciences, no. 37, 1937.
[3] A. P. d'Entrèves, *The Medieval contribution to Political Thought* (1939), p. 3.

to English political thinkers. I think it is true to say that in England constitutional progress is more closely bound up with the conception of political responsibility than with the more alien idea of democracy. In the subject now under discussion the responsibility can be expressed in financial terms, liability for payment of wages, service owed in return for wages.

It will be well to begin with a brief chronological survey of the history of the practice. 1258 is the earliest date for which there exist royal commands to the sheriffs to pay to the knights coming from their shires to the king's council 'rationabiles expensas suas in veniendo ad parlamentum, ibidem morando et inde ad partes suas redeundo'. The knights in question were those who had been chosen locally to receive in the shire courts the complaints brought against the local government officials; they were ordered now to come up to Westminster with their reports. It is very probable that whenever knights had come up to the king's courts on behalf of their shire courts, a common practice in judicial proceedings after 1166, their expenses had been paid locally, but there is no official evidence of this before 1258, and the well-known sympathy of the baronial council of 1258 with local grievances may explain the securing to the knights of their fair expenses.[1] Be that as it may, writs *de expensis* recur henceforward, in 1265, 1300, 1305 and 1307 and by the accession of Edward II they have become a matter of routine.[2] The rate of payment is for a long time left unspecified; the expenses are to be 'reasonable', but in 1311 the duration of the parliament is mentioned as a guide to estimating the amount to be paid; in 1315 a rate is enjoined; and after fluctuation from parliament to parliament the standard is established in 1327 as four shillings a day for the knight of the shire and two for the burgess, whilst the writ obtained by the member before he left the parliament stated the number of days for which he could claim payment, namely the duration of parliament plus the time allowed for travelling there—eight days from Cornwall or Cumberland to Westminster and eight days back; one day from Cambridge to Westminster and one day back. That the wages were still being paid under Henry VIII appears from the acts of parliament which gave Wales and Cheshire parliamentary representation in that

---

[1] *Close Rolls 1256–9*, pp. 332 f.; see also pp. v–vi.
[2] Details are given in W. Prynne, *A brief register of Parliamentary Writs*, Part IV, 1664; and, up to 1327, in F. Palgrave, *Parliamentary Writs*, 1827–34 (Record Commission).

reign and provided that their members should be paid:[1] the practice only died out in the second half of the seventeenth century. The payment of members' salaries to-day is based on an entirely different principle; the payment is made from national not local funds, and does not vary in relation to the duration of parliament or the place of residence of the member.

The king required the attendance of the local representatives at his court, guaranteed their expenses and ultimately fixed the rate of payment. That is the practice viewed from the centre, as the clerks of the chancery saw it when they filled in the writs from the lists supplied them by the clerk of the parliament. Our concern is rather with what happened in the shire, when the members returned to their homes and delivered their writ to the sheriff.

The writ commanded the sheriff 'quod de communitate comitatus tui habere facias militibus ejusdem comitatus nuper ad nos usque Westmonasterium pro communitate predicta de mandato nostro venientibus rationabiles expensas suas'. The process of assessing the county for payment was done in the county court, by the suitors of the court who had, in the days before the king had fixed a rate, to determine the scale of wages. In 1307, for instance, the sheriff of Westmorland said that at the next shire court held after the member, William of Goldington, gave him the writ, there was a discussion— *tractatus*—between William and the men of the community of the said shire, and the said men granted him 40s. for his expenses, and William expressed himself as well contented with that sum.[2] In 1308 one of the knights of the shire for Hertfordshire declared that the shire had *granted* him £10 for his expenses, and the sheriff says that the expenses had been *taxatae et agistatae* at £10; both say clearly that the shire court had determined the amount.[3] In 1322, just before the standard became fixed, there were two rates in use simultane-

---

[1] Stat. 6 Hen. VIII, c. 16; Stat. 27 Hen. VIII, c. 26; Stat. 34–5 Hen. VIII, c. 13.

[2] 'Predictus vicecomes bene cognovit quod hujus modi brevia Regis sibi venerunt, quod habere faceret dicto Willelmo [de Goldington] rationabiles expensas suas de communitate predicta pro labore suo predicto; set dicit quod in proximo comitatu suo tento postquam primum breve receperat, idem vicecomes ordinare fecit quid et quantum idem Willelmus habeat pro expensis suis predictis, et habito super hoc tractatu inter ipsum Willelmum et homines de communitate dicti comitatus, iidem homines concesserunt ei xl solidos pro expensis suis, de quibus idem Willelmus tunc temporis se tenuit bene contentum.' Plea Rolls of the Exchequer, 2 Edw. II, cited T. Madox, *Firma Burgi*, p. 101 f., note x.

[3] *Ibid.* p. 101, notes w, y.

ously; if the shire member was a knight he received 4s. a day, but if he were a *valettus* or yeoman he received 2s.[1] The sheriff of Derbyshire selected two knights without consulting the county, and when they came back from parliament with their writs the county found that it had to pay £20 for their expenses, when, if the election had been in their hands, they could have found two sufficient men to go to parliament for £10 or less.[2]

When the amount to be paid was determined, the shire court had to determine how it should be levied. In 1300 the sheriff of Leicestershire reported that 'per agistamentum totius communitatis in pleno comitatu' a rate of 4d. from every carucate of land in the county had been imposed.[3] I have not met any other instance of such a system as this: the usual method seems to have been to divide the sum among the different hundreds of the county, assessing each hundred at so much, and then to assess each village within the hundred at its contributory quota. In manorial accounts we find frequent statements of the sums contributed towards the wages of the knights of the shires in parliaments, and we learn also that the sums were collected by the bailiffs of the hundreds.[4] In 1444 this method was prescribed by act of parliament, but the statute was based on existing practice.[5] The same act, whilst reiterating the regulation of 1429 that only persons with forty shillings' worth of land should vote in an election, laid down that when the assessment of contribution to members' wages was taking place not only the suitors of the county court and the hundred bailiffs and constables should attend, but also all others who wished to be present, so that the assessment of contribution should be properly carried out, hundred by hundred and vill by vill, with no excess above the total due to the knights of the shire.

It was on the land that the burden of contribution lay, but the land holders were not always willing to pay the sum assessed on them. From the complaints of members who failed to receive the money due to them, of sheriffs who found difficulties in collecting it, and of the shires themselves that because certain persons or districts refused to contribute their neighbours were unfairly burdened, it is

[1] Prynne, IV. 54–6.   [2] Palgrave, *Parliamentary Writs*, II. ii, 315 b.
[3] P.R.O. Chancery, 219/1/8. See below, p. 248.
[4] E. C. Lowry, 'Clerical Proctors in Parliament and Knights of the Shire', in *Eng. Hist. Rev.* 1933, pp. 443–55.
[5] Stat. 23 Hen. VI, c. 14.

evident that there were differences of opinion as to who were morally or legally responsible for finding the wages.[1]

There was no serious dispute about the boroughs; if a borough elected its own representatives it was not expected to contribute to the wages of the shire members, but if it did not send members to parliament, the burgesses were liable with the other freemen of the shire.[2] Lords who themselves sat in parliament were exempt; and tenants on the ancient demesne of the crown were exempt. The real difficulty, both in law and in practice, arose in the case of those who dwelt in the liberties or who held land of the lords who were summoned to parliament.

From 1300 onwards the sheriffs are constantly reporting difficulties in collecting the contributions of the liberties—those areas within the shire where the king's writs had to be passed on by him to a bailiff appointed by the lord of the liberty for execution. In 1301, for instance, the sheriff of Leicestershire says: 'Part of the community of the county of Leicester is within the liberties of the honours of Leicester, Winchester and Peverel, and so this writ was passed on to the bailiffs of the said liberties in respect of the parts affected by the said liberties, and they replied to me that no one in the said liberties was bound to contribute to such expenses.'[3] The sheriff of Hampshire reports that he has passed on the writ to the bailiffs of the liberties of the bishop and prior of Winchester, who have done nothing about it.[4] The sheriff of Gloucestershire reports that the bailiffs of two of the liberties in his shire have paid a part of the money due, but that in the other six liberties no action has been taken.[5] In Wiltshire thirty-three liberties are named, in none of which have the bailiffs done anything.[6]

Perhaps as a result of such difficulties, from 1305 onwards the king's writ commanded the sheriff to levy the expenses 'tam infra libertates quam extra', within liberties as well as without. This made possible the use of the writ 'non omittas propter libertatem', by which, if the bailiff of a liberty failed to execute a royal writ, the sheriff might enter the liberty and execute it himself. But in England local government depended so much on the co-operation of the

---

[1] The subject has been treated very fully by L. C. Latham, in an article in the *Eng. Hist. Rev.* 1933, pp. 455–64, to which I am greatly indebted.

[2] *Rot. Parl.* IV. 76.   [3] P.R.O. Chancery, 219/1/8. See below, p. 248.

[4] P.R.O. Chancery, 219/1/9.

[5] Palgrave, *Parliamentary Writs*, I. 94–5.   [6] P.R.O. Chancery, 219/1/12.

countryside[1] that neither the authority of the king nor the efficiency of the sheriff could, in a matter like this, have permanently enforced an obligation that was not backed by custom and public opinion. There is abundant evidence that a strong body of feeling in the shires supported the demand that dwellers in the liberties should not be exempt. They were part of the community of the shire for which the knights went to parliament, as the sheriff of Leicestershire said in 1300, and men of the liberties were expected to attend the shire court at which the assessment of contributions took place.[2] When, in 1348, the phrase 'tam infra libertates quam extra' was omitted from the writs *de expensis*,[3] there began almost at once a series of petitions to parliament from the men of the shires which reflect clearly the point of view of the communities of the shires.

The first petition, in 1354, asked that it might be clearly stated whether the tenants of lords who hold by barony ought to contribute, with others of the county, to the wages of the knights who come to parliament.[4] The king's reply was that the existing custom is to be followed, and the same reply was repeated again and again until 1388, when a statute was passed which upheld old custom and added that no lord by purchasing new land could render it exempt if it had previously contributed.[5] But the real point at issue was what residents in a liberty, if any, were exempt by law, and as the king in parliament had refused to lay down the law, it was left to the law courts to interpret custom. This may have varied from shire to shire, but it seems to have been generally maintained that if a lord sat in parliament, he and his serfs were exempt from contribution, and the lords could apply for a writ at the end of parliament which ordered the sheriff not to levy any contribution to the knights' wages from their serfs.[6] As a writ of 1376, which forbids the sheriff to distrain on the *nativi* of the bishop of Chester for this purpose, puts it, it is not *juri consonum* that the goods of serfs, which are the bishop's own property, should be taken for this purpose.[7] In 1385 the lords declared they would not abandon their ancient privilege, and parlia-

---

[1] See A. B. White, *Self-government at the King's command* (Minneapolis, 1933).
[2] Palgrave, *Parliamentary Writs*, II. ii, 366. See below, pp. 248 f.
[3] It was reintroduced in 1365–76, and retained permanently from 1377.
[4] *Rot. Parl.* II. 258.
[5] Stat. 12 Ric. II, c. 12.
[6] Palgrave, *Parliamentary Writs*, I. 191; II. ii, 259; Prynne, IV. 437.
[7] Prynne, IV. 432.

ment explicitly recognized this right in 1377 and 1385.[1] Serfs, then, were exempt, but freeholders ought to pay, 'dedeinz franchise et dehors'. In 1391 a reason is given; 'les ditz Chevalers sont a chescun parlement pur tout la commune des countees et les seignurs des franchises soulement pur lour mesmes.'[2] In the early days of representation, about 1106, it had been said that a lord or his steward could discharge the responsibility of the vill which he held[3] and a parliamentary petition of 1379 shows that this theory was still accepted; 'les villes des Piers du Roialme qi tiegnent par baronie rien ne veullent paier a cause qe lour seignurs sont au Parlement pur eux et lours hommes en propre persone, et preignent si largement cel parol "lour Hommes" qe comment qil n'ad ne une ville qe iv ou v bondes et cent ou deux cents qi tiègnent franchement ou par rolle de court et sont frankes du corps, unqore ne veullent riens paier as dites Despenses'.[4] All the more ought those who hold by knight service of these lords of liberties be made to pay; 'les Chevalers en chescun countee sont esluz et viegnent si bien pur les ditz franchises come pur le remenant des ditz countes parmy tout le Roialme d'Angleterre' said a petition of 1415.[5] Sometimes the member was himself a tenant of such a franchise.

These petitions show clearly both the views of the community of the shires in the fourteenth and fifteenth centuries, and the attempts of the lords who sat in parliament to extend to their free tenants the exemption which all allowed their unfree tenants to enjoy. How far were the lords successful? In the later Middle Ages the English peerage were undoubtedly trying to use the great territorial power that they had accumulated to secure greater political privileges by usurpation and maintain them by force. They may have succeeded in some counties, but in one county at least the chief franchise-holder did not succeed in repudiating the responsibility of his free tenants for contributing to the knights' wages.

Cambridgeshire is divided into two almost equal parts by the river Ouse, and the northern part formed in the Middle Ages the very ancient and highly privileged liberty of the bishops of Ely, within which the bishop's bailiffs discharged almost all the functions of local government. The bishop of Ely sat in the house of lords as a tenant

---

[1] *Rot. Parl.* III. 25; II. 368; III. 212; and see the letter cited by S. B. Chrimes, *Eng. Hist. Rev.* 1934, p. 306.

[2] *Rot. Parl.* III. 293. Is this an echo of the *Modus tenendi parliamentum*? See M. V. Clarke, *Medieval Representation and Consent*, p. 383.

[3] *Leges Henrici Primi*, VII. 7.   [4] *Rot. Parl.* III. 64.   [5] *Ibid.* IV. 76.

in chief by barony. The bishop's tenants were exempt from attendance at the county court of Cambridge,[1] and at the courts held at Ely could obtain justice for which the residents in south Cambridgeshire would have to go to Westminster. None the less, it was stated in 1338[2] and again in 1379 that the Isle of Ely was always of old time assessed for a third of the wages due to the Cambridgeshire members of parliament,[3] and though the sheriff more than once reported difficulties in collecting and protests from the inhabitants of the Isle,[4] the bishop of Ely admitted liability when, in 1431, he agreed to pay £200 down, so that the residents in the Isle might be exempt thenceforward.[5] The money was to be spent on purchasing lands that would henceforth be responsible for paying a third of the wages of the knights of the shire.

The subsequent history of this bargain is of considerable interest and appears to be without a parallel. At some unknown date, the manor of Madingley, near Cambridge, was acquired and granted to certain persons at a farm of £10 a year, which £10 were to be applied to the wages of the knights of the shire of Cambridge. In 1542 'all the gentlemen of the said county of Cambridge, as well for themselves as for the whole inhabitants of the said county', asked the king to sanction the incorporation of the sheriff and the two knights of the shire for the time being as 'wardens of the wages', competent to receive the £10 annually from Sir John Hynde, king's serjeant and later royal justice, hereby recognized as lord of the manor of Madingley. The £10 was to be annually divided between the two knights, whether there was a parliament in being or not, until the election of their successors, and in consideration of this arrangement the county of Cambridge and its inhabitants were for ever to be discharged of the payment of wages to their representatives.[6]

---

[1] I owe this fact to the researches of Mr Edward Miller, who has also kindly transcribed the extract on p. 249 f.

[2] M. M. Taylor, 'Parliamentary elections in Cambridgeshire', in *Bulletin of Inst. of Hist. Research*, June 1940, pp. 21–6.

[3] In 1635–36, in connection with the levy of ship-money, the islanders asserted that a record of 18 Edward II had declared them liable for a fifth, not a third of county contributions. *Cal. S.P.D.* 1635, p. 375, 1635–36, p. 149. This record has not been traced.

[4] Prynne, IV. 517–18; P.R.O., Exchequer Plea Rolls, no. 99, m. 7d; no. 132, m. 1. See below, p. 249 f.

[5] *Rot. Parl.* IV. 382–3; V. 157.   [6] Stat. 34–5 Hen. VIII, c. 24.

A hundred years had passed since the Isle of Ely had paid down the £200. There is no record of any corresponding contribution from the rest of the county; it looks as if the liberty by itself had provided the funds which discharged the whole county from its financial responsibility. By 1542 it was not uncommon for members of parliament to waive their right to their wages,[1] and it must be remembered that with the rise in prices, the wages themselves were less valuable. It is quite possible that by this time a knight of the shire was well content to compound for his statutory salary at £5, year in, year out.

Thus the 'Shire Manor' of Madingley came into existence. It remained in the hands of the Hyndes, and of their descendants the Cottons, down to the nineteenth century, but the £10 a year had ceased to be paid long before 1774, when a politically minded antiquarian, or a historically minded politician, rediscovered the above facts and expounded them to the electors of Cambridgeshire and the Isle of Ely in a four-page pamphlet.[2] The writer agreed with Prynne in approving of the institution of wages for members of parliament, but 'until this constitutional and most desirable fashion of wages returns again' he thinks that, as a matter of common decency, something ought to be done about the £10 due from the Shire Manor. 'If no particular claim be made for the arrears, it will be right and look well for the present possessor [Sir John Hynde Cotton] to state the whole matter to the county and offer the balance in hand for some public work, such as building a county prison, establishing a hospital for poor children, cleaning out the river Cam, planning a navigation to Stortford, setting clear the Ely road, or whatever may be thought better.' The yearly value might, he thinks, be well applied henceforth 'in keeping the Ely road in repair, without turnpikes, in aiding the sheriff's expenses, in discharging prisoners for small debts and the like'. Such conduct, if pursued by the candidates at the approaching election, would be 'to our interest and their honour'. One of these candidates was Sir John Hynde Cotton, the lord of the Shire Manor, whose father had sat for Cambridgeshire

---

[1] E. Porritt, *The Unreformed House of Commons* (1909), I. 153. The borough of Cambridge continued paying wages to its representatives, if they were townsmen, down to 1660; it seems probable that if outsiders, like Cromwell, were elected to Parliament, they found their own expenses. C. H. Cooper, *Annals of Cambridge*, III. 206, 316.

[2] *To the Freeholders of the County of Cambridge and the Isle of Ely*, Cambridge, 14 Oct. 1774.

fifty years earlier. There is no evidence that any steps were taken either to demand or to make restitution of the revenues that had been so long withheld from the county. In the latter part of the nineteenth century the Cottons' estates were broken up and sold and the Shire Manor ceased to exist. But for four hundred years its name had preserved the tradition of the medieval method of assessment for parliamentary wages and of the bargain of 1431 between the bishop of Ely and the community of the county.

If the bishop of Ely, almost the greatest franchise-holder in southern England, acknowledged the liability of his tenants to contribute, it is safe to conclude that as a rule lords of liberties were not able to repudiate it; that they admitted that the dwellers in their liberties formed part of the community of the shire.

This phrase, 'the community of the shire', recurs constantly in the king's writs, in the sheriff's returns, in the petitions to parliament and in the law-suits before the barons of the exchequer when the knights claimed payment of their wages. It is the community which 'grants' the wages, though at the king's command, which adjusts the burden of payment among its members; it is the community which is represented. Can we regard this community as an estate of the realm, or as a social order?

The shire is not a community which has come into existence by a voluntary act of association, for it has been in existence since before the Norman Conquest. Its privileges are also older than the Norman Conquest; its ancient customs in some instances have been expressly recognized by a royal charter, but in most cases they are covered by the general promise of the king to uphold the ancient and established customs of the realm. The royal justices accept them as varying from shire to shire;[1] they will even ask the men of the shire to instruct them in these customs if necessary.[2] The collective financial responsibilities of the shire are first incurred in connection with its functions as a court, whose suitors find the judgments for which, if irregular, they will be collectively amerced, the amercements being assessed upon the county in some such way as the wages will be assessed later. The shire, in fact, has most of the features of the Swiss *landesgemeinde* as described by Dr Gasser and Professor Liebeskind.[3] But England is not a *Bundesstaat* or *Staatenbund*, it is a national monarchy, and

[1] Bracton, Lib. I, c. I.   [2] *Eng. Hist. Rev.* 1927, p. 119.
[3] *Etudes présentées à la Commission Internationale pour l'histoire des Assemblées d'états.* III (Louvain, 1939).

over against the shire court which embodies the *communitas* is set the royal agent, the sheriff, who exercises the royal authority in the county as does the French *bailli* in the *bailliage*.

Can the shire be taken to embody a social order? If the lords are in parliament for themselves, is it true to say that the knights of the shire are there to represent the country gentlemen, the successors of the Anglo-Saxon shire thegns, the forerunners of the 'squirearchy' of the seventeenth and eighteenth centuries, the equivalents, in some respects, of the Hungarian *Kleinadel*? As Professor Powicke has insisted, these country gentlemen are not only an essential part of social and administrative life, but they must be taken into account politically also.[1] In the *condominium* described by M. de Lagarde they are most certainly to be included as co-operating with the magnates, the burgesses, and the clergy in governing the realm of England.[2] But as a social order they merge at either end into the nobility and the burgesses. The younger sons of earls become country gentlemen, the burgesses purchase land in the shire, the country gentlemen come into the boroughs.[3] The overlap of borough and shire in Cambridgeshire can be traced from the eleventh to the eighteenth century. In the fourteenth century there are several examples of the same men acting as representative of a shire in one parliament and of a borough in another.[4] The fact that in 1322 a large number of shires preferred to be represented by a yeoman at 2s. a day rather than a knight at 4s. a day is, I think, evidence that the social category of knights was not of overmastering importance to the shire community.

The body that petitioned parliament about the wages of the Kentish members in 1414 consisted of 'gentils et autres gentz'.[5] The community of the shire which paid the wages included all those resident in the shire below the level of the parliamentary peerage and above the level of the serf—even the copyhold tenants are included, with the burgesses of an unrepresented borough, amongst those who share the financial responsibility. The feudal relationship of a man to his lord was less important than the fact that he was a free landholder

---

[1] *L'Organisation corporative du Moyen Age à la fin de l'Ancien Régime* (Louvain, 1939), III. 138. 　　　　[2] *Ibid.* p. 95. 　　　　[3] See above, pp. 19–26.
[4] For instance, William of Goldington represented the borough of Appleby in 1302 and 1305 and the shire of Westmorland in 1307, and Matthew of Crauthorne represented Exeter 1318–21 and Devonshire in 1328, while Roger of Harleston (see p. 249) was a burgess of Cambridge. 　　　　[5] *Rot. Parl.* IV. 49.

living within the boundaries of the shire. The community represented, though the country gentlemen might predominate, was the whole body of the shire 'inhabitants as well as gentlemen'. Nothing like class consciousness is traceable; even the exemption of the peers is rationalized on the grounds that they pay their own expenses.[1]

The statute of 1444 which laid down the procedure for assessing wages provided that it should be done in the presence of suitors and any others who wished to be present. Persons who could not vote certainly contributed to the wages of the members, and, as I have already shown,[2] the connection between wages and political responsibility was recognized by that anonymous fourteenth-century poet who wrote: 'We are sent from the shires to speak on their behalf, and if we are false to those who find our expenses, unworthy are we to claim our hire.' The community of the shire for whom the knights spoke, and which paid their wages was, I suggest, not so much an order or an estate as an organism—a unit held together by proximity, by local feeling and above all by common living traditions and common responsibilities.

[1] *Rot. Parl.* IV. 212.   [2] See above, pp. 229–235.

I. 1300

ENDORSEMENT OF WRIT 'DE EXPENSIS' DATED 6 MARCH 1300

P.R.O. Chancery 219/1/8

Quedam pars communitatis Comitatus Leycestr' est infra libertates Honorum Leycestr' Wynton' et Peverelli, per quod breue istud returnatum fuit Ballivis predictorum Honorum pro porcionibus predictas libertates tangentibus secundum tenorem istius brevis leuandis, videlicet de qualibet carucata terre tam infra libertates predictas quam extra in Comitatu predicto existente quatuor denariis, per agistamentum totius communitatis in pleno Comitatu factum, qui michi responderunt quod nulli infra libertates predictos existentes aliquam contribucionem pro consimilibus expensis in breui isto contentis facere tenentur, nec facere voluerunt. Ideo de hoc breue ad presens per istud breue nichil facere potui infra libertates predictas.

II. 1328

(Palgrave, *Parliamentary Writs*, II. ii. 366)

Edwardus Dei gratia Rex Anglie Dominus Hibernie et Dux Aquitanie Vicecomiti Midd' salutem. Cum nuper tibi precepimus quod de communitate comitatus tui tam infra libertates quam extra habere faceres dilectis et fidelibus nostris Rogero de Brok' et Henrico de ffrowyk militibus comitatus illius nuper ad parliamentum nostrum apud Westmonasterium in crastino Epiphanie Domini anno regni nostri primo (7 Jan. 1327) sumonitum pro communitate comitatus predicti venientibus ad tractandum ibidem super diversis et arduis negotiis nos et statum regni nostri tangentibus XXV libras et IV solidos veniendo ad parliamentum predictum ibidem morando et exinde ad propria redeundo videlicet pro LXIII diebus utroque predictorum Rogeri et Henrici capiente per diem IV solidos; ac jam datum sit nobis intelligi quod licet tu hujusmodi expensas super communitate comitatus predicti tam infra libertates quam extra virtute mandati nostri predicti prout hactenus fieri consuevit assideri velles et certos dies ad hoc faciendum pluries prefixeris; quidem tamen homines libertatum Westmonasterii et Walingford infra comitatum tuum coram te ad dies illos venire et hujusmodi assessioni interesse recusant ac expensis illis contribuere contradicunt in nostri ac mandati nostri predicti contemptum et ipsorum Rogeri et Henrici dampnum non modicum et jacturam. Nolentes igitur execucionem mandati nostri predicti per hujusmodi insolencias diucius retardari, tibi precipimus sicut alias precepimus firmiter injungentes quod predictos XXV libras et IV solidos de communitate comitatus tui tam infra libertates quam extra assideri et prout moris est levari et prefatis Rogero et Henrico sine dilacione habere facias juxta tenorem mandati nostri prius tibi inde directi, vel causam nobis significes quare mandatum nostrum alias tibi inde directum exequi noluisti vel non potuisti. Teste me ipso apud Eboracum XX die Januarii anno regni nostri primo (20 Jan. 1328).

(Endorsement)

Responsum Ricardi de Pons' Vicecomitis Midd'.

Quo ad levare faciendum expensas in brevi contentas levare feci de ballia mea xiii *li*. xvj *s*. quas solvi predictis Rogero de Brok' et Henrico de ffrowyk. Et quo ad levari faciendum residuum expensarum predictarum mandavi Ballivo libertatis Abbatis Westmonasterii que assessa fuit ad viii *li* viii *s*. Et Ballivo libertatis de Wallingford que assessa fuit ad lx *s*. qui nullum mihi inde dederunt responsum.

III

PLEA ROLLS OF THE EXCHEQUER, NO. 99, MICHAELMAS TERM, 1379

(P.R.O. Exchequer 13/99)

Cant' Pro Rogero Harleston' et Johannes Sybil' de debito.   m. 7 d.

Rogerus Harleston et Johannes Sybill', nuper milites electi pro comitatu Cant' ad parliamentum apud Glouc' tentum in festo Sancti Luce Evangeliste anno secundo Regis nunc (18 Oct. 1378), veniunt coram Baronibus huius Scaccarii xxviij. die Novembris hoc termino per Thomam de Herlaston', eorum attornatum, et queruntur per billam de Willelmo Moigne, nuper vicecomite Cant', de eo quod ubi predicti nuper milites habuerunt breve Regis de non omittatis etc. et de faciendo eos habere de communitate Comitatus predicti xiiij li. viij. s. pro expensis suis de tempore quo ipsi fuerunt milites ad Parliamentum predictum, videlicet per xxxvj. dies, quolibet eorum capiente per diem quattuor solidos, quod breve predicti nuper milites liberaverunt prefato nuper vicecomiti apud Cant' in pleno Comitatu tento ibidem die Jovis proximo post festum Natalis domini dicto anno secundo, predictus nuper vicecomes non solvit prefatis nuper militibus nisi tantum vj. li. viij. sol., et viij. li. residuas de dicta summa xiiij. li. viij. sol. penes se iniuste detinet et denarios illos eis solvere recusat in contemptum Regis. Et inde predicti nuper milites deteriorantur et dampnum habent ad valenciam x. li. Et hoc offerunt, etc.

9*

Et predictus nuper vicecomes presens etc., defendit dampnum et quicquid etc. Et dicit quod ex antiqua consuetudine semper usum fuit et adhuc est quod huiusmodi expense assideri debet per sectatores ad comitatum Cant'. Et dicit quod incontinenti post receptionem dicti brevis ad dictum comitatum tentum dicto die Jovis expense predicte assese fuerunt per dictos sectatores inter villatas comitatus predicti et quod tercia pars dicte summe xiiij. li. viij. sol., videlicet iiij. li. ix. sol., assessa fuit super villatas infra libertatem Episcopi Eliensis in Insula de Ely, sicut semper ab antiquo assideri solebat inter villatas infra Insulam predictam. Et dicit quod ipse venit ad homines dictarum villatarum infra dictam Insulam et cum dictam summam iiij. li. ix. sol. de illis levare voluisset, iidem homines dixerunt quod nunquam solverunt ad huiusmodi expensas nec modo volunt nec quod alique huiusmodi expense infra dictam Insulam unquam levare solebant. Et sic ipse nuper vicecomes fecit diligenciam suam ad predictas iiij. li. ix. sol' levandas. Et petit iudicium si ipse ad solvendas prefatis militibus predictas iiij. li. ix sol' aliqualiter impeti debeat. Et quoad residuum expensarum predictarum, videlicet lxxj. sol', dicit ipse nuper vicecomes quod summa illa assessa fuit super villatas infra libertatem predicti Episcopi in comitatu predicto extra Insulam predictam et quod quidam Johannes Dorele, ballivus ipsius Episcopi libertatis predicte, levavit eosdem lxxj. sol' et eos solvit prefatis militibus apud Cant' die Lune proximo post festum Sancti Michaelis anno tercio Regis nunc. Et hoc paratus est verificare. Et petit iudicium si etc. Et predicti nuper milites dicit quoad predictas iiij. li. ix sol' levandas infra dictam Insulam prout etc. quod ipsi per aliquam materiam per prefatum nuper vicecomitem superius allegatam excludi non debeant de solucione eorundem denariorum. Et inde petunt iudicium. Et predictus nuper vicecomes similiter. Ideo ad iudicium.

INDEX OF SUBJECTS

INDEX OF PERSONS AND PLACES

H. = Hundred; W. = Wapentake. The modern form of the name is given when known: (D.B.) = the Domesday form.

Date Due

NOV 12 '68			
NOV 27 '68			